PREACHER'S GIRL

Also by Jim Schutze

My Husband's Trying to Kill Me!

Cauldron of Blood: The Matamoros Cult Murders

The Accommodation: The Politics of Race in an American City

PREACHER'S GIRL

The Life and Crimes of Blanche Taylor Moore

Jim Schutze

WILLIAM MORROW AND COMPANY, INC.
NEW YORK

It is the policy of William Morrow and Company, Inc., and its imprints and affiliates, recognizing the importance of preserving what has been written, to print the books we publish on acid-free paper, and we exert our best efforts to that end.

ISBN 0–688–11934–4

Printed in the United States of America

BOOK DESIGN BY LYNN DONOFRIO

After the first year of work on this book I knew the story, but I still did not have a feel for the place. When my wife and son came and spent a wonderful vacation with me, prowling the state in search of roadside attractions, the face of North Carolina finally became familiar. So this book is dedicated to them—to Mariana and to Will.

From the very beginning, and through a very long process of gestation, this book has always owed its existence to my editor, David High-fill. He saw it. Without his guidance, and without the constant encouragement of my agent, Janet Wilkens Manus, it would not have gotten done.

PREACHER'S GIRL

Prologue

The old green humpbacked car scuttled down through the trees and tobacco fields on a shimmering two-lane North Carolina highway in high summer. The preacher's long waxy fingers coiled around the flesh-colored plastic steering wheel, squeezing the bumps and ridges. Cigarette-stained knuckles jiggled back and forth with little tremors. His eyes were big and fluid, black-brown like hers. His face was fixed ahead in a tilted, unblinking stare. Every five minutes or so, he reached down between his splayed rail-thin legs and lifted up a pint bottle for a poke.

She sat with her body pushed hard against the other door, chin on her arm up on the edge of the open window, gazing out over the nubby green fields, long soft hair blowing down the shiny side of the car. The radio said President Truman was on his way to New York by train. The preacher turned it off. They drove for a long while. She hummed the church songs they had been singing.

The whole family had been singing on the radio that morning. The engineer had grinned through the glass wall. The engineer had been drinking a Dr Pepper and eating a pickle while he read the newspaper, but he put his paper down and sat there grinning with the pickle in his teeth while they sang. All of them standing at the big round microphone, the tall lop-jaw preacher slapping his old guitar and jangling back and forth with his hips, the rest of the family singing and shaking tambourines: they jerked and smiled like marionettes for Jesus. Flonnie was still beautiful then, and Blanche was already beautiful.

They knew the preacher was drinking again before today. It always happened the same way. He opened another church, built it up, then the talk would start, some man in the church would come looking for the preacher with a gun, and it would all come down around their ears again.

When he was dry, when he was preaching, he pulled the people in by the droves. They heard him through the woods, that high quavering saw-blade voice crashing down in an angry tide of damnation and hellfire. They felt the black light from those eyes. They came out of the woods and the villages, mill hands and sun-leathered tobacco families, all to see this man who was a link with the beyond. They sat in his pews and moaned and shouted for him, hoping to touch some of his magic. Sooner or later, more often sooner, he started having sex with the women, and not much later he always started drinking again.

When he was on the bottle and out of a church, the preacher fixed looms in the mills and sold penny insurance to the gullible mill women who lived in narrow little wood houses on the poor side of the tracks in the towns of the North Carolina Piedmont. He was good at selling insurance, but all of the money he earned he lost gambling.

When he stopped drinking, he went back to preaching. He took the family out on the streets of the towns to sing hymns, to build up money for another church. That was hard, but it was better than the times between churches, when he was drinking.

The preacher had dropped the rest of the family off at home after the radio station and had taken her out into the country alone with him. Now he was stopped in the middle of the road with the engine running. She looked up, squinting against the purple glare of the sun on the windshield. She held her forearm up to shade her eyes. They were stopped at an intersection. The land was open on all sides, dotted green with recently transplanted tobacco seedlings. The plants had to be started in shaded soil and then replanted here in the open sun. The farmers treated their valuable plants like children.

Across the road at one corner of the intersection, purple in the heat, was a tall pine tree. Parked a few yards up the road on the red-dirt shoulder was a blue Ford coupe. She squinted and stared more closely. There was a man standing in the shadow beneath the tree, with his hips cocked out and his thumbs in his belt, grinning at the preacher's car. He wore a city hat. The sun made white speckles on his face.

The preacher leaned across the car seat, whiskey-breathing, and said quietly, "Honey, do you see that man over there?"

"Yessir."

"I'm going to pull up over there under that tree. When I do, I want you to go fuck that man."

"Why do you want me to?"

The preacher dipped his face down slightly, breathing. She could see the eyes flashing and the jaw rippling. "Honey, I want you to do what I tell you."

"Why?" she asked, pouting, coiled for the blow.

But he just stared at his fists where they gripped the steering wheel. He didn't want to hit her just then. "I owe that man a whole lot of money. If you don't help me, it's going to be real bad for everybody. He ain't a-going to hurt you, I can tell you that."

"How do you know he ain't?" she asked. A tear was trying to form at the eye on the other side of her face, the eye he couldn't see, but she flicked it away quickly, angrily.

"I'm gonna come watch," he said.

She looked up at him. He was smiling and drunk.

Chapter One

It was not yet the dawn of October 2, 1973. Dot Kernodle prowled the length of the half-dark bedroom, afraid to let her eyes adjust. The gloom made a tunnel. The bare gray wall on one side curved in over her, and on the other side she could see something like a double row of pearls grinning at her from the darkness. Her heart was beating hard, and her breath came short. Nothing could have prepared her for this.

Blanche Taylor, Dot's sister-in-law, had called her at five in the morning. In her little-girl-lost voice she had said: "I can't wake James. Will you come on down here?" James was Dot's baby brother.

Dot raced to her car in her pajamas and drove as fast as she could the short distance through Burlington to the little one-story frame house at 1014 Fair Street. All the way there, she tried to prepare herself for the possibility she would find James dead. You never knew with Blanche. You could never quite tell. James had been sick for weeks, and Dot had been secretly worried the whole time it was the heart attack come back, even though it had been four years. That could be just how Blanche would say it: "I can't wake James." She might mean James was dead. In the midst of her fear and in spite of an already looming grief, Dot was irritated with Blanche. It even irritated her to have to be irritated at a time like this. But why should this time be any different?

Dot had steeled herself as much as possible for what she might find. She had always been the toughest of the Taylors. If this was another heart attack, the rest of them would need her to take the lead. But no amount of inner resolve could have prepared her for this.

Blanche was sitting in the living room with Cindi and Vanessa, her fourteen- and twenty-year-old daughters. They were comforting their mother, who was dry-eyed and unemotional. When Dot came in the door, Blanche turned from the sofa and said simply: "He's in there."

Dot went into the room where James Taylor slept. Behind her at the front door, Dot heard Ralph, her brother, coming in. She stopped, leaned forward, and concentrated on the place in the darkness where she knew the bed to be. Gradually she recognized James, his body filling in like the Cheshire cat around the grinning rows of teeth. He was on his side, his eyes wide open and glassy, hands reaching up to her in a frozen motion of clawing. She could see now that his face was a deep purple. His lips were drawn back in a horrid grimace so severe that she could see every tooth in his mouth, all of them dry and shining in the morning window light.

But James's death had nothing to do with a heart attack. Rather, he'd been eaten alive, minutely and gradually, cell by cell, by arsenic. The secret of arsenic is that it loves life, races to life, embraces it, combines with it quickly and consumes it hungrily, converting it chemically, molecule by molecule, from life into death.

He had been extremely sick with flulike symptoms of sore throat and diarrhea for two weeks. He had seen the doctor several times and was worried about where the money to pay the bill was going to come from.

But then for a while the illness had seemed to be subsiding. For a day he was a little better. He still had not felt like eating with the family that night. His throat was sore. Blanche gave him ice cream, which he ate by himself.

After dinner he had felt well enough to go over to his minister's house and help him edit the tape recordings they were making of the hymn singing at church. Tape recording, at that time, was still a fairly high-tech hobby, and it gave James pleasure to know how to do it and to have the equipment.

At bedtime he was sweaty and nervous. James was always nervous anyway, fidgeting, jingling change in his pockets, fiddling with keys, but this night he had been worse than usual— jumpy and skittish, pouring sweat, distracted, as if he weren't quite sure what he was doing. Blanche announced she would sleep out on the sofa in the living room. She made him lie down and wiped his forehead with a damp cloth. No matter how bad James acted, whether he drank or lost money, even when he hit her, Blanche was always kind and gentle with him when he was sick. She was kind and gentle with all sick people.

She sat by the bed for a while holding his hand and humming hymns to him until he finally dropped off. Then she went out into the living room and fell asleep herself.

An hour later, the arsenic boiled off the inner lining of his stomach and bowel. He sat up straight in the bed, and a jet of vomit shot out of his mouth and splattered against the far wall. His bowels exploded in a volley of thin rice-water stools. He fell back flat on the bed, fully awake, eyes wide open, convulsing and totally unable to control himself.

But even as the toxin destroyed his muscles and nervous system, it already was sprinting even deeper into the physical and chemical structure that was his life. Moments after the vomiting began, his abdomen bulged and then drooped, horribly distending as the external tissues of the walled organs and the blood vessels turned to mush and all of his fluids began to leach into the open areas of his body cavity.

He was conscious and in his own mind for at least the first hour of his death process. He cried out, moaned, and screamed in agony. There were waves and explosions of pain as the basic synaptic chemistry of his nervous system began to pull apart. His body was flung about the bed and against the wall both by the pain and by the chaotic electrical storms taking place in his nerves and muscles. Then finally, as the oxygen-bearing cells in the blood began to collapse, he began to suffocate from within. His face turned a deep purple. His body went flaccid as the muscle cells ceased to be able to convert sugar into energy.

In the last hour of brain suffocation, the arsenic allowed him to escape into a universe of hallucinations. The ferocious grimace on his dead face told Dot his body had experienced wild pain to the very last instant.

His brother Ralph was walking up and down beside the bed, bent and gesturing up and down with the pursed upheld fingers of both hands. "I just don't understand, I just don't understand," he muttered, beginning to cry.

"It must have been a heart attack," Dot whispered. She walked out into the living room. "Blanche? Blanche? James is dead."

Blanche looked up. Cindi and Vanessa flanked her on the sofa. They looked at their mother.

"I know that, Dot," Blanche said.

Ralph broke into long deep sawing sobs in the death room behind her. Dot's lip was quivering, and she fought back tears.

"Blanche, was James dead when you found him?"

"I don't know," she said. "He wouldn't wake up."

"Mama," Cindi said, "don't you think you should call Raymond?"

Blanche reached for the phone.

Dot winced, in spite of her tears. "I don't know what the hell Raymond Reid has to do with this," she said. "What you need to do is call the damn coroner."

It amazed Dot that Blanche could find precisely the most inappropriate thing to do, even now, even at a moment like this. As always when she felt this way about Blanche, she wondered from what world Blanche really had come.

She had appeared from nowhere. James had come home with her one beautiful fall day twenty-one years ago, proud and excited with a striking woman on his arm. James was not bad-looking, before he got heavy, but Blanche was much more beautiful than any girl he had ever squired. Her face was sculpted in the high bird-boned features of the very prettiest Appalachian women. Shining black hair framed her head, and her large brown eyes were so dark they looked black, too.

Blanche had the kind of body most small-town men see only in circus parades—long, lithe, with generous breasts and a sleek round bottom perched on slender, perfectly shaped legs. She was beautifully dressed, in a way that was almost a bit much for Burlington, and she had a stagy presence that seemed overbearing at moments. He was twenty-four. She was nineteen.

They were married on May 29, 1952, at the Baptist minister's house, with James's older brother Ralph and his wife as witnesses. Naturally, the rest of the family was uneasy about things proceeding so fast, but Ralph would do anything for James. James was always funny, in his nervous, quick, twitchy way. James always tickled Ralph. The Taylor sisters were bound to be standoffish with a woman like this, but Ralph knew right away that Blanche was James's dream come true.

She was outgoing and funny, always on the go, always on the lookout for something fun, just like James. Her beauty was her invitation into the company of men, where she seemed very much at home. Blanche liked to talk about sports and crimes, Wall Street and politics right along with the menfolk, which was a good half of what the rest of the women mistrusted in her, Ralph thought. The other half was her looks.

She had grown up poorer than the Taylors, but they were all basically from the same stock—descendants of the tough Gaelic-speaking Scots who had fled Scotland for North Carolina in the eighteenth century. They were of a kind.

Blanche was born on February 17, 1933, in Brown Mill, the mill-hand section of Concord, eighty miles south of Burlington in the Piedmont region of North Carolina—a red-dirt plateau of 21,000 square miles stretching from the low-lying coastal region to the Blue Ridge Mountains in the west. She was the fifth of seven children born to Parker D. Kiser and his wife, Flonnie.

Parker Kiser ("P.D.") was one of the "primitive" preachers, as they proudly called themselves, who brought all the tradition of the old wilderness campgrounds down into the semi-urban world of twentieth-century North Carolina. He preached an intense monotonous singsong literal interpretation of the Bible, a mantra for visions and tongues. He always made money, from his churches or his jobs, but he never contributed much toward the support of his family.

Flonnie had to work full-time in the mills to keep rent paid and food on the table. Of the $40 a week she earned in the early 1950s, she had to give half to P.D., who never made any secret of the fact he was spending it all on young girls. Gradually, the work and the worry broke her posture, her health, and her face. But in her better years, even poor and tired,

Flonnie could make men stop and turn in the street, a fact of which P.D. was keenly aware.

The Kisers moved to Burlington in 1942, when Blanche was nine. Burlington was then, as now, a busy mill town in central North Carolina. Forty miles to the west was beautiful old Winston-Salem, home of the Reynolds family and R. J. Reynolds Tobacco Company, and west from there was Thomas Wolfe's Asheville and the green smoky grandeur of the mountains. To the east lay the college towns of Raleigh, Durham, and Chapel Hill, and farther east from there was the pirate mystery of the Atlantic coast and the Outer Banks. But Burlington was where poor folks went to work when they could no longer make a living on the farm.

It had started like all of the tiny little settlements around it—as a place on a stream where there was enough fall in the water to drive a mill. Many streams and creeks poured down into the long bend of the Haw River that ran through Alamance County, each one providing a hospitable site for a mill hamlet. As the hamlets grew at the end of the nineteenth century, they pressed together and formed the small city of Burlington—a center of employment where, by the middle of the twentieth century, a rounder like P.D. could find just enough employment and just enough movement to keep himself going and cover his traces.

P.D. was ferociously strict with his children, especially the girls. He reviewed their ragged clothing regularly to make sure it was sufficiently modest. They could take part in no activities after school and were expected to rush straight home. As soon as she was old enough, Blanche began to work in the stores downtown, spending most of the money she earned on clothing, which she had to hide from her father.

When she reached puberty, she was already a striking girl and clearly destined to become a beautiful woman. P.D.'s glowering watchfulness grew all the more intent and forbidding when boys began to follow her home from school.

She had quit school when James brought her home. James's mother, Isla, was kind to Blanche, as she was kind to all people. Blanche quickly took a place at Isla Taylor's side and talked with her as if they had known each other for years, monopolizing her at family gatherings so that Isla barely had a chance to speak with her own flesh and blood.

"James is so funny with his cameras, don't you think, Miz Taylor?" Blanche said in her singsong voice, always scanning her listener's face closely. "He fusses with those things so much, you'd think they were pretty girls."

Mrs. Taylor didn't like references to sex, even oblique, and Blanche never spoke without drifting into some kind of coy or joking reference, but Mrs. Taylor always kept her feelings to herself. Watching from the far corners of the room, Dot and the other sisters could tell their mother was uncomfortable.

But even the sisters saw, as did their brother, Ralph, that Blanche was right for James in many ways. James doted on his mother and always behaved carefully in her presence, but out of her sight he was a loud ribald man with a dirty joke at his lip and a bottle never too far from reach.

The Taylors grew up in the Mill Hill section of Burlington—the parallel of Brown Mill in Concord, where Blanche had been born. James was the next to the last of eleven children. His parents, William and Isla, raised all of their children in the same three-room house and were married for sixty years. They were a warm, solid family, serious of purpose. James was far and away the least upwardly mobile of his siblings. The rest became professionals and successful business people. He was the least educated, having dropped out of high school. The rest of them attended college, which most of them completed.

James was, in effect, the family ne'er-do-well, although none of them ever said it, and the others were always pitching in to "help James get started." They lent him money so he and Blanche could make a down payment on the house on Fair Street, and they frequently made smaller loans to tide him over. But the family trait of seriousness never rubbed off on James. He drank a great deal as a young man, and he was a gambler, often losing all the money he had to his name in the friendly games at the Burlington Moose Hall.

He was sentimental, childish, and given to eruptions of violent temper. But he hid most of that beneath a veneer of laconic wit, small-town savoir faire, and a penchant for what most people suspected was racy behavior.

Even though James was not college-educated, he did work that commanded a measure of respect, rebuilding and refinishing fine furniture by hand, a trade much admired in this region, only a few miles from High Point, the fine-furniture capital of the nation.

The year after Blanche married James, her first daughter, Vanessa, was born, and she started working at the Church Street Kroger store in Burlington as a checker. Blanche was never just a Kroger worker. From the moment she started at Kroger, she was always the main attraction. Men lined up behind her register just so they could look at her. Many women liked to get in Blanche's line, too. She sang to each one in her busy little chittering bird voice, always with some expression of concern for their personal affairs. She never forgot a name, never failed to use it.

Kroger itself was something of an upbeat experience for Burlington at that time. Most grocery stores in smaller communities were still locally or regionally owned, especially in the South, and still had the look and feel of their owner's idiosyncrasies. But Kroger was national. There was a modern snap and sparkle to a Kroger store that made shoppers feel they were taking part in something smart.

Behind the scenes and away from the eyes of the customers, Kroger was a more tangled web than it appeared to be on the surface. It was an anomaly in the South—a successful business whose employees were members of a fairly tough union. The company spent endless man-hours and a great deal of money teaching its managers how to deal with union employees. The managers were carefully drilled in the art of building up a paper file on an employee who needed firing, and they were taught to be especially careful in even the most outwardly casual conversation with union stewards, who could be counted on to play their own games and build up their own paper trails, too.

Adding to the complexity of daily life in a store was the predatory masculine sexual ethic of the 1950s, perhaps stronger in the South than elsewhere, perhaps not. If there was any definite difference in the South, it was the length everyone went to, male and female, to maintain an outward appearance of Christian propriety and to camouflage the sex games in the store from public view.

Blanche was the grand master there, too. She flirted hard with her bosses, kept close tabs on all of her coworkers to know who was sleeping with whom, and always seemed to be ahead of the game.

Blanche was enjoying what would have to be described, at least in terms of typical personnel practice at Kroger, a meteoric rise. Management posts in a Kroger store were strictly segregated by sex in the 1950s. The jobs open to women were all at the front of the store and involved dealing with the public. The actual management of the store was the exclusive preserve of the men.

But within the realm open to women at Kroger, Blanche began to rise steadily toward the top. The top job for a woman at Kroger was head cashier. The head cashier was the day-to-day operational boss of all the other cashiers and of the bagboy/stockers. She was responsible for training new cashiers, and while she did not have formal authority to hire and fire, she was virtually responsible for those decisions under normal circumstances. It was a woman's job, but it was a woman's job with clout. From the day she set foot in the store, her coworkers saw she was the kind of person who would set her eyes on the head cashier's post and never turn from her course.

Some of her coworkers suspected that Blanche was involved in things that were much more serious than office politics. In particular, Mary Sharpe was worried about some of the odd sleight of hand Blanche seemed to practice with the cash registers. Blanche had a penchant for using "loaner" registers and for moving around, using other checkers' drawers, rather than following the safe and sure procedures designed so that each cashier would check out on a register that was entirely her own responsibility for each shift. Mary suspected Blanche of embezzling money.

Blanche's mother, Flonnie, filed for divorce from P. D. Kiser in 1959. She had to go to the courthouse with a lawyer and file papers explaining in detail what the preacher had done to deserve such a fate—a very public event in the Burlington of the time, even for such humble people as the Kisers.

She told the court she had seven children. The preacher had abandoned the family at Christmas in 1956, four years after Blanche had left home to marry James. He had left no money in the house, no food, the bills unpaid, the house unheated. He had told Flonnie he was leaving "to find him a younger woman" and that he would not pay a cent for her support—an entirely empty threat, since he never had supported her anyway, instead taxing her meager earnings $20 a week in order to augment his own takings. The court awarded her $25 a week in support for one year, dropping to $10 a week for a second year and then ending. The preacher, surprisingly, paid it faithfully.

Cindi, Blanche's second daughter, was born in 1959, the same year that Kroger made Blanche a head cashier. When Blanche announced to Mary Sharpe she was going to promote Mary to be her assistant in the booth, Mary made up an excuse about the hours involved and declined. She didn't want to be within a hundred miles of Blanche and the safe. Blanche shrugged it off and gave the job to another woman.

During the same period, James Taylor's life had begun closing in around him. Almost as soon as he settled into domestic life, James Taylor's stomach began to grow, and it spread across him like a second body hugging his front. His hair started to fall out in front while he was still in his twenties, leaving a patchy, uneven line as if the hair had been snatched out by the fistful. The boozing and the gambling that had seemed rakish and wild when he was still half a boy had quickly grown less amusing as he entered what was supposed to have been responsible manhood.

James did not have much to feel good about. By 1959, James's sex life with Blanche had cooled to little more than the occasional. Blanche's attitude toward him was cool at best. At the same time, James could hardly fail to see the clues and hints all around him of Blanche's flamboyant infidelity.

When she announced plans at dinner one night to visit her mother the next morning after church, James said, "How you gonna get over there? I'm going to Winston with Eddie."

"To play cards," she said.

He sat up straight. It made James very angry for Blanche to talk back to him in front of the girls.

"It don't make a damn what it's for, Blanche. I'm going, and I will have the car. So how are you going to get over there?"

"I'll get there," Blanche said. She spooned chocolate pudding daintily into her mouth.

"In one of your boss's company cars."

"Maybe," she said, looking him straight in the eye.

James said nothing for a while, noisily slurping his pudding and staring at the spoon between bites.

"I just wonder how it is," James said. "I just wonder how it is that a supervisor lets one of his damn checkers have his company car all the time for her personal use. I never heard of that. Maybe you could tell me how that is, Blanche?"

Blanche said nothing. She concentrated on her own dish of pudding.

"Blanche, maybe you don't hear me when I'm talking to you? Is that it? You can't hear me?"

James lifted a generous dollop of the rich brown chocolate pudding on his spoon, held the spoon back with a forefinger, and flicked the entire spoonful of pudding into Blanche's face. It was a perfect bull's-eye. The huge blob of pudding hit her right between the eyes and began to drip down over her nose and mouth, plopping onto the table in front of her. Blanche sat hunched forward, not moving or looking up.

"I thought maybe you didn't notice I was talking to you, Blanche. I was asking you why it is your boss lets you drive his car all over town like you was married to him instead of to me. Would you mind giving me an answer about that?"

She did not move. James dipped the spoon down into his pudding again. He lifted it, tipped it back, and shot another huge gob of it, this time hitting her in the forehead. Vanessa ran from the room, and Cindi, who was still a baby, began to howl.

"It's not because you're fuckin' him, is it, Blanche?" James hissed. He dipped the spoon again, but this time instead of flicking it at her he simply reached across the table and heaved the contents onto her cheek and mouth.

Blanche finally lifted her face. The pudding was still sliding down out of her hair and over her eyes like mud. A tear was trying to form at the corner of one eye, but she flicked it away angrily with one finger. She stared at James without speaking, her eyes dark and angry. She stood up and went into the kitchen, where she wiped her face clean with a towel. She began to clear the table and wash the dishes. As she turned on the hot water to fill the sink, she heard the angry screech of James's tires on the street; he was making his escape to the Moose Hall.

Chapter Two

For several years in the early 1960s, James managed to do better, at least as a father. He brought his drinking under control and broke off contact with his old gambling buddies. James joined the Baptist Church and became an active member and began devoting his spare time to photography.

Blanche filled her own spare moments selling Tupperware, or "tumbleware" as the ladies of Burlington tended to call it— a new kind of plastic food container for the home, sold by housewives to housewives at events called Tupperware parties. Tupperware was a domestic wonder, right up there with Kroger stores and electric hair curlers as an artifact of modern life and the national culture.

Blanche was good at selling Tupperware when that was what she was actually doing, but most of the time she used Tupperware parties as an excuse to cover up evening meetings with men.

She could be outrageously flirtatious, for Burlington. When a new deliveryman with the right kind of body came into the store, Blanche would turn immediately and give him a frank up-and-down appraisal. She might be in midsentence, talking about Jesus and the Bible, and she would stop and mutter to a coworker, "Man, I'd like to see the dick on that guy."

In spite of Blanche's growing promiscuity, the period of the early 1960s was a time of relative peace in her life. James was beginning to come into his own. Even though William and Isla Taylor's children were now grown and had children of their own, their lives still seemed to center around the little three-room house on Mill Hill where William and Isla still lived. On many an evening most of the siblings might be present— Dot, Oley, Rachel, Ralph, James—attending to various chores and distractions around the home of their parents.

Dot's husband had drowned in 1954, two years after James and Blanche were married. James descended on Dot's two young children whenever he came across them, picking them up and carrying them upside down and shrieking, out into the yard, where he hung them from the trees like squirrels. His love for Dot and his devotion to her children were forces that seemed to help draw James out of his earlier self-indulgence and into manhood. He began to spend more time with his own daughters, too, often taking them with him to his parents' home, where he whiled away long hours making home movies of all the children while they played with their grandfather and listened to their grandmother's stories.

One evening in 1962 at his mother's house, with the rest of the family around, James told Blanche she was not to go out. She was stunning in a dark, low-cut, full-skirted dress and high heels. Blanche had used up the Tupperware excuse earlier in the week and hadn't had the foresight to invent something else. Before she could make good her escape, James said, "Blanche, you stay here with us tonight. I'm making movies to show at Christmas, and I want you in 'em."

She wilted visibly, took a sullen look around the room, and slunk to old Mrs. Taylor's side. Isla made friendly inquiries about Blanche's own parents and siblings, to which she made perfunctory responses.

"Oh, fine. Just fine, Mama Taylor."

Isla took a long look at Blanche. Quietly, so the others would not hear, she said, "It won't hurt you, Blanche, to spend a night with the family."

Blanche gave a disconsolate little sigh and pushed herself deeper into the sofa next to Isla. She was quiet for a while. "James is spending too much money on all this movie film," she said.

"It makes him so happy to do it, Blanche. He seems to be doing so much better. I get the picture he's not drinking at all now."

"He quit." She surveyed the little scene of togetherness balefully. "He spends all our extra money on cameras and movie film, and those girls need clothes, Mama Taylor. I did the wash last night, and I couldn't find no more than two pair of socks for either one of them that matched or wasn't stained or full of holes."

"Well, Lord knows I've got drawers full of little-girl socks still around here somewhere, Blanche, that I'd be proud to let you have."

"Look at him. How much weight he's put on."

The smile evaporated from Isla's face, giving way to a look of deep worry and concern. Dot's daughter, Vicki, who was in her early twenties, was sitting still, watching Grandma Taylor and Blanche carefully. Of the entire family, Vicki was least fond of Blanche, most protective of Grandma, and least likely to take any grief.

Vicki and the others got up and went out into the kitchen to look for something. Isla turned and looked straight into Blanche's face. "Blanche, you may not know it, but you have a good husband in my son, and you have a good home. You always seem so restless, so fidgety, always on the go. I wonder where you go sometimes. It can't all be tumbleware that you're doing."

"I stay busy, Mama Taylor. I don't like to get bored. I want to do something with my life."

But Mrs. Taylor was on the hunt. "Blanche," she said, "I want you to look up at me. Blanche, honey, are you doing right by my son?"

Blanche lifted her face slowly. She perused Isla Taylor's face intently but coolly. "Whatever do you mean, Mama Taylor? I have tried and tried to give James a good Christian home and to bring him to Jesus. If James is closer to Jesus today at all, it's my doing. I am about as good a Christian woman as you are going to find in this house."

But Vicki had dipped back around the corner and was listening. She stepped out into the room. "If you're such a Christian woman, Blanche, why don't you stay home and take care of those girls at night instead of driving over to Winston with your boss, and why don't you stop bringing those children over here and dumping them on this poor woman who's too old and too frail to be spending her time nursing your babies for you while you run around on your husband?"

Blanche turned the same masked face up to Vicki. "Well, Vicki," she said, in an exaggerated tone of condescension, as if speaking to a five-year-old, "I have work to do in the evenings, honey, and James knows how to take care of the children, too."

Vicki shrugged and stepped back into the kitchen. The others had gone out into the garage, still hunting for whatever it was they wanted. Vicki sat down at the kitchen table alone and opened a loaf of bread to make herself a sandwich. A shadow came over the table. She looked up. It was Blanche.

Blanche reached down and gripped the loaf of bread in the middle with one fist. She squeezed it to paste, lifted it, and shook the loose pieces into Vicki's face and hair. Her face was working, twisting.

"Don't ever talk to me like that again!" she screamed at Vicki.

Vicki leaped to her feet and shoved her own face right up into Blanche's. "Shut up, Blanche," she said. "Just shut up. If you got a problem with me, let's just take it out in the yard and let's take care of it."

Blanche recoiled. Her face was working a new puzzle now. The threat of a physical fight had taken her aback. Vicki moved in on her to capitalize.

"Blanche, I am on to you. I am on to you. I know what you are. And I am gonna tell you this. You stay away from my grandma. All you do is nitpick and worry her to death and stir her up and take advantage."

Isla had come to the door and was watching silently. Blanche whirled and looked at Isla, as if hoping for support. But Isla said nothing. Blanche pushed past her brusquely and rushed out the front door.

"Stay away from my grandma!" Vicki shouted after her.

Blanche sped away in a borrowed Kroger company car.

Isla and Vicki watched her depart.

"Vicki," Isla said quietly, "I want you to watch out for her. I want you to watch out for that woman. Don't never turn your back on that woman."

The place in Blanche's life where there was order and satisfaction was at the Kroger store. Day-to-day operations at the store had improved with the arrival in 1962 of an eager young management trainee named Raymond Reid, who had come from the Danville store to be assistant manager.

Even though he was still very young and only an assistant, Reid seemed to bring a new spit and polish to the Burlington store. At twenty-six years old, he was handsome, decisive, mature beyond his years. He managed to be a tough boss and a fairly nice guy at the same time.

He was Kroger through and through, a fact that was inconvenient for Blanche, since Reid was one of the few Kroger managers who took the company's official rule against in-house sexual hanky-panky seriously.

Reid was born in Danville, the only child of poor, stern, decent people. He was third in his class when he graduated from high school, and the University of Virginia offered him a scholarship, but the family needed him to work and bring home a paycheck. He stayed at Kroger, where he was already working as a bagboy.

He had gone to work for Kroger at age sixteen. The manager of the Danville store, who had spotted him early as a serious boy, took him aside in his senior year and told him he could stay on full-time after graduation and expect to be a candidate for the company's management training program after a few years.

Kroger became Raymond Reid's alma mater and mission in life. Everything another man might pour into book studies or hobbies or relationships Raymond Reid poured into Kroger. He was a quick and close student of what went on around him. He mastered all the policies and the practical ins and outs of the store early on. And he took all of it very, very seriously.

In 1960, when Raymond was twenty-five years old, Kroger put him in the management training program in a store in Durham. The first thing he did was go back to Danville and marry Linda Thompson—a beautiful girl with a lively figure and big brown eyes who was seven years younger than he. Linda had been dreaming of Raymond Reid since she first met him at a dance, when she was fourteen. They first dated when she was sixteen. Raymond's family was not especially religious, but Linda's parents were strict Methodists. Raymond and Linda had to sneak in order to go out together.

Linda was a top student and wanted to finish high school. Her parents wanted her to go on to college. But when Raymond Reid came back with the management training position in hand and a nice pay raise to boot, there was no question in her mind what she was going to do with the rest of her life.

They moved to Durham, and Linda became pregnant with their first son, Ray Jr. A few months later when Raymond was transferred to a job in High Point as a manager trainee, they were delighted with the move. Linda stayed in Durham, while Raymond went ahead. He found a house, rented it, and then came back for her.

The management style Raymond was learning in the store carried over into his home life. He was very much the boss there, too. Linda did not have access to the checkbook and had to ask for whatever money she needed. The good news was that Raymond Reid was a fair, good-spirited boss, at work and at home.

In the store he operated strictly by the book. The Kroger book. Right and wrong for Raymond Reid were defined entirely by company policy and the interests of the store. Every regulation, from punctuality to dress code, was as important as every other regulation. He missed nothing. He forgave nothing.

For all of that, the people who worked with and for the young Raymond Reid liked him. They could talk to him. The fact that he had come up from bagboy, that he wasn't one of these managers who parachute in straight from college without a clue, made him seem real and approachable.

Raymond knew exactly what the deal was with Blanche and some of the other young male assistant managers in the store. He found none of it surprising or even terribly interesting. Blanche was good-looking and ambitious. It was no big deal.

Reid liked Blanche right away. He made it plain he was not interested in sleeping with her, but they hit it off as coworkers.

Blanche even made friends, after a fashion, with Linda Reid. In 1964 when Linda was pregnant with her second boy,

Stevie, Blanche threw a baby shower for her.

Six months later, James got drunk one day and decided to confront Blanche about an affair she was having with one of the assistant managers. Blanche was at work, running a register for another checker who was on break. It was midmorning, and the store was fairly busy. All of the customers were housewives, most of whom had babies or very young children with them.

At a few minutes after eleven, James appeared in the front of the store. Blanche was in the back. James asked one of the checkers to get her. He lurked awkwardly at the front window, standing and rocking with his hands folded while he waited for her to come.

Blanche came forward warily to see what he wanted. James almost never visited the store. The other checkers saw Blanche exchange a few quick sentences with him, and then they saw Blanche shake her head sharply no and begin to walk away from him toward the back. James followed her, saying loudly, "Get him! Get him out here right now!"

The young assistant manager, who had been up in his office and seemed to be unaware of any problem, sauntered out into the store and passed James with a somewhat pompous "Good morning, Mr. Taylor."

But James caught his sleeve at the elbow and stopped him. All of the people in the front could hear shouting now, as James began to ask in progressively louder tones, "Are you fucking my wife? I said, are you fucking my wife?"

"James, shut up!" Blanche shouted. "Get out of here! How am I gonna support those children if you lose me my job?"

The young man began by ordering James off the premises, but as James pursued him, keeping his face inches from his face, he grew panicked and imploring, begging Blanche to get him out of the store.

"You are drunk, James," she said. "I don't know what some-body told you, but it's a lie. You are making a real mess for us with this shit."

Muttering something to the effect of "You ain't heard the last of this, either one of you," James shambled from the store, his face patchy white and red, his expression grim, humiliated to the bone. Blanche never mentioned the incident to any of the coworkers who had watched it happen.

Shortly after James's drunken scene at the store, Raymond

Reid was made store manager. Blanche immediately launched a more deliberate campaign of seducing him. She stayed away from the bawdy oral-sex jokes that had exerted a voodoo-like power over other young management types and experimented instead with subtler approaches. She found that Reid was developing an interest in religion and watched some of the television evangelists like Rex Humbard and Jimmy Swaggart, just then becoming popular. Blanche was taken with them, too, and had become a faithful viewer. She talked about them with Reid whenever she could, but the occasions when Blanche could succeed in slipping friendly Bible chatter into the conversation with him were few and far between. He was mainly all business.

In September 1966, P. D. Kiser died. The cause of death was diagnosed as a heart attack, triggered by chronic emphysema. And, indeed, it was a heart attack, ultimately, in the sense that his heart stopped. Like so many findings recorded on common death certificates, the diagnosis really was only a restatement of the fact that he had died. It missed all the chemical drama of what really had happened, and certainly it came nowhere within hailing distance of the cause.

Within half an hour of the time the preacher received his dose, his breath took on the stench of garlic. An old country doctor, schooled in medicine by lore and by experience, might even have leaned down and known what that scent meant. The breath of a sick person can tell his tale: scent of bitter almonds for cyanide, vinegar for glacial acetic acid, wintergreen for salicylate. Garlic for arsenic.

But a country GP would have to know a lot. The scent of garlic on the breath of a dying old man can also mean he has been poisoned by phosphorus, tellurium, parathion, malathion, selenium, dimethylsulfoxide, or thallium.

The most obvious symptoms present the strongest evidence—the terrible gnawing stomach pain, rice-water diarrhea, projectile vomiting, deep blue face, brain swelling and delirium, cold clammy skin, and lethargy. But grotesque as those symptoms may seem to the layman, they would barely raise the eyebrows of people accustomed to dealing with the very sick and the dying. Those same symptoms could just as easily steer a doctor toward acute alcohol poisoning, Guillain-Barre syndrome, diabetes mellitus, vitamin deficiency, lupus, blood disease, diphtheria, multiple sclerosis, or any of a host of other common diseases, including tick bite.

In fact, it is the ability of arsenic to duplicate the symptoms of other diseases that makes it so difficult to detect. Arsenic is the fiftieth most common element on earth. It is everywhere, in dust and in water, in plants and in animals. And yet, common as arsenic may be and common as are incidents of arsenic poisoning, it remains one of the least accurately diagnosed of all afflictions. For some reason, the possibility of arsenic poisoning simply is not a thought that leaps easily to the minds of physicians.

Arsenic poisoning can be stopped and reversed by a chemical therapy called chelation. The problem in the case of a serious dose is time. Half an hour after the preacher's dose was given to him, while he was writhing in pain and holding his stomach, the arsenic was already moving out of his stomach and into his bloodstream, where it bound itself chemically to his red blood cells. Within twenty-four hours, it had left the bloodstream. And by then, given the size of the dose, it was too late.

By then the arsenic already had made itself a part of the molecular structure of cells in the liver, lungs, intestinal walls, and spleen, where it bonded with the sulfhydryl groups of tissue proteins. Within twenty-five hours, the preacher's bones had stopped taking on sulfur as a basic building block and were accepting only arsenic instead. In thirty hours the arsenic had begun to enter his hair.

The one place the arsenic did not penetrate was across the blood-brain barrier, so that the preacher was more or less conscious for most of his death, slipping in and out of the madness caused by slow oxygen starvation. Eventually, as the death certificate reported, his heart did stop. What the death certificate did not reflect was that between the time he received his dose and the time when his brain finally released him and his heart stopped beating, the preacher lived whole lifetimes of hell.

If anyone should have had a chance of being properly diagnosed, it might have been the preacher, because he died in a small hospital. Arsenic loves a big hospital. Its signs—the things an attending doctor can see with his eyes—and symptoms are a signature of arsenic only when they are taken together. The garlic breath, the projectile vomiting, the violent diarrhea, the oxygen starvation, the burning sensation in the hands and feet, the numbness of the hands and feet and creeping paralysis, the violent irritation of the nose and throat, the incredible distension of the stomach as the body fluids spill out into the body cavity, and then the unbelievable overall bloating of the body, so ferocious that the features of the face are lost in swelling—all of these things together can mean almost nothing but acute arsenic poisoning. Throw in a few other clues such as the Mees lines or white horizontal stripes across the fingernails that are time record of earlier doses and there can be no question. The condition can only be arsenic poisoning.

But in big modern hospitals, nothing is taken together. Everything is taken apart. A specialist is called to the bedside to consult on each symptom, on each organ system and syndrome. In that sort of contest, arsenic is almost invincible. It attacks life in so many ways and at such a fundamental biochemical level that each of its effects on the body perfectly mimics the effect of some other disease or problem. The lungs fill up so that they act and sound emphysematous; the blue-purple cyanosis of the face and cardiac arrhythmias mimic heart attack; the blood chemistry is that of a body under severe bacterial attack; the headache, dizziness, muscle weakness, convulsions, delirium, and coma can all look like the work of a savage onslaught against the brain, such as a tumor or severe infection might cause; and each specialist can be valiantly wielding his sword against his peculiar type of foe while none of them sees the larger foe looming over the entire horrible symphony of death.

If there was any single place in the United States where doctors might have been expected to be on watch for arsenic poisoning, it should have been North Carolina. Statistical studies done by the FBI's National Center for the Analysis of Violent Crime at Quantico, Virginia, have revealed that arsenic poisoning historically has been more common in the Southeastern United States than anywhere else in the nation. Nationally, murder by poison is an extremely rare crime, accounting for between five and fifteen of the fifteen thousand to twenty thousand murders that take place each year in the country. And of those five to fifteen poisonings, only a tiny share involve arsenic.

And yet, in North Carolina alone there have been more

than forty-five confirmed arsenic poisonings since 1940.

Nannie Doss of Lexington, North Carolina—a frumpy grandmother with curly hair, big black glasses, and a chipmunk smile—died in prison in 1965 while serving a life sentence for the arsenic poisoning of her husband, Sam Doss, a fifty-eight-year-old Tulsa, Oklahoma, highway worker she had married three months before killing him. A suspicious coroner found what he said was enough arsenic in Doss's body "to kill a horse."

Rebecca Case Detter, of Kernersville, North Carolina, just between Burlington and Winston-Salem, is still in prison on a life sentence for killing her husband, Donald G. Detter. She used Terro ant poison, which was arsenic-based at the time.

Sally M. Holloman of Smithfield, North Carolina, is serving a life sentence for the arsenic murder of her husband, Jasper Talton Weaver. He was dead eleven years before she was suspected. She had dosed him slowly, giving him the last few doses while he was dying in the hospital.

Susan Broadaway of Greensboro, next door to Burlington, is serving a life sentence for attempting to kill her husband by putting arsenic in his coffee in 1978.

The vast majority of North Carolina's long line of arsenic poisoners have been women, many of them in the image and style of Velma Barfield, or "Death Row Granny" as she was known in her final years. Velma Barfield looked a good deal like Nannie Doss—a large, sausage-armed woman with a friendly smile behind thick glasses. When she died by lethal injection in 1984, Velma Barfield was the first woman executed in the United States in twenty-two years. Reporters came from all over the world to interview her and invariably painted her as a pleasant, kindly, and decorous old woman.

In North Carolina's long gallery of arsenic murderers, there are the faces of few men. Robert F. Coulthard is one. Coulthard was a social climber from the wrong side of the tracks who married into a prominent High Point furniture family. Not long after marrying Sandra Lyn Coulthard, he began an extramarital affair and then took out a $351,000 life insurance policy on his wife without telling her.

One of the ironies of arsenic poisoning is that it's such a sneaky crime, and yet the people who do it often do such a clumsy job. Coulthard ordered his arsenic from a commercial supplier, had it delivered to his office and paid for it by personal check. He dosed his wife by salting it on the fast-food hamburgers to which she was addicted.

One of the most awful aspects of Sandra Coulthard's death—a slow and brutal process—was that it could have been stopped. Soon after the thirty-year-old mother of two was admitted to High Point Regional Hospital on June 26, 1988, doctors decided her symptoms "strongly suggested the possibility of heavy metal arsenic intoxication"—the medical phrase for arsenic poisoning.

The doctors ordered a blood test, even though a urine test is the accepted way to look for arsenic. They sent the blood sample to the wrong lab—to a lab that wasn't able to examine it for arsenic—but that lab sent the sample on to a lab in Van Nuys, California, that was able to test it, even though the wrong fluid had been collected.

On June 29, Sandra Coulthard was transferred to nearby Duke University Medical Center. Two days later, the California lab sent results via computer-telephone link to the High Point Regional Hospital, which she had just left, showing lethal arsenic levels in Sandra Coulthard's blood.

When the results came into the High Point computer, a technician made two hard-copy printouts. He put one of them in the mailbox of one of the doctors who had been attending Sandra Coulthard when she was at High Point, and he sent the other copy to the nursing station where she had been treated.

No one sent the results on to Duke.

In spite of the massive doses she had received, Sandra Coulthard might have lived. Once it is known that a person is suffering from arsenic poisoning, there are chemicals and drugs that can be used to stop the arsenic dead in its tracks.

But the people at Duke never found out. Neither the doctors at Duke nor Sandra Coulthard herself ever had suspicions that might lead them to the real cause. Robert Coulthard sat with his wife in the hospital and fed her the last and fatal doses in her bed.

Chapter Three

Outwardly, James Taylor was a man remade by 1969. He had stopped gambling and drinking. He worked hard and spent all of his spare time either with his family or in church work. He was heavier, balder, and a little grayer about the eyes than he had been just four years earlier, but these were the prices all men pay for the underlying calm of maturity.

Unfortunately, in James's case there was no calm beneath his surface. Inwardly, the sexual tensions of his marriage and the humiliation of being a cuckold gave him no inner rest. Finally, the forces gnawing at him within began to erupt.

One Sunday the family was dressed for church and James was helping put the girls in the backseat of the car. Blanche had not come home until four that morning and was late getting ready. Finally, she hurried from the front door of the house, still arranging the belt of her long camel-hair coat. James was standing by her side of the car. Up and down the street, other families were climbing into cars for the drive to church.

"Get in," he said. "We're late."

"I'll get in when I'm ready," she said, not even looking up, still fussing with the coat.

"Hurry up, Blanche."

"Shut up, James."

The girls watched from the backseat.

"Blanche," he muttered, "where in the God damn hell were you?"

"James," she said, "I will not have you cursing the Lord's name on a Sunday in front of these children."

James stared at her. He reached out, yanked open the car door, and shoved her inside hard with one hand. She fell into the open car and banged her face on the metal frame. She struggled to right herself, but James was pushing her with both hands now, fighting her into the car. She screamed and fought back. The neighbors stopped moving, stood by their cars, and stared.

James kicked the door shut with one leg, but Blanche had scrabbled back out by the time it latched. She was kneeling on the drive next to the car with the bottom of her coat caught in the door. She reached to get a grip on the door handle, but the angle at which she was pinned by her coat made it impossible for her to get her fingers on the handle. James stalked around to the other side, yanked open his door, got in the car, and started it up. He backed down the driveway into the street, turned the car, and then began to drive.

Blanche finally had gotten enough grip on the handle to enable her to hold her head up off the pavement, but the coat was dragging her so that her knees were scraping and banging horribly and her dress was up around her waist. The girls in the backseat could just see her shrieking face as it bobbed up into view and then disappeared under the car, over and over, over and over, all the way down the block, while the neighbors stood by their cars in their Sunday best, staring silently.

James stopped the car. He stalked around to the other side, pulled the door open, lifted Blanche by the front of the blouse, and shoved her into the car seat. Then he got back in the car and drove back home.

There was racial trouble in Burlington. The streets downtown were blockaded. The police stopped James in his car. The police officers, all of whom he knew by first name, told him he could not come through downtown without a pass. They told him there was shooting going on, and the blacks were doing a lot of it themselves.

Always emotional and excitable anyway, James went into a frenzy. He drove home as fast as he could. He didn't intend to stay home. He intended to get a gun and go back out. To do what? He didn't know. Just to be there. But by the time he got home he was pouring sweat, his hands, neck, and face were cold and clammy, and his breath was coming short. He began to feel sick and rushed to the bathroom, where he was overcome by vomiting and violent diarrhea.

The doctor told him the next day it had been a fairly serious heart attack and that he would have to slow down and take it easy if he wanted to stave off the next one.

Blanche had made some personal headway with Raymond Reid—they enjoyed talking and felt comfortable in each other's company—but they had not become sexual partners. Blanche, meanwhile, stayed on a friendly basis with Linda Reid and hired her boys to mow her lawn, a domestic chore James could no longer perform.

The walls of Raymond Reid's marriage to Linda were beginning to crumble. It was not all Raymond Reid's doing. Linda recognized her own need for some independence and had her own strong feelings about life. She was beginning to chafe under Raymond's increasingly dictatorial and impersonal style. Somehow in that shadow language married couples develop with each other, Raymond Reid conveyed to her that he would not be heartbroken if their marriage ended, and Linda Reid was close to deciding she needed to make the best of a new reality.

Blanche believed more and more strongly she had found in Raymond Reid what she always had been looking for in a man. She had a theory about it. She told a friend at work:

"I'm strong, I just always have been, I can't help it. I need to be, my family needs me, real bad, not just my girls, my brothers and sisters and my mother, they all need me, they always have. But men can't handle that, they can't handle a strong woman, they're too weak themselves. I hate a weak man. A strong woman like me needs a very strong man who can step in and ain't afraid of it, ain't afraid to take the lead of a strong woman. I think Raymond's like that."

Isla Taylor began to weaken and became bedridden midway through her eighty-third year. By November 1970, she was in and out of the hospital with an array of problems typical in elderly people, most of it heart- and lung-related. Finally on the night of November 25, with her sons and daughters beside her, she passed away. She had been slipping all day, too weak to raise a wrist. Moments before she died, Isla Taylor sat bolt upright in her bed and seemed to survey her family. In her eyes there were no pupils. Her entire eyes, including the whites, were solid balls of a brilliant cobalt blue. The arsenic had only knocked at the door of her system. Most of it lay undigested in a pool at the pit of her stomach.

The next year, in 1971, Raymond and Linda Reid separated and filed for divorce. Blanche immediately became Raymond's principal nurse-protector, counselor, and suitor. She stepped up the religious aspect of her approach to him, urging him to watch various television preachers whom she believed capable of helping him in his moment of loneliness and confusion. When Reid moved out of his house and into a small apartment, Blanche was suddenly rushing off from her own home in the predawn hours to take Raymond breakfast, "because the poor man is just helpless by himself."

None of this, of course, was lost on James Taylor. In a period of months after Raymond Reid's divorce became final, it became obvious to the other people working in the Kroger store that he and Blanche finally were having the full-blown affair she had sought for so long.

James Taylor had lived four years after his first heart attack, all of that time under its shadow, as if it were a sword suspended over him. There had been no warning of the heart attack, no reason for it. It had struck from the blue sky. So who could know what might trigger the next one? The fatal one. He could not afford rage.

In September 1973, James Taylor began to suffer symptoms of what he took for the flu—a bad sore throat, swollen glands, and the worst case of diarrhea he had ever had in his life. He finally went to the doctor when some of the symptoms seemed to be beyond what even the worst strain of flu could cause. He was developing painful blisters on his hands and feet, his hair was falling out in patches, and his face was puffy and swollen all the time. One night there was even blood in his urine and stool.

The doctor had no idea what was wrong. He ran tests, which cost money, and the bill was beginning to worry James almost as much as whatever was wrong with him. He asked the doctor several times if it could be related to his heart, and the doctor said no.

The night he died, his throat was swollen and sore. Blanche had cooked dinner, but he said he didn't think he could get it down. She came to him, felt his forehead, and comforted him. It was a rare moment of tenderness in a marriage that had gone sour years before. She talked him into eating some ice cream. He sat at the end of the table spooning it down gingerly while the rest of them ate their dinners.

Within an hour of eating, he was on his bed writhing in pain, as if an animal were within him gnawing to get out. He sat up, eyes wild with fear, and a jet of vomit shot across the room and splattered against the ceiling and wall.

His eyes went glassy and slow; he mumbled nonsensically; violent attacks of abdominal pain wrenched his body.

Vanessa, then twenty, had already moved from the family home. Cindi, fourteen, still lived with her parents. Blanche told Cindi she would have to call the doctor in the morning. She sent her to bed and made a bed for herself on the sofa in the living room. She had been suffering from diarrhea, too, in recent weeks. It was an old and familiar adversary. She lay on the sofa and listened to his long gut-rending moans and wild shouting cries of pain in the next room. Eventually, she fell asleep and dreamed.

While she slept, James died. She went in to him in the early morning and shook him. He was on his side, with his hands reaching up as if clawing the air. His face was a deep blue, almost purple. Blanche stepped out of the room and closed the door. She woke Cindi and told her her father had died. Then she went to the phone. She called Vanessa. Then she called Dot.

"I can't wake James. Will you come on down here?"

Cindi and Vanessa sat with her on the sofa while the family arrived. "Mama," Cindi said, "don't you think you should call Raymond?"

Blanche agreed that she needed to tell Mr. Reid she would not be in that day. She called him at home.

While brother Ralph was still sobbing in the room with James and the sisters were consoling each other in the living room, Raymond Reid showed up at the house. Blanche was off somewhere at the moment, not there to greet him. He motioned to Dot not to bother herself about him.

"Will you have a cup of coffee, Mr. Reid?"

"Yes, that'll be fine, Miz Kernodle," he said. While she fussed with the pot on the stove, Raymond Reid walked to the kitchen cupboard, opened a door in the middle of a long over-head cabinet, stuck his hand into the cabinet, and retrieved a cup. When he turned around, Dot was standing there with pot in hand, staring at him.

"I guess you found a cup for yourself," she said.

"Yes," he said. He put it forward to be filled. "This is a terrible thing."

The several years after James's death were the best time of Blanche's life. She and Raymond Reid grew closer, but each held on to a measure of independence. Reid kept his apartment for a while, then moved to a trailer home in Kernersville near Winston-Salem. Blanche kept her house. They worked together, slept together when there was time, and left each other alone the rest of the time. It was in many ways an ideal balance. During those years in the early 1970s, life afforded Blanche both the reassurance and the freedom she needed in order to hold her life and her personality on center.

But there were some bumps along the way. In early 1976, a money bag came up missing at the store and the police had to be called. Blanche, as the person most immediately responsible for the cash, had to be considered under suspicion by the local police and by Kroger's private investigators. But nothing ever came of it. The bag was never found, no one ever found a clue to what had happened to it, and the incident was forgotten.

Blanche was jealously private about her relationship with Raymond. One day a woman who was one of Raymond Reid's neighbors came in to shop at Kroger and stopped on her way out to trade gossip with the women at the cash registers. Blanche was not in view.

"Well I guess y'all know who Miss Blanche is spending her free time with by now?"

They did, but they pretended not to. They looked around quickly to see if she was anywhere near.

"No, who?"

"I can't believe y'all don't know. You mean she's not brag-gin' on him to you? La! She's over there 'most ever' night."

"Who is it?"

"It's your boss. Raymond Reid."

The older checkers had guessed at the affair long ago, of course, and they enjoyed knowing that the customers knew what was really going on, but they knew better than to mention any of it to Blanche.

A new, younger checker who had listened to the customer's gossip made the mistake, however, of thinking she could tease Blanche gently about it.

"I hear you and the boss are an item."

Blanche whirled, her face already dark.

"That's a lie. Who told you that?"

"A little bird," she said, trying to pass it off. But Blanche was already inches from her face, eyes wide and black.

"I said, who told you that?"

"Nobody, Blanche. Who cares? A customer."

"What customer?"

"Blanche, just forget it."

Blanche planted herself right in front of the younger woman, so that she was physically trapped against her register. The only customer in the store, an elderly man buying a loaf of bread, looked over, ducked his head, and hurried out.

"If you want to keep your goddam job, honey, you better tell me who told you about Raymond and me."

The other women watched in silence. Blanche could make good on her threat. It was the one threat they had seen her carry out before.

Most of the time, the cashiers accepted the deal with Blanche. She would pry and pry into their lives, dredging for juicy details. Sometimes she would adopt the role of a com-forting mother, helping them deal with the problems she had uncovered. Sometimes she would use her knowledge to ridicule them. But if any of them ever made the mistake the young one had made and expressed any curiosity about or knowledge of Blanche's life, it would be hell to pay. The best thing to do with Blanche, they all believed, was stay as far away from her as possible. Let the men have her.

In spite of the poverty of James Taylor's estate, Blanche was able somehow to come up with enough cash to make a down payment on a new split-level brick house at 341 Hamilton Street in the Greenacres subdivision of Burlington. She always managed to dress herself and Cindi in new, expensive-looking clothing, and she always managed to drive a new car.

From the moment James died, Blanche never visited, called, or had another thing to do with the Taylor family. She had been a member of the family for twenty-one years.

The Taylors still saw Cindi and Vanessa around Burlington and sought them out whenever possible, even asking them to family events on rare occasions. They made a number of efforts to reach Blanche in the first year after James's death and then stopped trying.

It was a dark time for Raymond Reid. He got along badly with his ex-wife for a while after the divorce, which put some inevitable strain on his relationship with his boys. Whatever else might come his way, Raymond Reid was never going to give up his sons.

Raymond Reid always made time for his boys. He started a coin collection for them, and each time he brought them to the trailer to show them an acquisition, he always made a point of showing them he had two identical specimens of whatever new coin he had bought.

"See," he'd say. "Here is one for Ray. And here is one just like it for Stevie."

He kept the collection in his strongbox. It was understood but unspoken that the coins would come to the boys only when he died.

Raymond Reid was a man of strict routines and very focused interests. Almost all of his focus was on work. His idea of a terrific day was to go to work early, work very hard all day long, go home, watch television and eat dinner on a tray, and then go to bed with Blanche.

Blanche coaxed him out of his rut whenever she could. North Carolina offered engaging distractions. On weekends she drew Raymond into her car, put the girls in the backseat, and made the hour-long drive to the mountains. In the fall, the Blue Ridge Mountains could be a whirling circus of color. Little roads wound through snug villages where people sold apples out of baskets.

They were both loyal parents to their children. Raymond Reid always found his way to his sons and always succeeded in convincing them he loved them, no matter what problems there may have been in his marriage to their mother. The Reid boys were growing up handsome, smart, and well-behaved.

Raymond Reid played cards down at the Moose Hall, the way James Taylor had. And he drank. But there was a big difference. Raymond Reid was not a drunk. And when Raymond Reid played cards, he won.

Raymond regretted the distance he sometimes felt between himself and his sons, but, with that exception, his life was what he wanted. He had his work. He had a good-looking woman. Everything in Raymond Reid's life was right.

The only exception to that rule was the Church Street Kroger store. It was not producing the numbers the company believed it needed to see in order to keep it open. The regional manager, Kevin Denton, came down several times to go over the books and see if there was any obvious problem he could spot. But there was none. The store wasn't doing well. It was just one of those things.

Kevin Denton enjoyed his trips to Burlington. Visiting the troops and letting them feel a shudder of foreboding when he arrived at the door was part of what Kevin Denton liked about his job. He was Kroger all the way, too, like Raymond, but he was the other kind of Kroger executive, a college man—distinguished, handsome, with a distinctly military air. There were only two modes in his relationship with his underlings. He could be chilly and formal, which he was most of the time. Or he could be raunchy, randy, football-player-raucous, in an aggressive fashion that obligated his underlings to laugh uproariously while they still felt a shudder of fear.

He bragged to Raymond Reid about his own looks: "A guy with my looks can usually fuck just about any woman he wants to."

Raymond told Blanche later: "It embarrasses me so much for a man in his position to talk like that about himself. I just would think he would know how to act better than that."

Denton was especially aggressive with the women who worked in his stores. He was the kind of man who liked to repeat jokes he had heard elsewhere—the more sexually explicit the better. He was famous for reprimanding a cashier harshly one minute and then telling her a bawdy story and waiting for her to laugh the next.

Blanche couldn't stay away from him.

When people dropped off film to be developed that included shots of naked people, the development company returned the negatives with a prim red tag notifying the person that his or her film was "Unsuitable for Printing." Blanche made it her hobby to watch for those tags and pry open the envelopes as soon as they arrived.

On one occasion, a resident of Burlington who recently had visited a nude bathing beach in Europe took his film to the Kroger store to be developed, and it was returned with a red tag on a day when Denton was visiting the store. Raymond Reid stood by grinning sheepishly while Blanche and Denton held the negatives up to the overhead fluorescent lights, grinning and giggling like adolescents at the images.

In 1977, Denton decided to close the Burlington store. He demoted Reid to an assistant manager and sent him to Martinsville, Virginia. Blanche was given a job as cashier, but not head cashier, at the Kroger store on High Point Road in Greensboro, just a half hour west of Burlington.

It was a very brief demotion. Kevin Denton didn't know Raymond Reid very well or care much one way or the other about him personally, but he knew he was a good store manager. The problem in Burlington had to do with real estate and the surrounding market, not the store manager.

Three months after the transfer to Martinsville, Denton moved Reid again, this time to Durham, forty miles east of Burlington, where Denton gave him command of his own store again. He left Blanche where she was.

Blanche took the whole thing badly. She schemed and finagled until she got herself transferred to Durham with Raymond—a long commute, for North Carolina, almost an hour each way from her house, but she was a head cashier again.

In 1983, Kroger built a large beautiful new store on Battleground Road in Greensboro. The store, named after the road it was on, was a major new facility for Kroger, built with an eye toward consolidating management and distribution operations in the area around Burlington, Greensboro, High Point, and Winston-Salem. The offices of the regional management staff were moved to the store from another older building on Kung Avenue.

Raymond Reid was one of three men brought in as coman-

agers, just beneath the manager. It was a small step backward for
Raymond, but he brought Blanche with him as head cashier,
which made her very happy. It meant that Raymond, Blanche,
and Kevin Denton were now all working together at the same
location.

Whenever Denton was in the store, Blanche fluttered to
his side like a moth to a lamp. Raymond saw it but ignored it.
Denton was Raymond's boss, two tiers up.

Finally one day Denton asked her. "Hey, Blanche, honey.
What's the deal with you and Raymond now, anyway?"

"Raymond?" she said lightly. "He ain't my boyfriend anymore, if that's what you mean. He's too short, and he's let
himself get too fat."

It was true that Raymond Reid was putting on weight. He
was in his late forties. He wasn't the type to run or play tennis.
Raymond Reid worked and watched television. He had become
more focused on his job as the years went by. He had taken to
carrying a concealed voice-activated tape recorder on his person
so that he could document all conversations, with employees,
customers, and his own superiors. He kept copious personnel
files and maintained an immaculate record of all his own memos
and other official intercourse with management. He thought
about work a great deal of the time.

He also wanted Blanche to marry him. Raymond had
grown tired of their arrangement. He didn't understand why
Blanche wouldn't want to cement their relationship, and he
sometimes lost his temper over it in conversations with her.

Blanche, in the meantime, was circling Kevin Denton, with
intentions that were difficult to read. Denton had taken her
remarks about no longer being Raymond Reid's girlfriend as a
serious come-on, and a serious come-on with Kevin Denton was
serious business indeed. He thought nothing of walking up to
women employees in the Battleground store who had never
given him the slightest encouragement and grabbing their bot-
toms or their breasts. Denton was one reason Raymond was
spending so much time lately worrying over his tapes and his
files. The women in the store were growing restive.

Some of the women had sex with Denton. Some of them
made it obvious to Denton that he had better keep his distance.
Blanche was always somewhere just in the middle, hovering
and flirting but drawing away.

That was more than Denton could understand. In his book, Blanche had come on strong. That meant she wanted him. His favorite ploy, when he wanted sex with one of the women in the store and had decided she wanted him, was to call her to his office. When he sat at his desk, he kept his back to the door. He would wait until the woman he was after was in the office, tell her to shut the door, and then swing around laughing in his chair with his erect penis in his hand.

Some of the women complied. Some told him to stay the hell away or there would be major union trouble. But Blanche, fine-looking Blanche, was always a question mark, giggling and coaxing but never putting out.

Sometimes the teasing between them got very hot. She caught him at the back of the store one day and said, "Mr. Denton, I thought about you last night."

"You did? What were you doing when you thought about me, Blanche?"

"I was over at Linda Lambert's. I spent the night over there to get away from my girls and from Raymond."

"Whaddja do over there? Have a pajama party?"

"Yeah, we did. Only we didn't wear no pajamas. We just walked around in our bras and our panties all night. We were looking at *Playgirl*."

"*Playgirl*? What were you looking at in there? Pictures of men's things?"

"Maybe."

Denton looked around. They were alone at the back of the store. He splayed his legs a little and nodded down toward a bulge in his own crotch. "You want to feel something big, feel of that, why don't you?"

Blanche stepped forward to him and ran the fingertips of one hand lightly over the erection inside his pants.

"You want to see it?" he asked.

"No, I'm afraid if I saw it and told these other girls around here, they'd never let you alone."

He dropped his hand down to the pants of her uniform and clutched her between the legs. She giggled, pushed away, and flitted back to the front of the store.

Chapter Four

In early 1985, Blanche's old nemesis of merciless diarrhea returned, and she had trouble sleeping. She thought it had to do with money, in part, and with her station in life. She complained to other women at the store that Raymond would have a generous retirement income and money in the bank waiting for him when he retired but she would have little to show for her years of loyal service.

After her father's death, she had begun attending the church of an odd, pudgy little preacher who conducted exorcisms in a farmhouse far out in the country, surrounded by tobacco fields on three sides and a bare dirt yard in front. The preacher disappeared in 1984, just after Christmas, abandoning his wife and small children.

Blanche was riven when the man reappeared months later and, in asking his flock to take him back, confessed that he was a homosexual.

"Oh my good God almighty," she wailed on the phone to another woman in the church. "The man's a queer! How can

they be so wicked? How can men be so wicked and vile before
the Lord? Preacher men! Preacher men! And the man is a
damned queer!"

Just after the Christmas season, in January 1985, Blanche
called Raymond and told him her new split-level house was on
fire and that she had called the Burlington Fire Department.
He jumped into his car and raced over. He could smell the
smoke five blocks away, and when he rounded the corner, yellow flames were lighting up the night sky.

Raymond rushed to Blanche, who was standing on the lawn
in her work clothes. She was trembling, her eyes wild but dry.
She turned and entered the house, which was still burning, but
the fire was under control. All of the firemen and police officers
knew her, and none of them had the nerve to tell her not to
enter her own house. Raymond followed.

She walked down the smoke-blackened corridor to her bedroom in the back. She stood in the door with Raymond behind
her, staring into the room. There, scorched and blackened,
soaked from the hoses and splotched by falling soot, were all
of Blanche's fancy brassieres, silk panties, and sexy teddies,
dozens of them, strewn around the room.

"It was a pervert done this, Raymond," she said in an oth-
erworldly monotone. "I saw him out in the yard. He was a man.
He was in my yard today. I asked him what he wanted. He said
he was driving a three-wheeler up in the woods with his son
and lost his wallet. He kept looking at me. He's the one done
this, I'm sure."

"Did you know him, Blanche?" a young police detective
asked, notebook in hand.

"No, Bob, I didn't. I never seen him before in my life.
That's the reason why I think his story about the three-wheeler
was a lie. I never saw nobody out there on a three-wheeler, or
heard it even."

The police and the arson investigators from the fire department agreed it was a deliberately set fire with sexual over-
tones, probably set by the unidentified stranger Blanche had
seen in her yard.

A few weeks after the fire, Blanche went to Raymond at
work and told him she would have to take time off.

"The fire has just upset me so bad. I can't sleep, I can't
eat. The diarrhea is so bad, Raymond, I just can't be out on

the floor five minutes. My hair is coming out in hanks. It's terrible."

"So you're going to take off."

"Well, yes, for a little while. Until this gets better or calms down or something."

"You're taking sick leave then."

"I'm taking off, Raymond. I can't work."

"So that's sick leave. You'll have to get a note from a doctor to say you can't work."

"Well, you know I can't work."

"Blanche. Honey. I cannot put you in for the time if I do not have a note from a doctor to put in the file, and even then, it goes straight to Denton, who sends it straight to headquarters for evaluation."

"Well, I'll see a doctor, then."

She told Raymond a week later that her doctor had confirmed she needed to take a sick leave and had also told her to move out of her house permanently, rather than try to rebuild it.

"Well, where are you going to live, Blanche?"

"I'm gonna buy me a trailer house up in that park off Deep Creek Church Road near where Cindi lives."

"What are you going to use to pay for it? I thought you were broke."

"I have a little bit. I got paid for the fire, you know."

"No, I didn't know. You never told me."

"I got paid a little bit."

She had received a considerable settlement from her insurance company. She sold the house as it stood, paid off her note, bought the new mobile home northwest of town off Deep Creek Church Road, and still had enough left to invest in a small business venture. She decided that she, her daughters, and her new sons-in-law would buy a few used house trailers, refurbish them, and sell them at a profit.

In addition to going into business with her children, Blanche pressured her daughters and sons-in-law to come to her house trailer for family get-togethers. On one occasion, one son-in-law attended a Sunday lunch and brought a male friend along.

Over delicious scratch-made chicken and dumplings, Blanche chattered away to the handsome young stranger about things she had heard Jimmy Swaggart say the night before, about the love of Jesus and how you can see it in a person's face.

Then after the meal, as the young man stood next to her, alone with her in the kitchen, dish towel in hand, Blanche said: "You know what you really need? You need a really good blow job."

The man paled, stuttered, backed away slightly.

"Pardon me, ma'am?"

"You heard me right, honey. A young man like you, probably running with these young girls, they don't have no idea how to give a man a good blow job. If I went down on you, it'd probably kill you. You probably couldn't handle it."

The young man made a stumbling, embarrassed escape from the trailer house, leaving Blanche's daughters and sons-in-law wondering what she had done this time.

Raymond was beginning to grow restless. He had no business telling her what to do—she wasn't his wife. She had always been odd in certain ways. But something about Blanche was no longer adding up.

One night barely a month after the fire, while she was still on sick leave, Raymond came to pick Blanche up at the trailer home. She had been pressuring him to attend evening church with her, and Raymond finally had caved in and agreed to go. It was a major concession.

She was still on sick leave. It seemed odd that she could attend long raucous church services and sing hymns with the familiar Kiser family gusto and still claim to be unable to work, but Raymond said nothing about that. On this evening, as on more and more occasions recently, however, he was not in a chipper mood when he came to pick her up. He waited while she fussed in the bedroom, and he reminded her they were late.

The sun was just setting as they drove off. Raymond looked in his rearview mirror and suddenly jammed on his brakes. Blanche stared straight ahead and said nothing, as if waiting for him to get going again.

"Blanche! Your trailer's on fire!"

"No, it's not," she said, without looking.

"Blanche, there's flames coming out of the bedroom window!"

She made a half turn and said, "No, I think that's just the sun reflecting on it. Let's get going or we'll be late."

Raymond stared at her. He began to wrench the car around in the middle of the road. "Blanche, are you crazy? Your damn trailer is on fire! Look, there's smoke!" He gunned the engine and raced back toward it.

"Oh, dammit," she said. "It must have been that pervert again."

When they got back to the trailer, Raymond pushed his way cautiously inside and was hit by a blast of heat, smoke, and noxious gases coming from the bedroom end. He let the air clear and then forced his way back to the bedroom. He found the fire licking up from a circle at the foot of the bed. He raced back to the kitchen, grabbed an extinguisher, and put it out.

A fair amount of damage had been done already by the fire and the smoke. There, in a little pile in front of Blanche's open closet, were the remains of a large wax candle. Around it were the black ropy remnants of melted synthetic-fiber undergarments that had been piled around the candle.

A month later, Blanche came into a second tidy settlement from her unlucky fire insurance carrier.

Eventually Raymond told Blanche she had to come back to work. Denton had told Raymond to cut off her leave and get her back in the store. When she did return, she ran straight to Denton.

"Oh, Mr. Denton," she said, "I tell you. I just feel so sexy today. I can't stand it. I don't know what's wrong with me lately. I just feel so horny all the time. I swear. I feel like if I was a man, I'd have a hard-on."

"Well, let me see, Blanche," he said, grinning and swaggering up. "Maybe I better check and see if you do." He cupped his hand between her legs and rubbed up and down. "That feels too soft to me to be a hard-on."

"Oh, Mr. Denton," she giggled, yielding slightly to his hand. "You shouldn't ought to be carrying on like this."

A week later, Blanche presented herself at the law office of James F. Walker, Douglas Hoy, and John R. Kernodle. Hoy listened to her long chronicle of incidents in which she felt she had been sexually harassed by Kevin Denton. She told him that Denton frequently made references to her job security and her ability to retire, while making sexual advances. After some consideration of her claims, Hoy and Walker suggested to Blanche that she needed to seek counseling from a licensed psychiatrist.

They also agreed to take Blanche's case on a contingency basis, meaning they would sue Kroger and not charge her any money unless they won. By visiting a psychiatrist over a period of months, Blanche would be able to establish a medical record of physical and emotional complaints—a record that would help the lawyers in their own efforts to amass ammunition for a trial.

Blanche chose Dr. Jesse McNiel of Burlington, a big, pleasant, slow-talking man with a manner that was much more good-old-boy than Freudian. She didn't tell Raymond that she had seen the lawyers or that she was seeing McNiel. She told him nothing.

Whether or not Raymond had entertained any doubt about the first fire, he knew Blanche had set the second one. But he could not discuss it with her. Any mention of the fires was across that line she defended so ferociously, the line that separated her own prying curiosity about everybody else from her extreme, often angry defense of her own secrets.

There was one woman at work, Helen Dearman, with whom Raymond could speak as a friend.

"I know she set it," he said. "I don't know what's wrong with Blanche. I wish sometimes she'd just marry me, and maybe that would settle her down, whatever's wrong with her."

Helen was a big woman with dyed bright yellow hair that she wore in a spray-lacquered helmet. Her face was pudgy and rough, but her eyes were a clear and friendly green. "Raymond," she said, shaking her head slightly and looking down, "you need to watch out for Blanche. Blanche just ain't all there."

"Oh yes she is," he said. "Blanche just needs to settle down and quit being so nervous and high-strung."

The visits to Dr. McNiel put Blanche in an unaccustomed posture. The arrangement called for her to talk and for him to listen.

"My husband, James, had a heart attack when he was forty," she told him on the first visit, "and then he died of another one when he was forty-five. I have been quite religious all my life, or I was. I was very active in the First Disciples until the fire. After that, I just lost my interest in religion.

"On January 23rd, somebody broke into my house. The only thing they bothered was my underwear, my panties and my bras and such. Whoever it was, the fire broke out while they was in the house. It started from an oil lamp that the robber dropped. I had to stay in that house myself after that. Dr. McNiel, I just can't imagine why somebody would do something like that to me.

"Then I started having this sexual harassment on my job. I'm not staying in my house even at present, I'm staying with my daughter. I'm just too upset. I have diarrhea all the time, my hair's falling out."

On Monday of the week before Easter Sunday, one of Blanche's sisters called. Her husband had been in the hospital for several weeks, dying of cancer. Every year over the course of their long marriage, Blanche's sister and her husband had gone back to the little hamlet of Carolina where he was born, just outside of Burlington, to attend the Easter-morning sunrise service at the Carolina United Church of Christ.

Now this year, for the first time, he would be unable to go back. Blanche's sister wanted to attend the service for him, and she asked Blanche to accompany her.

The annual Easter sunrise service that year was going to be a major occasion for the Rev. Dwight Moore, who had taken over as pastor of the Carolina United Church of Christ earlier that year. He knew the service was especially important to the people of the little mill village high on the bluffs above the Haw River—more important sentimentally, perhaps, than the Christmas service.

It was very important to Dwight Moore to make a good impression. He felt he had been gaining the confidence of the parish, and he wanted to cement the relationship.

It would be an occasion when he could lead his flock in a moment of special personal and religious communion. They would gather in the dark in the cemetery at the top of the high hill. As the sun rose over the headstones, lighting up the silver billows of fog rising off the Haw River far below, he would begin to preach the story of the Risen Lord.

It would be a moment when blood and soil and religious

faith all flowed together. There would be tears of joy. Later, there would be breakfast back at the church hall—laughter and joking. The experience would fill and strengthen the souls of the members.

He loved them. They were just what the doctor had ordered for his own wounded soul. They were his people, and he understood them from the ground up, knew what made them tick and what they needed.

With the sharp eye of a seasoned clergyman, Dwight Moore had quickly figured out the basic social geography of his little church. There were 134 members in seventy households. A good many of the members were elderly people, widows and widowers who lived alone in their own homes, watched over and assisted by the extended family of the church.

One had to know the history of the community to understand that these would be somewhat defensive people with just the slightest tinge of an inferiority complex, a mill-town mentality, fearful of the outside, resistant to change, but sharply protective of anyone attacked or affronted by an outsider. Just beneath that level, the church was divided into four or five typical North Carolina clans.

When the day arrived, the weather, the sunrise, and the setting conspired to provide Dwight with a flawless backdrop for his moment of magic. He preached the story of Simon Peter, who denied three times on the day of the Crucifixion that he even knew Jesus Christ. The moment he denied Jesus the third time, a rooster crowed. Peter remembered Jesus had told him, "Before the cock crows, you will deny me three times."

From her seat near the back, Blanche watched intently while Dwight preached. He was not at all the kind of preacher she usually liked. As soon as he opened his mouth, telling the story of Simon Peter in a soft, thoughtful voice, Blanche was certain that Dwight Moore had never cast out a demon in his life.

"Imagine how unusual it was for a rooster even to be there, right in the middle of a big city," Dwight said in hushed dramatic tones. "Have you ever heard a rooster crow in the middle of a big bustling city?"

Dwight paused to allow the silence of the graveyard to fill in around his audience. But in the middle of the silence, Blanche spoke up loudly from the back:

"Yes," she said. "In fact, I've heard roosters in cities a lot. A lot of people in cities keep roosters."

There was a rustling in the crowd as people turned and stretched to see who had spoken. Through an open channel in the little crowd of heads, Dwight Moore caught his first glimpse of Blanche Taylor, who at fifty-two years was still beautiful and unusually youthful in appearance.

Dwight did what he could to pick up the thread again. He beat a hurried retreat to the end of his sermon. But the service and setting were so beautiful that few of the flock even noticed he had lost his rhythm.

He made a beeline for her at the breakfast in the fellowship hall following the service. Above the clatter of dishes and scraping of chairs in the little hall, he said, "Hello, I'm Dwight Moore."

"Blanche Taylor, Reverend Moore," she said, extending a hand and smiling sweetly. "So pleased to meet you."

"It's a pleasure to have you."

"This is my sister, Temperance. She and her husband come every year for the sunrise service."

"It's a great pleasure to have you here, Temperance."

"Don't waste too much time on that one, preacher," a man cracked from the end of the table, nodding at Temperance. "She's married. It's her sister there that's single."

There was an explosion of mirth, giggling, and pretended shock at the man's joke.

"Well, they're both so attractive, they'd have to be sisters, I guess," Dwight said.

"Now Reverend, I already told you once what the difference is between 'em."

There was more laughter and tittering. Dwight smiled his broad, beaming, boyish smile and then moved off through the crowd to play host and preacher to the multitude. Blanche watched with a frank eye on his behind.

Chapter Five

By Tuesday, Dwight had found out where Blanche lived. In the accepted custom of small-town and rural preachers, he appeared at her house that day unannounced to pay a pastoral call. But she was not there. The sky was dark and threatening. He left his card in the door. He decided to postpone the rest of the morning's calls and return to his little parsonage behind the church.

He sat at the desk he kept in the parsonage, away from the church office and the church telephone. He looked out the window. Rain was beginning to melt against the glass. He remembered that long funeral he had conducted at his last church, the Warwick United Church of Christ in Newport News, Virginia.

A storm had come up suddenly. One minute, the only sounds had been the soft dovelike sobbing of the old women standing nearest the edge of the grave and the creaking of the winch, lowering the coffin down slowly into the waiting concrete vault below. Then booming thunder had erupted high over the horizon, a wash of purple had flooded the sky, lightning had split the air above them, and thick bullets of rain had come driving down all around, splashing in the raw red dirt at the grave's edge, speckling the brilliant blue surface of the coffin as it descended beneath their feet.

They all looked up from the coffin to the rain. They all hesitated for a moment, staring at Dwight Moore, waiting for him to give a sign whether he was through or not. The tears of those who had been crying were lost in the rain on their faces. Lorene, his wife, looked at him. He nodded to them through the driving rain. He was finished. He had completed the funeral service and burial of his oldest parishioner. Now the congregation were gathered around his wife, waiting. Waiting for Dwight to leave. It had been almost two weeks since he had stood before the assembled church on a Sunday morning and resigned. Now, with uplifted faces, slick with rain, at the edge of the grave, they waited for him to go away.

He drove back to the home of the parishioners who had been putting him up for the last several days. It would be awkward. They would offer to help him pack his car. He would decline. It would be awkward, but everything had been so awkward. It had been ten days since he and Lorene had met for lunch. They had discussed what needed to be done concerning the children, Doug and Deborah. As all their meetings had been in the last month, the lunch was quiet, polite, very somber, and, they thought afterward, when each of them was able to think about it, terribly sad. Everything had been so sad.

They had driven together to the home of the chairman of the board of trustees. He had asked Dwight to give him all of his keys to the parsonage and the church, and he had asked Lorene to do the same. But the moment they arrived, the chairman had greeted Dwight with the news that his loyal and beloved old parishioner had died. It is not easy for a minister to leave, even in disgrace.

Perhaps it really was not disgrace. Perhaps that was why they held on to him, persuaded him to stay and conduct this last funeral. He was the one who had said he could not stay with them, in view of all that had happened. He and Elaine had broken the news of their relationship to the parish. It had not been the other way around. They hadn't been found out, ferreted out of hiding and held at bay. Dwight had even imagined somehow, back when he and Elaine had first made the decision to go public, that he was going to be able to remain the minister.

People who are not familiar with the Protestant denominations often take the United Church of Christ for a fundamentalist church. It actually is a descendant of the old Congregational Church and is quite liberal. But in his heart of hearts, Dwight knew how little that really meant. He was one of the church's pastors out in the far provinces where the real battles had to be fought. When he stopped kidding himself, he knew how little bearing the intellectualism and liberalism at the center of his church had to do with life in the parishes, life in the real world.

It wasn't as if the real world were such a shock to him, either. Born in 1934, Dwight Moore was the son of a tobacco farmer in Rockingham County in North Carolina. He and his brothers and sisters had squatted in forty-eight-hour shifts outside the ancient log tobacco barns on his father's farm, tending the wood-fired furnaces that nursed the tobacco leaves hanging inside through their delicate curing process. When he completed Bethany High School, he went off to Bible College in Cleveland, Ohio. He came back to North Carolina, to Elon College just outside Burlington. It was a good religious school of Quaker origins. He met Lorene there. She was studying music. They graduated together, then Dwight went on to divinity school at Duke.

At Duke his teachers worked hard to make Dwight Moore a complicated man. It was a task they knew well. They saw these bright, sturdy lads and young ladies come down from the tobacco patches all the time, and they knew that some of them had potential, some were capable of being shaken and jolted free from the blinders forced on them by their country fundamentalist backgrounds. Dwight was the perfect case. He left Duke and went out to his ministry with far more doubt and much less religious certainty than he had brought with him to Duke. His teachers were gratified. He would do well someday.

Dwight Moore didn't have to tax himself to remember what real life was really all about, here in Virginia or two hundred miles south in Rockingham County. His revelation to the parish of his sixteen-year affair with Elaine, the church secretary, and the mess that had followed the revelation—all of it together was more than any small middle-class Protestant church was going to live with for long.

In those long fevered meetings with Elaine when they were working it all out, the plan had been that Lorene and the children would move out of the parsonage after a time, and Elaine, after leaving her husband, would move in. It was one of those completely cockeyed ideas that somehow look believable when two people have been putting each other under intense pressure over a period of years to resolve a situation that is absolutely and fundamentally insoluble.

There is no way to solve the dilemma of a minister who carries out a clandestine relationship with his secretary for sixteen years. There is no way to resolve the dilemma of the secretary, who is married and has children of her own but nevertheless resents being the minister's concubine and servant, instead of being his wife. No way to solve the problem of the two families, who have always been close and have spent a great deal of social time together; no way to fix things for the church people, who always have taken their minister for a kind, very proper, shyly intelligent paragon of virtue.

But they kept talking about it, kept talking about ways they would fix it. Finally they came up with this crazy plan. They would make a clean breast of it. Dwight would tell Lorene he had been having an affair with his secretary for sixteen years. Lorene would be angry. Eventually, however, Lorene would see that she was the one, with her teaching job in the public schools, who could afford to go out and rent a new home. Dwight would need to stay in the parsonage.

Elaine would tell her husband. He would be angry. But what was he going to do about it? And Elaine had said repeatedly that their marriage had ended in spirit years before.

The church members would be upset for a while. But they all loved Dwight, especially some of the older members, who were so important to the church. Who would forget his long years of service, the nights spent sitting hand-in-hand with the dying, the marriages and the late-night counseling? Surely Dwight would be able to ride out the initial shock and keep the church, but with Elaine as his wife instead of Lorene.

So they made their announcements. And no sooner had it been done than all of it began to crumble around them. Dwight wasn't sure how. He had become panic-stricken at one moment

and tried to go back to Lorene. She refused. When he returned
to Elaine, she accused him of making her his second choice. In
the meantime, Elaine and her husband had reconciled.

No such luck at the Moore residence. Lorene made it plain
to Dwight that his announcement had ended their relationship
forever. It made no difference what the church secretary decided. Lorene was moving out immediately, she was taking the
children, and there would be no reconciliation.

And then all of a sudden it was obvious—so obvious—that
there was absolutely no way the church was going to live with
this situation. The parishioners did love Dwight enough that
they were not going to come to him and tell him right away.
But they were people who came from the same soil and the
same blood as he. This was too much for them. They would
wait for him to see it.

He did. He saw that he would have to leave, of course. He
and his wife made all the necessary arrangements, concluding
with their last lunch together and the drive over to the home
of the chairman.

Then this final funeral had come up. He had to stay. A
lady in the church who always had cared especially for him
offered to let Dwight stay at her house until after the service.
He had hoped it would all be taken care of and the dear departed would be safely interred in a couple of days, but of course
this turned out to be one of those situations where the relatives
were all scattered to the winds and were not able to get to
Newport News quickly. The deceased parishioner had lan-
guished at the funeral home while Dwight was down the street,
languishing in the church lady's house, waiting to get this last
burial done so he could begin his exile.

Finally he was on the road, 220 miles of it through the
mountains of Virginia and northern North Carolina. The rain
never slowed. The storm grew more dense and angry as he
drove. The windshield wipers beat a hissing tom-tom on the
body of the car, as the car scuttled low-backed and wet down
two-lane highways between dense walls of forest. In the dry
interior of the car, his eyes were clouded with tears.

His life felt completely empty. It was all gone. He thought
back through all of it, his entire life. His father, Robert Lee
Moore, had wanted him to stay on the farm. Dwight had a
green thumb, his father said. But he had devoted himself in-

stead to his ministry, and now that was gone. His church was gone—the sixteen years of intricate building, nurturing, weaving of relationships that make a parish—all of it vanished somewhere behind him in this awful storm.

His wife. His bright, purposeful son. His funny, warm, adorable daughter, always having a time with this or that, always finding her way around whatever it was. His family was gone.

But in all of it, the worst was Elaine. He kept trying to work the puzzle again and again. It had been she, he felt, who had sought him out in the first place. It had been she who had pressed and pressed for an end to their marriages and an open relationship. It had been she who had vowed they would make it together.

And then, just when he was at his most exposed, when he had risked everything, when he was absolutely naked before his God and humankind, she had dumped him. Just like that. Or had it been his fault for faltering? He kept trying to work it out, plunging on down through the storm toward North Carolina, biting back tears and stooping his head to see through the rain.

At eleven o'clock that night he pulled up the long dirt drive into his father's farm in Rockingham County. The headlights of his car caught corners of the old log tobacco barns lurking beneath the trees. He saw his new brother-in-law Howard's bee boxes out under the sourwood trees and found something comforting in them. Dwight was a beekeeper, too.

Dwight's elderly father and his stepmother both came to the door at the side porch and threw on the light when they heard his car. His father hobbled out through the rain and helped Dwight carry in his things. His stepmother offered him soup, which he declined. His father offered him the leathered hand of an old tobacco farmer, holding his hand and keeping it there for a moment, just long enough to let the warmth and support of a loving father pass through without words.

Dwight's siblings had found careers and positions in life that were either more lucrative or at least more stable than the life of a preacher. The tobacco farm his father had hoped Dwight would stay and work was now being farmed for rent by a stranger. But Robert Lee Moore was equally proud of all of his children. He himself had started with nothing, had married a woman who had a piece of land in her dowry, and with this meager start he had built one of those wonders of rural North Carolina—a clan-strong family, possessed only of purpose and fiber but as good and respectable and well educated a family as any a rich man might engender. He took Dwight back into his house without a question.

Dwight stayed with his father for a week. He walked the old farm, surveying where grass and young trees had reclaimed land on which his father had raised crops. Tobacco is a demanding crop that has never quite surrendered to mechanization. The new plants have to be raised in sheltered soil, and then when they have achieved a certain amount of strength, they must be dug up one by one and transplanted to larger fields.

Later the mature plants are harvested by hand, a leaf at a time as they ripen. The leaves are tied together, two or three in a bundle, and hung upside down from poles across the rafters of the curing barns, where they are cured in intense heat for one to two days. In the old days, when Dwight and his brothers and sisters were growing up, the heat in the barns was from wood-burning stoves. Farmers in North Carolina often use the same old log barns their great-grandfathers used, but the wood-fueled heating systems have been replaced with natural gas heaters.

When the leaves are cured, they are graded and taken to auction, where a buyer chooses them a leaf at a time. The long rigorous process, when it works well, yields the finest cigarette tobacco in the world. Nearby Winston-Salem is headquarters of the R. J. Reynolds Tobacco Company, namesake of two of its most famous brands, and site of a huge cigarette-making plant. Sometimes on a humid evening, all of Winston-Salem smells like a newly opened package of fresh unfiltered American cigarettes. It's a sweet-smelling bouquet that has set the standard for tobacco products all over the world. North Carolina tobacco, raised by hand on little farms by descendants of the pioneers, is worth enough to send large families of children to college and to provide retirement and decent health care for their parents. That's what they mean when they call it their "cash crop." Small wonder the tobacco farmers hold on to their industry with ferocious loyalty, no matter what the Surgeon General says.

But farming was out of the question for Dwight. He was a

minister, a priest, a preacher. No matter what had happened, he could not simply walk away from what he was.

His sister Nola made a proposal. She had only recently married Howard Halbrook. Both of them had houses, and they were living in hers. Howard's house in nearby Reidsville was vacant. It was a pleasant ranch-style brick home just outside of town, with some acreage in the back and with Howard's bee-keeping and honey-bottling shop in the basement. Dwight could stay there and putter around until he found his direction again.

Dwight lived in the house for a year. The national denom-inational leadership of his church suggested he take a pastoral training course at North Carolina Baptist Hospital in Winston-Salem. It really was a combination counseling course and ther-apy: he counseled patients for three months, during which time he was interviewed himself by trained counselors.

North Carolina Baptist Hospital is encamped on a hill. From a distance, on a cool fall day when its stacks are blowing white steam, it is Dickensian, a cross between a hasty military fortification and a medieval village. It is the teaching hospital associated with the Bowman Gray School of Medicine at Wake Forest University. Like most megahospitals, it is actually a com-munity of many hospitals linked together by color-coded lines on the floor and a central billing system. Beneath its jumbled external appearance, North Carolina Baptist is by every mea-sure a state-of-the-art medical kingdom, in terms of both the basic technological plant and the faculty of doctors, nurses, and technicians who work there—all of whom have been gathered from around the nation and world, from wherever people on the medical and scientific A-lists may be found.

It was an exciting, challenging atmosphere for Dwight, and he responded to it with energy and commitment. The church was pleased with his performance there.

Invitations began to come his way to do what is called "sup-ply" in the church business—that is, he was asked to fill in for vacationing ministers around the area or to assist ministers on special occasions. It got him out and around, put him back in the pulpit preaching to people and back in the churchyard pumping hands and listening to an occasional problem or com-plaint. In the course of that long year, Dwight Moore healed.

Toward the end of that time, Dwight began to date. Women liked Dwight. Church women adored him. But any woman would have given him a second look, once he shook off his stoop-shouldered grief. Over six feet tall, graceful and rangy, well-spoken, blessed with an easy Jimmy Stewart grin, often witty, always plain, never coarse, with impeccable manners, capable of telling a sharp joke with the best of them, Dwight Moore was what Southerners really mean when they call a man a gentleman. Dwight Moore was a manly man who used his wisdom to help other people feel better about life, and that made him irresistible to females.

Finally at the end of his long mourning, his bitterness and self-recrimination, the sun shone through to Dwight Moore's path, and he was given another parish. The Carolina United Church of Christ had been without a minister for some time, and the church people heard there was a United Church of Christ clergyman in the area who was without a church. Shyly, they invited him, and just as shyly he showed up to be interviewed by the board.

The tiny community of Carolina was typical of the cotton-mill settlements surrounding Burlington. Ossipee, Glencoe, Alamance, Haw River—they were cotton mills first, at the turn of the century, and next to each mill the mill owner had built a little town for his employees. At some time in the 1920s, the economics of owning a company town changed, and most of the mills deeded their towns to the inhabitants.

For a long time, Carolina was known as Carolina Mill. The mill had long since closed, but the village had changed little since it was built. The biggest house in town was still the former home of the supervisor. Most of the inhabitants were descendants of the original mill employees and themselves worked in the modern mills of the Burlington area. The community had never incorporated formally. It was only a community in name and spirit. Legally it was just another stretch of map in Alamance County.

The United Church of Christ was a modest but pretty 1950s structure at the top of a hill, a stone's throw from the crossroads at the center of the village. A small frame home was next door. The membership of the church was less than half what the membership of Dwight's church in Newport News had been. For these few families of modest income, maintaining a church and a house and paying a minister a salary was both a considerable burden and a matter of profound pride.

Some of the older people in the church realized, of course, that Dwight was a man in his early fifties, with a hiatus in his career and a family left somewhere behind him in other circumstances. Of course, they could have pried. But they liked Dwight. Whatever he had been through, he bore the scars well. They asked him to become their pastor. He accepted and rushed back up to Rockingham County to tell his father.

In his darkest moments, after the divorce, he had told himself to accept forever that he had lost his calling and his family. Now he was a minister again. And now this very attractive, if somewhat odd, woman had shown up in his life.

After leaving his card at the door of Blanche Taylor, Dwight had assumed she would call within the next day or two to return his greeting. But she did not. He went back at the end of the week to leave another card, but when he looked in the crack in the door he saw that his first card was still there.

Raymond had become so concerned about Blanche's erratic behavior that he had decided now was the time to make his move. He drove to her mobile home in Burlington and handed her a little velvet-lined box.

"What is this, Raymond?"

"It's just a ring."

"What kind of a ring?"

"It's just a ring, honey."

"It's expensive."

"Don't feel like I'm trying to pressure you. I just wanted you to have something nice from me. And here. I got us something else."

He reached in his pocket and produced a fat envelope from a travel agency in Winston-Salem. In it were airline tickets and hotel reservations for two in Florida, scheduled for a couple of weeks away.

"How will I get the time off, Raymond?"

"I'm your boss, remember. You've got the time."

She called Dwight Moore the next day. He said he would like to see her. They had trouble working out their schedules, but they finally agreed that she would drive to Carolina, on the far side of town from her home, and pick up Dwight the following evening after his prayer meeting.

The parishioners were still dawdling out in front of the

church when Blanche pulled up. They pretended not to stare
when Dwight walked out to the car and left with her. But once
Blanche's car was out of sight, there was a lot of buzzing and
winking and excited nodding in the group.

Dwight and Blanche drove to Mayberry's, one of a local
chain of restaurants named for the Andy Griffith/Don Knotts
television situation comedy that had been set in a fictional North
Carolina town of that name. They ate ice cream and spoke about
religion for the most part. Dwight quickly picked up the signs
of fundamentalist belief in Blanche, but it was a difference of
opinion from his own liberal beliefs he had worked with in
people all his life.

On the surface, she was congenial and warm. Just beneath
that surface, Dwight sensed something more magnetic. The
longer he sat across the table from Blanche looking at her, the
more inclined he felt to overlook any possible theological differences they might have.

For a month or more, Blanche had been uncharacteristi-
cally reticent at work. But in the few weeks that intervened
between Raymond's gift of the ring and the scheduled depar-
ture for Florida, she was back to her old chatty, nosy self.

"You know," she told a small assemblage of cashiers, "I
think I'll probably get married within the next couple years."

"To Raymond?" one of the bolder ones asked.

"No, I don't think so," she said cavalierly. "I think if I
remarry, it'll be to somebody who's from a higher class than
Raymond. I might marry me a preacher-man if I found the
right one."

Before she left for Florida with Raymond, Blanche visited
Dr. McNiel again, delivering another long peroration while he
scribbled the notes. Sometimes in the high chittering bird voice,
sometimes in a tougher, harsher voice, she delivered her version
of everything.

"I've made a sacrifice of myself to Raymond Reid for ten
years. But I'm an outgoing person, and I can't be with him. He
doesn't ever want to go anywhere. But I don't want to hurt
Raymond's feelings, that's my problem."

During the trip to Florida, Raymond paid for everything.
They flew to Sarasota, where he had booked them an expensive
room. The weather was perfect. They swam and beachcombed

by day and went out dancing at night. Blanche was lighthearted
and girlish. Toward the end of the two weeks, Raymond begged
her to marry him, and she said no. She said she had things on
her mind. He looked into her face and knew better than to ask.

While they were in Florida, Kevin Denton called their
room. Raymond answered, and Denton made a few snickering
inquiries about how things were going on his trip. Then Denton
asked to talk to Blanche.

"Blanche, this is Kevin Denton. How you doing down
there?"

"Just fine, Mr. Denton. How are you?"

"Everything's fine. Blanche, I've been going over some of
these schedules the store managers have been showing me, and
I see where we're going to be taking on quite a large number
of new checkers at my other Winston stores. You're so good at
training, I wonder if I could talk you into transferring to one
of these other Winston locations while we're breaking in these
new people?"

"No," she said quickly. "I'd really rather not. I'm happy
where I am."

"Well, there's no pressure, Blanche. If you want to stay at
Battleground, well then that's fine."

"That's what I'd like to do."

"Okay, then, that's how it'll be. Sorry to interrupt you all.
Don't do anything down there with Raymond you wouldn't do
with me."

She laughed. "I guess I know what you mean. 'Bye now."

Back in Burlington, Dwight was having his own romantic
difficulties. He received a phone call one afternoon at his church
office from Elaine, the woman he felt had broken his heart in
Newport News. He was shocked to hear her voice. It was their
first contact in almost two years.

Elaine told him she was calling from a motel barely a mile
from Dwight's church.

"What brings you here?" he asked very tentatively.

"I came because I wanted to see you."

"Does your husband know you are here?"

"Yes."

He promised to come right away. He hung up and sat at
his desk. The church building was empty. It was midafternoon.

The village around the church was deserted. He could hear only the faint rolling chatter of a mockingbird somewhere outside in the trees. He stared at his desk. Incredible, how a life can be so completely healed over, how the pain of an ancient wound can be completely forgotten, and then, in an instant, in the timbre and rhythm of "hello" on the telephone, it can all fall in on itself again like a house of cards. He rose slowly, went out to his car, and drove the short distance to see her.

She stayed in the motel in Burlington the entire time Blanche was in Florida. She and Dwight met and talked every day. She had brought him some books that she badly wanted him to read. They were books of poems about and for women, by Susan Polis Schutz: *I Want to Laugh, I Want to Cry,* and *I Want You to Be Happy.*

Dwight took the books back to his house. But he was not eager to read them. Things had changed for him. He had a very attractive, completely presentable woman interested in him—a woman a man could be proud of both socially and sexually. A looker. A woman with some color and snap to her. He was no longer Hamlet in a clerical collar. He was free to make decisions on his own behalf.

Blanche had been back in Burlington only a day when he made contact with her again. They agreed to meet at a walking track that had just been completed in a city park in Burlington. It was a spring evening, and they walked slowly around the track, deep in conversation. Blanche was subdued and somber.

"There's something about me, Dwight, that I need to tell you that might change how you feel about being seen in my company."

"What is that?" he said, with his clerical antennae tuning in closely.

"I am involved in a situation at Kroger that could possibly result in a lot of publicity at some point and maybe even a scandal. My zone manager there has been sexually harassing me for some time."

"I see."

"He's turned on by me or something. He does all kinds of things I'm too embarrassed to talk about. You know, like he tries to put his hand in my panties or he exposes himself. Once he came up to me right in the store and rubbed his hand on my vagina. He asks me to have oral sex with him all the time."

"I see."

"I have a lot of years invested in Kroger and in my retirement, and I can't afford just to walk away from the place. So I've been seeing some lawyers who are advising me, and I am in the process of building evidence for a lawsuit. I'm even seeing a psychiatrist here in Burlington, because my lawyers told me I should."

"Well, Blanche, that sounds like a very difficult and painful situation for you. As far as any potential embarrassment to me, of course I am a clergyman and I have quite a bit of experience with this kind of problem. Maybe not this exact problem, but I have often been involved in people's personal difficulties, so I'm not worried about that."

"I appreciate that, Dwight."

"I do wonder if the best thing for you to do might not be just to go straight to the top management at Kroger, because they certainly would not approve or condone such behavior, and tell them what this man has been putting you through, and say, look, I either want this situation stopped, or I am seeing lawyers and I am fully prepared to file a lawsuit if it isn't stopped. Why not just go right over his head and do that?"

"I don't think that would work."

They walked on in silence for a few minutes, Dwight feeling a little nonplussed.

"Blanche, I think you may be mistaken, if you don't mind me offering an opinion. For one thing, a lawsuit like the kind you are talking about would cause a great deal of very damaging publicity in a community like this, and I just don't believe Kroger would ever want to put up with that. And, also, I am concerned, frankly, for you. If this man is capable of doing the things you describe, well then, frankly, not to frighten you, but a man like that could be dangerous."

Blanche let a little snicker escape. "Oh, I think I can take care of myself," she muttered. Dwight looked over to see her face, but she was walking with her face down and her eyes already were lost in the deepening shadows of evening.

She returned to Dr. McNiel.

"I feel real guilty when I tell Raymond not to come over. He's always wanting to come to my house. In my personal life, I can't bring myself to hurt anyone. I need to tell him goodbye.

"The zone manager, the one who's harassing me sexually? He asked me to go to another store. I had diarrhea so bad after I talked to him, I just about couldn't stand it. Soon as I went back to work, he started trying to get me to go up in his office with him. I know what he wants up there. I just don't know about men. When you're dating them, they seem like the perfect man, a dream come true, and then as soon as you finally get together with them, it all comes out. The ugly truth.

"James, my husband, he was like that. He was so nice and handsome and kind when we were dating. I never had no idea until after we were married about his gambling. My father gambled terrible. So did James. He was just obsessed with it. He would steal money from me all the time. He played poker. He gambled away everything we had.

"Raymond is just like James. Everything about Raymond is just what James was. James caused me a lot of grief. A lot of grief. Maybe that's why I didn't remarry. Maybe I was afraid to take another chance."

Back at work, Blanche sought out Denton in his office. Denton asked how her vacation had gone.

"Me and Raymond's over with," she said matter-of-factly. "Hey, lookit what somebody gave me down there. It's real silly."

She handed him a fuzzy photocopy of a crudely drawn cartoon. In it a man was depicted lying on his back on the floor with a huge erection. Above him, suspended from a ceiling fan and apparently about to lower herself onto the man's penis, was a naked woman. The caption was "Turn Me On."

"Mm-mm," Denton said. He looked Blanche in the eye with a frank expression of curiosity and interest. "What do you think?"

"Well, there's all different kind of ways for people to get turned on, I guess."

"Yes, I expect there is."

"The zone meeting's coming up, I guess. I'll probably be stuck around here late tomorrow night getting the conference room ready."

"You think you'll be here late?"

"Pretty late."

"Well, I might see you then. I might have to come back in tomorrow night to get some work done for the meeting."

"I might see you."

On the afternoon of October 16, 1985, Blanche was working in the front office of the Battleground store with Betsy Reamer.

"I'm going to have to clean up the conference room upstairs for the regional meeting," she said.

Betsy nodded. Blanche had told her the same thing three times already that afternoon. It was just like Blanche to worry something to death. Betsy shrugged it off.

Just then David Dieboldt, another comanager, came into the office. Blanche turned to him and said, "I'm going to be up in the upstairs conference room straightening it up for the zone conference tomorrow, if anybody needs me."

She hurried out onto the floor of the store and grabbed Willis Upthegrove, a stocker. "I need your help," she said in a theatrical voice. "I have to go straighten up the upstairs conference room."

Dieboldt watched her depart with the gangling Willis Upthegrove in tow.

"What was that all about?" he asked.

"Oh, who the hell knows," Betsy said. "Just Blanche."

The conference room was a Spartan windowless affair of tile flooring, folding tables, industrial-strength fluorescent lighting, and gray metal folding chairs. A shipment of new uniforms had come in, and the boxes were stacked around the room, along with some stray boxes of groceries. Blanche had Willis carry out the groceries. They moved most of the uniforms to a small storage room and coat closet just down the hall. When that was done and the room had been swept, Blanche dismissed Willis.

"I'll just stay up here by myself and finish up," she said. She picked up her purse and walked downstairs with Willis. Willis Upthegrove went back to his duties, stocking cans of soup, but Blanche went to the back room where the hourly employees' lockers were. She removed the car keys from her purse and locked the purse in her locker. Keys in hand, she returned to the upstairs conference room.

At about that time, Denton showed up downstairs, wearing beltless stretch-waist trousers, a shirt and tie, and a light windbreaker. As he walked toward the back, he told David Dieboldt he would be working late upstairs on some paperwork for the next day's zone meeting and did not want to be disturbed.

When Denton entered the conference room, Blanche was picking up the pants of a woman's uniform, left in a jumble in the corner.

"What size are those?" he asked, tossing his jacket on a table.

She looked at the tag attached. "Twenty."

"They sure are big-butted. Do they have to make 'em big-butted for the kind of women we have working at Kroger?"

"I don't know, Mr. Denton," Blanche said, leaning around to look at his behind. "Do you think you could fit in 'em?"

"Let's just see about that," he said. He kicked off his loafers and undid the button and fly of his pants with a swashbuckling flourish. The pants fell to his ankles, and he stared at her for a moment, grinning with his eyebrows at the top of his forehead. He kicked his pants off, threw a hand behind his head, and did a wild little hula, and then slipped on the female uniform pants.

Denton minced around the room with the pants pulled up tight against his crotch, then kicked the pants off, pulled off his underpants, and stood facing Blanche with his erect penis gripped in one hand.

"Don't you want some of this white stuff?"

"Much as I can get," she said. "Let me make sure the coast is clear. Just a minute."

Blanche stepped out of the conference room, closed the door behind her, and tiptoed down the stairs. At the bottom of the stairs, just before the door that opened into the meat department, was an area where employees took their breaks. Betsy Reamer was sitting at a table sipping a Dr Pepper. Blanche walked halfway across the area, stared at Betsy without speaking, and then, as if she had forgotten something, turned and walked back up the stairs. Not wanting to know what was going on, Betsy Reamer rose and walked back out to the office at the front of the store.

When Blanche reentered the conference room, Denton was still naked from the waist down with an erection in one hand, beginning to say something breathless and chuckling about "white milk," but Blanche turned quickly, flipped off the lights, grabbed up his pants and underwear from the floor, and grabbed the woman's uniform pants. "Mr. Denton, I've got your clothes. I'm leaving. You've treated me like a damn whore all you're going to." She bolted from the room and slammed the door behind her. Outside the door she threw the woman's pants into a trash can.

Blanche raced down the stairs gasping for breath and fumbling in the pocket of Denton's trousers with one hand. She stumbled, fell, gashed an elbow on the banister, kept going. She ran as fast as she could for the front of the store. As she passed the open door of the store office at the front, she hurled Denton's billfold into the office.

"Call someone," she screamed. "I've got his pants. Mr. Denton is up there naked!"

She ran out of the store, still shrieking, "He's up there naked!" A gaggle of customers stood at the door with their jaws gaping. A few seconds later they heard a screech of tires as Blanche raced for her lawyer's office with the pants.

Denton stumbled in the dark. "Son of a bitch!" He banged a naked shin on the edge of a metal folding chair. The chair went crashing over in the pitch darkness. "Son of a bitch!"

Denton finally found his way to a wall. He leaned with his palms against it and did not move for a long moment, breathing deeply. He saw a crack of light at the bottom edge of the door. He palmed his way down the wall toward it. Once there, he found the light switch. The lights came on like thunder. He looked down on himself. "Son of a bitch!" He looked around. Blanche had left not a shred of clothing or other cover anywhere in the room. He raced to the closet/storage room at the back. Locked!

"Oh, son of a bitch!"

He ran over and pulled the curtain away from the little window halfway down the wall that looked out into the meat-cutting area. Below were two butchers, one a young man and the other middle-aged. The younger one was feeding round steak into a shredder, while the other one cut up chickens with quick loud whacks on a wooden cutting table.

"Hey!" Denton shouted through the window. "*Hey!*"

They could not hear him above the steady moan of the walk-in freezer.

"Son of a bitch!"

Denton went to the door, stuck his neck out, and surveyed the staircase. He took delicate naked footsteps, pointing his toes as he went, down the narrow staircase to the break area. It was empty! At last a tiny little bit of luck! He poked his head out of the door into the store.

"*Hey!*" he yelled at the meat cutters. "*Hey!*"

The younger one looked up. Denton was leaning out of the door, holding the door against his naked lower body as a veil.

"Yessir?"

"Get me a smock. Bring it right here right now."

"Yessir, just let me finish—"

"*Bring me the goddam smock right now, asshole!*"

The older man, without looking up, reached up with one hand, snatched a clean smock off a hook, and threw it in the younger man's face. The younger man hurried over and handed it to Denton, who took it and slammed the door. He ran back upstairs to retrieve his loafers.

A moment later Kevin Denton came strolling out into the Kroger Battleground store, cool and collected as ever, every hair neatly in place, very much the man in charge again. His tie was cinched up beneath his chin, and around him a large white butcher's smock was tied. He made his way coolly but efficiently toward the front door. Only as he was pushing his way out the door did an observant customer gasp, hand flying to her mouth as she saw the exposed crack of Kevin Denton's naked behind disappearing into the night.

Chapter Six

Raymond Reid slept late the next morning. In all his years with Kroger, it was the first time he had ever been late for a zone meeting. He shaved sloppily, threw on clothes, and drove fast to the Battleground store. When he walked in, Betsy Reamer leaned out of the office and motioned for him to come over, but he waved a hand to show he didn't have time. She watched with alarm as Raymond walked to the back.

He knew the minute he walked in that something was wrong. Sitting at the table with Kevin Denton and all the regional managers and comanagers were two people from the Virginia office.

Denton told him he was late.

"Sorry." He took his seat. Everyone stared at him in silence.

Denton said they had a problem. Another man at the table introduced himself. He was a company lawyer. He gave Raymond a brief sketch of what had happened the night before. Two thirds of the way through the lawyer's speech, Raymond

Reid jumped out of his chair. A lifetime of devout company loyalty snapped.

"You filthy son of a bitch!" Raymond snarled, moving around the table to get his hands on Denton.

Several comanagers jumped up to restrain him.

"She set me up, Reid!" Denton shouted back. "It was a setup pure and simple."

Reid whirled to the lawyer. "You better hope she don't sue your ass for a million dollars, because if she does what's gonna come out is that this dirty damn animal over here's been stickin' his paws all over these women and forcing them to have sex with him for years. It's about all we can do to keep any women on the payroll!"

The lead man from Virginia stood up slowly, lifted both palms up in the air next to his face, squinted his eyes, and shouted for them both to shut up.

The lawyer looked as if he might rise at that point, then sank back in his chair instead, drumming on the table with the eraser end of a yellow pencil. "The realities are these. Whether we have been set up or not, this woman clearly was interested in creating a situation where she would have witnesses and physical evidence, to wit, the unfortunate Mr. Denton's pants.

"What that means is that we are probably looking at a lawsuit. If we are looking at a lawsuit, it will probably be for much more than a million dollars."

It was for $14 million. But much more was at stake than that. Blanche Taylor was going to tell the community of Winston-Salem—the entire Piedmont, for that matter—that their nice shiny Kroger store was a place where women were poked and prodded and assaulted sexually by their male superiors. Instead of representing everything bright and modern, Kroger was going to be made to look like everything old, familiar, and ugly about the world.

By early afternoon of the next day, the Kroger people were convinced Blanche had set them up. Too many things about "the incident," as it already was known, did not ring true. Her fellow cashiers were full of little inconsistencies. She never locked her purse in her locker; she always kept it with her. And why would she carry her car keys in her hand? She had been the one who took the cartoon about the ceiling fan to Denton. She had led him on.

But Denton's admissions were staggering. He quite freely admitted to a long history of sexual contact with his female employees—all of it directly in conflict with the frequently disseminated official policy of the Kroger company. The Kroger lawyers pressed a deal on him, right away.

Denton made $60,000 a year. He had college-age kids, $16,000 in a retirement account, $10,000 in an IRA, a $3,000 equity in a VW Rabbit automobile, $52,000 with his wife in equity in their house, $125 in checking, $822 in a money market account, 2,500 shares in Occidental, $25,000 worth of shares in First Union Bank, and $5,000 in furniture and odds and ends. The Kroger lawyers made it plain to him that everything he had and ten times more would not be enough to pay for his own lawyers, if he chose to strike out on his own and fight. If he resigned, the company would defend him and do what it could to protect his personal assets.

He saw the light. At the end of that day, a shaking Kevin Denton scratched his name to a dictated letter of resignation. The record would show that Kroger had demanded his resignation within three working days of Denton's phone call advising the company of the incident. The actual effective date of resignation would be delayed four months so that Denton would be able to collect full retirement benefits. In the meantime, even though he soon would be officially off the payroll, Kroger would handle his defense for him.

In the next few weeks, Blanche's lawyers papered the store with a blizzard of subpoenas. But on the other side, beneath the scrutiny of their bosses and the company investigators, the cashiers were eager to supply small circumstantial pieces of evidence that pointed to Blanche's deceit. They continued to offer the same testimony under oath, but Blanche's lawyers brushed all of that aside and went for the big stuff.

A male employee said he had walked in when Denton was touching the breasts of an employee. Several employees reported advances. One cashier said she had been forced to engage in nonconsensual sex with Denton. Blanche's attorneys asked the woman how many times. Without missing a beat, she said, "Fifteen."

And then came Kevin Denton's deposition. Kroger had tried to soften the blow by having Denton "stipulate to" or freely admit certain parts of the charges against him in Blanche's lawsuit, figuring that would be better than letting Blanche's lawyers wheedle it out of him. The Kroger strategy early on was to paint Denton as a rogue employee who had chosen to violate all of the company's guidelines and policies on sexual contact but to paint Blanche also as a slut who had freely engaged in sex with Denton and then turned on him and entrapped him for money.

But when they got to the actual process of taking his deposition, Blanche's lawyers knew there was much more than that to be found beneath the rug of Mr. Kevin Denton's long career. Prodding and pushing him, they got Denton to admit it was much more than a matter of friendly and encouraging pats on the back.

Denton said under oath that he had engaged in "sex acts" and had "fondled the vagina" of one cashier "on Kroger property." He said he had "engaged in oral sex" with a second cashier, "fondled" a third. Asked about Blanche's story in which Denton stood grinning maniacally with his erect penis exposed in one hand mumbling about "white milk," Denton admitted that he had so presented himself to Blanche and to three other cashiers.

While the legal wheels were whirring, Blanche was busy improving her own supporting evidence for the lawsuit. She demanded an emergency session with Dr. McNiel the day of the zone meeting.

He scrawled quickly in his notebook while Blanche poured out her story. McNiel's notes said: "Last Thursday Mr. Kevin Denton took off his pants and stood with erect penis, took patient by shoulders and said, 'Don't you want some of this white stuff?'

"On another day he ran his hand up patient's dress and pinched her. Last night found Mr. Denton trying on one of girls uniforms. Later patient came back to get uniform and he was nude except for shirt.

"He locked door, and patient said he wasn't going to treat her like a whore. Ran off with his clothes and left billfold with a girl. Patient told authorities (at Kroger). Patient brought the pants and jockey shorts to office. Patient extremely upset, asked for emergency session today. Lawyer James Walker."

* * *

A few weeks after "the incident," Blanche came home one evening and found Raymond's car parked in her driveway. He walked around from the other side of her house trailer.

"Hello, Blanche."

"Hi, Raymond. C'mon in."

She had a small bag of groceries in her arms. She fumbled with the lock and then let him in. He sat at the small table in the dining area, drumming his fingers. She put the groceries away and then walked back out to him with a quizzical smile.

"I wanted to see you, honey," he said. "I've been worried about you."

"I know. I've been real busy with the lawsuit. I'm so worried about everything, Raymond. I'm worried about money. That car out there isn't worth a damn no more. But I can't be buying a new automobile now with no job. The lawyers tell me I can't expect any money for at least two years."

"Can you sit down, Blanche?"

"Sure." She sat across the table from him and smiled.

"Blanche, I miss you."

"I miss you, honey. My lawyers and my psychiatrist say I need to not have anything to do with a man for a while."

"Because?"

"They just don't think I should."

"Because it would be bad for you? Or because it would look bad?"

"Both, I guess."

"Blanche, I'm under a lot of pressure here. I have to go up to Roanoke tomorrow and see them. They're going to grill me."

"Well, I know it. They're plain mean. But you just do what you have to do, Raymond. I know how you are about your job. Come and tell me about it after."

At Roanoke, Raymond was questioned closely about his relationship with Blanche. The Kroger lawyers already had figured out that Blanche was going to claim Denton had marred her sexually and that she no longer could enjoy a full sexual relationship with a man. It was a bone-crushing interview for Raymond, who was torn by his loyalty to Kroger and his feeling that it was ungentlemanly of the lawyers and the detectives to expect him to divulge details of his intimacy with Blanche. Luckily, he was able to tell them truthfully that they had not been having sex for some time.

The lawyers could see Raymond Reid's discomfort—the pain of an honest man caught in a conflict of loyalties. They made another appeal to his company loyalty and then suggested a few things he might ask Blanche about in order to satisfy his own curiosity.

He went to see her again a few nights later and told her some of what had gone on. That night Blanche was warm and welcoming. He wound up in bed with her for the first time in several weeks. While he slept, Blanche slipped out of bed and went to the dresser top, looking for the slim sound-activated microcassette recorder she knew he always carried.

Raymond didn't have to work the next day. He and Blanche drove to Greensboro, where they found Blanche a beautiful new blue Honda Accord. Raymond wrote a check for it. She hugged him, and he hugged her back as hard as he could. "I care about you, baby," he said, with tears in his eyes.

"I know you do. I know you do."

Dwight had heard Raymond Reid's name for the first time a few weeks before he bought the Honda for her. Blanche had told him Raymond was a dear friend who sympathized with her in her legal battle with Kroger.

In the days after Raymond's name was first mentioned, Dwight had pursued Blanche even more ardently than before. She invited him to dinner one night, and after the dishes were washed, she turned and kissed him passionately. Taking him by the hand, she led him to her bedroom.

In the weeks ahead, they slept together often. Neither one of them gave voice to the possibility of marriage, but for Dwight, their sleeping together meant they were thinking of getting married.

But Dwight still wanted to understand Blanche's relationship with Raymond.

Standing on the small wooden porch at the door of her trailer home, staring at the new car on the gravel drive, Dwight said: "I thought you were worried about money."

Blanche was in the door of the trailer.

"I am, Dwight. I don't have a job. I don't know when this lawsuit will ever be over. Wouldn't you be worried about money?"

"Well then, how did you buy a new car?"

"Raymond bought it for me."

"Raymond?"

"Raymond Reid. My friend. I told you about him."

Dwight complained that he didn't think it was proper for Blanche to accept such a large gift from a man who was only a coworker and friend. Blanche said the car was none of Dwight's business and he was not going to get anywhere trying to stick his nose in her affairs.

Dwight dropped the matter, but at the same time the conversations about marriage took on a new dynamic. Dwight was now in earnest about it. It was Blanche who seemed always to dance away.

Raymond Reid was called on the carpet.

"How in the hell did Blanche Moore ever get tape recordings of our meetings, Reid? Have you been taping us?"

"Of course not," he lied. "Why would I do that?"

"Denton says you tape everybody. Did you give tapes to your girlfriend?"

"No, of course not. Why do you think she has tapes?"

"Because she told us she did. She told us to watch out, because she had us on tape planning what to do."

Raymond went to the trailer that night.

"You need to call and not just come over, Raymond."

"Blanche, what are you talking about? We've lived together almost like man and wife for twelve years."

"I told you the lawyers don't like it. I'm supposed to not be able to stand the sight of a man."

"Well, what is this anyway, Blanche? Is it a setup?"

"Are you gonna stick up for Denton now?"

"No, but that doesn't mean you didn't set him up. Why did you tell them you had them on tape? I was missing a tape after I spent the night here last month. Did you steal tapes from me?"

"Raymond, I think you better leave."

He pointed a finger at her. "If you've got tapes you took from me, you better get rid of them, because if you try to use them, I have certain things I could tell them about you."

The eyes came up black and round. "Get out, Raymond."

"Give me back the tapes."

She handed them over, and Raymond left.

* * *

Blanche showed up a few days later at Raymond's house trailer in Kernersville. She was remorseful. "I'm so sorry, honey. I've just been under a strain."

"I know you have, Blanche."

"I don't even know what I'm doing half the time."

He reached out and held her.

The next week Raymond flew to Denver, rented a car, and drove up to Boulder to see his elder son, twenty-five-year-old Ray Jr., who had been working on a ranch in Colorado the last six months. Ray Jr. had struck out for Colorado after college, not at all sure what he wanted to do. His parents' divorce had bothered him less than some of the bitterness that followed it. But he had great respect for both his father and mother and realized they had dealt with their own problems the best way they knew how. He had been homesick for both of them, and he was delighted when his father called and said he was coming.

Ray Jr. had seen little of Colorado outside Boulder in his time there. He and his father decided to take a road trip in Raymond's rental car. They struck out toward the east, down out of the mountains and across the perfectly flat tabletop prairies. Nothing in the crooked hen-scratch roads of North Carolina had prepared them for the ruler-straight ribbons of highway across the Great Plains, stretching from horizon to horizon like bridges between blue bluffs of sky.

They drove just to drive. Not far into their adventure, the radio in the rental car stopped working. After an hour or so of awkward silence, they began to talk. Ray Jr. told his father about some romantic disappointments he had suffered since college.

Raymond talked about Blanche. He told his son about the lawsuit, about how much he hated Denton for what he had done, about how Blanche's lawyers had told her not to have anything to do with Raymond and what pain that had caused him.

"I love her, son. I really love her."

On a place mat in a restaurant in Kansas, they read about a man who in the late nineteenth century had left a will demanding that his body be mummified. The place mat said the body was still on view in a glass coffin a couple of hundred miles from where they were.

Raymond and Ray Jr. looked at each other.

"Hey, we gotta see that," Raymond said.

Ray Jr. laughed and agreed. They piled back in the car and drove fast down those straight flat skyways through perfect walls of grain. Ray Jr. thought to himself that he had never imagined he would one day ram around the countryside in a car spilling his heart out about girl problems to his father. The thing that amazed him even more was hearing his father talk about his own girl problems.

At the end of the visit, they embraced at the airport. It had been a wonderful time for both of them. They were both loners. Now each had a friend.

On the day Raymond returned to North Carolina, Dwight called Blanche and said he wanted to see her that evening.

"I'm afraid I can't, Dwight. My friend Raymond Reid is coming in to the airport, and I need to go pick him up and give him a ride."

"The airport in Greensboro?"

"Yes."

"Well, that's thirty-five miles from your house. Didn't you tell me he lived in Kernersville?"

"Yes."

"That's fifteen miles the other way from you. And then you've got to turn around and drive fifty miles back home?"

"Yes."

"What time?"

"He comes in at nine P.M."

"Oh, Blanche, I just think that's ridiculous. What's wrong with the fellow? Why can't he just get on a bus or an airport limousine? Surely he can't expect a friend to get out in the middle of the night and drive all over North Carolina just to run him home from the airport?"

"Dwight, he's my friend. He's done for me, and I just have to do for him. It's what's right."

Her reunion with Raymond was emotional. He told her several times how much he loved her and how much he had missed her. On the way to his house, he begged her to marry him. He told her he was well fixed, that he had saved his money over the years and could provide for her. They slept together that night.

When Raymond got to work the next morning, Betsy Reamer pulled him aside to give him all the latest developments in

Blanche's lawsuit. He listened silently, nodding his head at the significant pieces of information.

"And Raymond," she said shyly at the end, "there's something else I just think you should know."

"What, Betsy?"

"I don't like being the one to tell you this. But Blanche has got her a preacher man she's interested in."

"What do you mean?"

"She's been telling us she's going to marry him."

Raymond was still standing in the office, trying to absorb this latest bit of news, when another cashier came up.

"I don't like these afternoon shifts, Raymond," she said.

He looked up absently and said in a monotone: "I can't help you. Somebody's got to work them, and it's your turn."

"Well, I don't like that. I need to be home for my children."

"I can't help you."

"Yes you can."

He looked up quickly. A note in her voice had caught his attention. "What are you talking about, Monica?"

"Blanche is telling the company she can't have no sex no more because of what Mr. Denton done to her. I know better. I know about you and Blanche. I know a lot."

"How do you know?"

"I just do. Now I want days. I want off afternoons next time the schedule is posted. I put in too many years here to have to work afternoons while Blanche is always the little queen bee. I'm not gonna take it no more, especially not now that Blanche has found herself a way to get rich off the company to where she don't even have to work no more."

The company lawyers called Raymond back to Roanoke later that week. This time they put the pressure on him. He was either with them or he was against them. They were convinced from all the evidence they had been able to gather that Blanche was scamming the company. Denton was an idiot who had broken all the rules. Denton was out. They had to defend him in order to defend the store, but the minute the suit was settled, he was gone.

Raymond called Blanche and talked to her for three hours on the telephone. "I'm just under an awful lot of pressure, Blanche."

"I know that, Raymond. So am I. Look what I've got to go through."

"Blanche, they think you set him up. They say they can prove it."

"How?"

"All kind of ways. The way you did your purse and all that."

"Well, my lawyer says that's nothing."

"I just..."

"You what, Raymond? You what? Raymond, I hope you know I'm counting on you."

"What about this preacher man I hear you're going to marry?"

There was a long silence.

"Oh, Raymond. You sit up there in Kernersville by yourself in that trailer and you think up all these things. Can you just come on down here and see me? I'll cook you a decent dinner. Come on down after work tomorrow."

Money worries were beginning to weigh heavily on Blanche. She had spent all of the money from her insurance settlements after the fires and was most of the way through the small amount she had set aside before the settlements. She was not working. The lawyers had told her not to expect to see cash in hand anytime soon. It could go on for years, they told her. She worried not only about herself but about her daughters, who still needed money from time to time.

Raymond lent her small amounts. So did Dwight.

"If you would marry me, I could take care of you," Raymond told her on the telephone. "I have some money put away."

Dwight told her the same thing.

By early 1986, Blanche's lawyers finally felt confident enough to show more of their hand. They filed the necessary motions and went through the steps necessary to firm up the suit for trial. As new legal papers were filed with the court each day and as the case folder grew thicker and hotter, the lawsuit became a popular topic of conversation in Winston-Salem, much to the dismay of Kroger.

The case was set in Superior Court in Greensboro, seat of Guilford County. The preliminary motions were heard by a young judge, William H. Freeman, then forty-one years old. Born in Virginia, a graduate of Wake Forest University in Winston-Salem, Judge Freeman had a reputation for being bright, charming in a very offhand Southern way, attractive to women, and easily bored. He had back trouble and often got up out of his chair behind the bench to pace and take some of the pressure off his spine.

Judge Freeman had presided over a dozen dramatic death-penalty cases. At one point six people on death row in North Carolina had been sent there by the crack of his gavel. While the Kroger sexual harassment case was hot stuff for the local news hawks, it was tepid fare for Judge Freeman. After the preliminary hearings were over, the regular rotation of judges put the case before Judge Julius A. Rousseau. Judge Freeman was not disappointed. He assumed he would never hear of Blanche Taylor again.

The Kroger side offered Blanche $25,000 in cash to take a walk. When her lawyers passed the offer on to her, she turned it down flat without a moment's hesitation.

Two weeks later Raymond Reid began to suffer stinging pains in his arms and legs and a terrible skin rash. He went to see his regular physician, Dr. Norman S. Garrett, Jr., of Greensboro. Dr. Garrett was the Kroger company doctor. He had first met Raymond when he gave him a company physical in 1981. He had treated him privately over the next several years for various ailments, including blood-pressure problems and a bad respiratory infection that had been aggravated by Raymond's heavy smoking.

On this occasion Dr. Garrett made a diagnosis that was perfectly logical and fully supported by all of the evidence he could see in an office visit. He told Raymond Reid he was suffering from shingles.

Shingles is basically a recurrence of childhood chicken pox. The gross effects of shingles are similar in type to the early effects of arsenical peripheral neuritis—skin eruptions and blisters that are red at the base and white at the center, painful stinging and itching along the path of the affected nerves.

What was actually happening to Raymond Reid's body was quite different from shingles. The ingestion of arsenic had caused a chemical change in the long nerve fibers of his extremities, causing the nerves to absorb their own protective

outer coating of myelin. As the myelin was resorbed, the bun-
dled tubes inside the myelin sheaths, through which nervous
impulses were supposed to travel, were damaged and eaten
away. The result was a combination of severe crippling pain
and a numb tingling in the fingers and toes.

The pain of arsenical neuritis is much more severe than
the pain of shingles, but the degree of a patient's pain is difficult
for doctors to measure, especially since some patients under-
state their pain and others overstate it. Shingles is a common
misdiagnosis of the early stages in what the medical texts call
"chronic" arsenic poisoning—arsenic poisoning by small regular and repeated exposures or deliberate doses. Dr. Garrett
put Raymond on cortisone. The painful attacks subsided.

Raymond continued to work through most of the three-
week bout, but toward the end he had to stay at home by himself
at the trailer park for several days. Blanche did not call or visit.
On the third day at home, Raymond hobbled outside the trailer
and sat in the sun on the little metal stoop, with his back against
the warm wall of the trailer.

Merrilee Stryker looked up from the dishes she was wash-
ing and saw him through the kitchen window of her trailer.
She rinsed her hands, dried them on her apron, hung the apron
on a hook, and straightened her hair in the mirror. At twenty-
seven and single, she was a very pretty woman, with blond hair
and humorous green eyes. She had an older woman friend at
work to whom she talked about Raymond. Merrilee thought he
would be a great catch for her friend. She sometimes wondered
if she shouldn't be interested herself. She poured a cup of coffee
and carried it outside.

"Raymond, how are you doing today?"

"Better," he said. "C'mon over."

She came over and sat sideways on the step at his knee.

"Better?"

"Yeah. Much less pain. The stuff the doctor gave me
worked, I guess. Boy, last couple days was pretty bad. But I'm
feeling good this morning. Physically, anyway."

Neither one of them spoke for a long moment.

"I haven't seen Blanche over," she said, looking away.

"No. She hasn't been over."

They were silent again.

"What are you going to do, Raymond?"

"I don't know. I should break up with her."

"What does she say?"

"Oh, Blanche has got her a preacher man she's seeing."

"I didn't know that. She was over a week ago."

"She never told me. The girls at Kroger told me."

"She never told you?"

"No."

Merrilee looked up at Raymond and smiled. "Raymond Reid, I know any number of women who'd be proud just to go out with you. You're a good-looking man. You're a good man. You have nice manners. You have a good job and a career."

He smiled. "Thanks. It doesn't hurt to hear somebody say nice things about you."

"Well?"

"I should break up with her. But I love her. I love her a whole lot. She's odd and eccentric. But she's just as good as the day is long. She brought me to Jesus. She's . . . she's beautiful. Good to me. She's everything I want in a woman."

Merrilee rose. "You ever change your mind, just give me a knock on the door. I got a list of women who'd jump at the chance."

Dwight was visiting Blanche. She came from the back of her trailer home where she stored cleaning fluids and utensils in a closet. She was holding a small bottle. She sat next to him and held the bottle up for him to see.

"I need some of this stuff," she said. "I can't find it around over here."

"What is it?"

"It's ant poison. It's called Anti-Ant. See?"

She handed it to him and waited for him to inspect the label. "They'll have it at that mini-mart over by you."

It was a two-ounce bottle. It contained a colorless, odorless liquid, slightly sweet to the human palate. A warning on the bottle said it was poisonous and should be kept out of the reach of children.

Dwight did as Blanche requested. He went to the mini-mart and bought her a bottle of Anti-Ant. The solution of arsenic was 2 percent. The bottle Dwight brought home and gave to Blanche contained enough arsenate to kill five to ten adult human beings, depending on their conditions.

Chapter Seven

Blanche's lawyers informed her that they were getting ready to file the final papers that would bring her suit to a focus and force the court to set a trial date. They were tying up last-minute details and wanted to make sure she had crossed all the t's and dotted the i's. They asked about Raymond. Could she handle him? Was he under control? Blanche called him up and said she wanted to bring dinner over to him at his trailer.

"The pressure is real bad," Raymond said. "They say they'd fold their tent and pay you off in a minute if it was just Denton that it was all about. They think he's a sorry son of a bitch. But they're convinced you set him up anyway, and they intend to fight you."

"Well, I didn't set him up. You know that, Raymond, don't you? I hope you're still on my side."

"All I can tell you, Blanche, is that it's real hard for me. And I guess I don't know yet what to do."

"Let me just bring you over a good hot meal."

When Raymond went back to Dr. Garrett, he was in terrible

pain. He was suffering severe diarrhea, nausea, wracking abdominal pain, and projectile vomiting. The longer and more intimately his body engaged this most recent dose of arsenic in battle, the more pernicious a poison it became.

In order to get rid of the arsenic, his kidneys first had to break it apart into other, slightly different substances. Most of what the kidneys turned it into could be readily, if painfully, excreted by the body, and his body had been working overtime doing just that.

But even while Raymond's kidneys were hammering away at the arsenic molecules in order to get rid of them, they also were holding back tiny amounts of an even more poisonous form of arsenic. The stuff that came in was arsenate—the molecule in its pentavalent form. The stuff the renal tubules produced and then held back was arsenite—the far more poisonous trivalent form. In trying to get rid of the arsenic, then, his body actually had distilled it and made it more potent. The more potent the arsenic became, the more violently his body worked to expel it.

Since his body was not as capable of excreting the trivalent form, the body tried to seize it instead and bind it up in parts of the body where it would do the least immediate harm, particularly in the bones, hair, and nails, where it would reside harmlessly though permanently, or until the hair or nails were cut.

Dr. Garrett put Raymond in Wesley Long Community Hospital in Greensboro for observation. He prescribed Phenergan suppositories for the nausea. Phenergan is a form of promethazine, a powerful antihistamine used to suppress nausea and vomiting in animals and occasionally in humans. Garrett told Raymond the therapy would work fairly quickly and he would be able to go home. But instead of responding to the therapy, Raymond continued to grow dramatically worse. Garrett next treated Raymond with powerful Septra antibiotics.

But after the Septra, an examination of his blood showed a distressingly low white cell count, along with evidence that some agent was simultaneously attacking the basic structure of all of the elements of the blood. A bone-marrow scan showed something was going haywire with the chemical structure of the marrow. Garrett decided that something invisible was tearing at Raymond's system.

Over the next week, Raymond developed an acute urinary-tract infection, the tip of his penis became badly inflamed, his intestinal tract seemed not to be working, his heartbeat was too rapid, his kidneys were failing, and his body was beginning to swell alarmingly.

A consulting neurologist was called in. He found that Raymond was suffering a general weakness and a curious numbness and tingling in his hands and feet. Neither Dr. Garrett nor the neurologist could come up with any definitive clinical explanation for what was happening to him. Raymond had begun coughing up large amounts of phlegm. He kept repeating a little dully to whoever was standing nearby, "I feel rotten."

Blanche was often at his side. She had worked out a busy routine for herself. She awoke with Dwight each day and sometimes lingered for breakfast. Then she drove to Greensboro to see Raymond for a while during the day. At Wesley Long, she questioned Dr. Garrett closely about his condition. She took care of whatever other business she had—often a visit to the lawyer or to her psychiatrist—and then she returned to her trailer home in Burlington in the evening and awaited Dwight's arrival.

The infection at the tip of Raymond's penis seemed to grow worse and was impervious to antibiotics. Dr. Garrett hoped removing his uncircumcised foreskin might help to clear it, which meant that in the midst of his other agonies, Raymond had to undergo a painful circumcision.

But nothing helped any of his symptoms. On July 13, 1986, Raymond's kidneys stopped producing urine. Dr. Garrett could think of nothing to do for him. He called Blanche and told her what was going on. He said he thought Raymond should be transferred to North Carolina Baptist Hospital in Winston-Salem. She agreed that whatever Dr. Garrett thought was appropriate should be done. Dr. Garrett called Dr. Robert Hamilton at North Carolina Baptist.

Dr. Hamilton was a specialist in internal medicine and in nephrology—the functioning of the kidneys. At Dr. Garrett's request, Dr. Hamilton agreed to become Raymond Reid's attending physician and to have him admitted to Baptist. And so Raymond Reid was packed in an ambulance and sent to the same hospital where Dwight Moore had repaired his soul in chaplaincy training after the agony of his divorce.

The fact that he was not producing urine meant that Raymond Reid was in immediate if temporary danger of dying, and the fact that he came from another hospital with no diagnosis meant that he would have to be subjected to extensive biochemical testing. The failure of his kidneys would soon throw his heart into panic, which meant that at any moment heroic measures might be needed in order to keep him alive. Raymond Reid was taken immediately to the intensive care unit.

Moving swiftly down the long low corridor on a litter, Raymond was conscious and more or less aware of the scene around him—a Brueghelian hubbub of the lame and the halt, young doctors cantering along laughing and infants wailing, a gray-faced man alone on a litter next to the open door of the cafeteria kitchen, a long-stemmed bouquet on the floor by the dangling receiver of a pay phone, long lines of pasty-faced people with checkbooks waiting in front of young women at video display terminals, up the elevator, off the elevator, Muzak and clatter, soft fetid food smell and the astringent odor of antiseptic. Swinging doors opened before him, doors closed behind him, and he was suddenly high on a cloud of near-silence. He could hear regular mechanical gurgling noises, muted conversation, and the scratchy tinkle of a cheap radio playing at the far end of the ICU.

Most of the ICU patients at Baptist were too sick to eat or even breathe for themselves. They were kept alive by the big boxy machines the nurses called "vents"—automatic ventilators that force air through tubes down into a patient's lungs. Baptist had both the fully mechanical Bear I and Bear II vents, covered with adjustment dials and gauges, and the newer Puritan-Bennett 7200 computerized vents, with consoles that looked more like the control panel on a microwave oven.

In order to make a human throat stop trying to vomit out a plastic breathing tube, the throat muscles must be paralyzed. For decades the drug commonly used to paralyze a patient for intubation had been Pavulon, a synthetic version of curare—the poison that Amazonian Indians put on the tips of hunting darts. Pavulon has no effect at all on consciousness. A patient totally paralyzed with Pavulon and not provided with a vent would lie perfectly awake and aware of all of his sensations and feel himself slowly suffocate, unable even to blink an eye, let alone cry out. Even with a vent, Pavulon paralysis is a terrifying experience for most people, so that ventilated patients in ICUs almost always are given hypnotic drugs, too—Valium and, more recently, Ativan—so they will not remember the experience.

The patients closest to death in the ICU at Baptist were the ones with the most tubes running in and out of their faces and arms. As more systems of the body failed, and as more and more testing and monitoring were necessary, the more the body had to be threaded with tubes. The "Salem Sump" was one— a wide-bore tube that went in through the nose and down directly into the stomach. It carried food the consistency of baby food, along with crushed pills and other medications that normally must be given by mouth.

If a patient's stomach was not working at all, a narrower-gauge tube would be inserted all the way through the stomach into the duodenum. Patients whose gastrointestinal tracts were not functioning properly had to be fed by the process usually called hyperalimentation, which means vitamin and mineral super-dosing through intravenous tubes in the arms or elsewhere. The other purpose of the IV tube was for administering medicines and also for maintaining a watch on blood pressure and oxidation.

Some patients, for various reasons, had all or most of these types of tubes in them at once. A patient with severe heart problems also at times had a Swan Ganz catheter stuck down through an opening in the jugular or another large vein directly into the interior of his heart, producing a readout that showed exactly how the heart looked and was working from the inside out.

In addition, there were tubes that were inserted only for cleaning purposes, for suctioning sputum up out of the lungs or for cleaning the mouth.

Most of the tubes were fitted with stopcocks, so that they could easily be disconnected from the monitors and feeding devices. The Salem Sump, for example, was prone to getting clogged with feeding solution and had to be flushed. The practice at Baptist was to keep a beaker of diluted Coca-Cola or sterile water nearby for flushing.

A host of other wires and electrodes were attached to some patients—a red LED glowing at the tip of what appeared to be a bandaged finger in one bed, white wires running from the chest area of another patient—all watching and reporting on special functions and problem areas of the body.

The beds themselves were technological marvels, fashioned of many small separate inflated cushions under each part of the body, each cushion maintained at its own air pressure, all monitored by a bank of gauges at the foot of the bed. By regulating every square inch of the bed, the nurses could prevent or slow down the terrible process of bedsores and decomposition that usually began at the shoulder blades, coccyx, and heels and then spread over a patient's entire body.

The overall arrangement was a curious mixture of extreme orderliness interrupted by little islands of messiness—a tray with a well-thumbed drug manual dumped on top of a jumble of medications in cardboard boxes, a photocopied article from a medical journal left behind on a stool, and everywhere the rubber gloves that symbolized what AIDS had done to hospitals.

The ICU was a world of women. Almost all of the doctors were male, but they were only visitors. The nurses were the natives of this island, the ones who stayed and tended the fires through the long nights and days. Especially in the ICU, it had always been a nurse's instinct to rush to the blood and phlegm of a life in crisis and reach in to save the spark. Now it was a nurse's instinct to stop first and put on gloves. In the case of some patients, as in Raymond's case when he first arrived, a condition of sterile "isolation" was maintained, which meant that anyone who went near the patient, including doctors, nurses, and visitors, was required to wear gloves, mask, and smock.

While the patient's bodies raged inside, warring against whatever diseases were tearing them apart, the patients themselves were silent. The eyes of some had been taped shut. Because of the Pavulon paralysis, they would be unable to close or blink their eyes themselves and might stare until the air and light had eaten away the outer coating of their corneas. Beneath the tape, glistening with drops and ointment the eyes rocked back and forth fitfully in whatever Valium-fogged version of life had presented itself.

Some kept trying to draw the instinctual breath of life, pulling down with what strength their dose of Pavulon had left in the diaphragm. The vents breathed for them in the opposite way the body breathes on its own: the body sucks air down by negative pressure, but the vents blow it in with positive pressure.

The ventilators were programmed so that if a patient was able to achieve enough negative pressure to draw an effective breath of air, the vent would pause and let him take a breath. The bodies of some patients kept trying but were too weakened to achieve what the vent's sensitive instruments measured as a legal breath of air. Therefore the vent kept blowing and the patient's diaphragm kept taking tiny little gasps. The war between the two made the skin on the patient's chest jiggle like sailcloth luffing in a light wind.

Dr. Hamilton bent over Raymond Reid's litter and said hello. Hamilton was in his late forties and slightly pudgy, with small intelligent features and short brown hair.

"Can you figure out what's wrong with me?" Raymond asked in a raspy voice. "They were stumped at Long. It's pretty bad. I feel real bad."

Hamilton noted that Raymond was having difficulty breathing while he spoke. "We'll do some things right away that should make you feel better," Hamilton said. "We'll be doing extensive testing, meanwhile, to see if we can't get at the cause of all this."

Raymond was wheeled to an open bed. Nurses and an orderly helped him climb from the litter to the bed. When Raymond lifted himself, Dr. Hamilton's quick eye saw that his lower legs were swollen. As soon as Raymond was flat, the nurses folded away his robe. It was a sight that would have made a layman fight for his breath. But Hamilton and the nurses scanned Raymond's body without so much as a lifted eyebrow.

Raymond Reid was an intriguing puzzle, indeed. It was as if all the diseases known to man had been drawn together for a unified attack on a single human being. The arsenic was erupting his skin in open lesions on his legs and trunk. Large patches on his chest and stomach were a deathly white. Hamilton noted that the recently circumcised end of Raymond's penis was still very inflamed.

He was beginning to wheeze, even while they examined him. His stomach seemed to bloat and distend before their very eyes. A quick listen with the stethoscope revealed only weak whispers in the bowel where normally there should be growling and gurgling noises.

Blood was taken immediately. The early reading on the blood was very bad. The salt level in the blood was way low, meaning the body was retaining abnormally high amounts of water.

The blood itself was worse. The arsenic was tearing apart Raymond's red cells, making him anemic and threatening him with chemical suffocation, and his white cells, making him vulnerable to massive infection. The acids his kidneys were failing to excrete were piling up in the body. Another test showed the liver was beginning to fail, too.

Immediately the tubes began to enter his body. The first was a catheter stuck up through his inflamed penis. In fact, the kidneys had not completely shut down, and there was urine in the bladder, trapped there by the inflammation of the urethra. Dr. Hamilton was able to get that urine out quickly, which brought Raymond some relief. Dr. Hamilton was able to use other techniques to jump-start the kidneys and begin clearing Raymond's system.

But on Raymond's second day at Baptist he was worse. He was agitated and restless, jerking around on the bed. Thick-tongued and hard to understand, he kept asking, "Where is this? Where am I? Where is Blanche? Where is this?"

On that second day, the specialists began to float into the ICU like white moths—a hematologist to study Raymond's blood and bone marrow, a urologist to examine his penis and urinary tract, a neurologist to check his nervous system. More needles and tubes went in.

A spinal tap was performed to see if something in the spinal fluid might explain Raymond's mental confusion. But the results only confused the doctors. There was too much pressure in the spinal canal and protein levels were elevated. Dr. Bradley T. Troost, chairman of neurology at the Bowman Gray School of Medicine at Wake Forest University, came to see Raymond and to read the chart.

Blanche appeared at ten in the morning, beautifully dressed in a yellow knit suit, with her hair freshly coiffed at shoulder length and her makeup perfectly done. She introduced herself decorously to the nurses.

"I'm his girlfriend. I'm very worried, of course. Can you tell me anything?"

Lisa Sue Hutchens, the assistant head nurse, stepped forward to handle Blanche. At twenty-four, small and even younger-appearing than her years, she was not prepossessing physically, but her eyes were direct and bold. She gave Blanche a measured version of the truth. She told her that Raymond was in very serious condition and that the doctors had not had any early luck figuring out what was wrong with him. She said the doctors and staff of the ICU were doing everything they could for Raymond, and then she explained the rules of the ICU, including the visiting hours. Blanche looked in on Raymond, who was asleep. Then she left.

Blanche reappeared in the afternoon, with cookies for the nurses. Raymond was asleep when she first showed up. She gave the nurses a long, high-pitched, funny account of her morning of shopping.

"I finally said to that girl, 'Is there some way you can just close the drawer and we'll start over,' but I guess she couldn't, she couldn't back out of it, and she was all flustered and wouldn't let me help, I swear, I usually know better than to do that with them, you know, give them a quarter to keep from getting a dollar's worth of change back, because the poor things just cannot count anymore, but it makes me so mad, I mean, I've run cash registers all my life, and I always figured I was expected to be able to add and subtract, isn't that something?"

The nurses munched on the cookies and laughed at Blanche's stories. The people the nurses saw all day long were either dying patients, hurried doctors, or the relatives and close friends of the ill fighting back tears.

Blanche was funny. She was bright and nice. And she was something else the nurses liked. She was tough. She could be near it and be steady. She was a little zany at times, with her trilling rambling monologues, but that only made her more diverting. And she brought food. In an atmosphere of constant stress and fatigue, where people cannot drink or take drugs to relax, where most of them will not smoke cigarettes to relax, snacks are the vice of choice. Put something tasty on a tray on a counter, and the white uniforms will come buzzing around like happy little bees after sugar.

Raymond was awake. Blanche walked to a wire table on wheels where sterile supplies for visitors were kept. Without asking assistance, she slipped on a paper hat, mask, and smock and pulled plastic gloves over her hands. She went in to him.

He was groggy and incoherent. She sat in a chair next to him and attempted to speak to him. The nurses watched from the corners of their eyes. They were instinctively watchful whenever someone not of their tribe came near one of their charges. They also were trying to gauge the relationship.

Blanche called him "Honey" and "Raymond," to which he made groggy replies. She walked out to Lisa Sue Hutchens.

"Is it all right if I mop his brow with a wet washcloth?"

"Yes, certainly, Blanche. There's water over there at that sink."

Blanche sat for an hour, cooling Raymond's head, whispering through the paper mask over and over again, "I know, honey, I know."

Raymond's sons, Ray Jr. and Stevie, appeared at the door to the ICU. Ray had come back from Colorado and Stevie had left his classes at East Carolina University in Greenville. Blanche looked up, saw them, and rushed out to intercept them.

"Raymond's real bad," she said. "Your daddy's real bad. They don't know what's wrong with him. The Kroger doctor couldn't do him any good, and these doctors don't know yet what it is. He's real serious. Boys, I'm afraid he's not going to make it."

Ray and Stevie were thunderstruck. Blanche had called the day before to say he was sick and was going into the hospital for tests. She ushered them to his side. When Raymond saw his sons standing over him, he smiled and lifted up both hands to be squeezed by their hands. The boys bit back tears and spoke warmly to him, coaxing him, encouraging him to get better. They stayed at his side until visiting hours ended.

That night, Raymond improved. His sodium levels corrected, and by morning he looked better and was sitting up and speaking clearly to the nurses. When Dr. Hamilton came in, he reintroduced himself to Raymond and filled him in on what had been happening. He said the evidence indicated Raymond may have suffered from a herpes infection.

It also was possible Raymond had reacted to the Septra antibiotics given him at Long. The doctors still needed to do some very careful monitoring and testing, but Raymond obviously was feeling better, and that was a good sign. They wanted him to try to eat some things by mouth so they could get the GI tube out of his nose.

Blanche came in later that morning, clutching her purse to her side, and went straight to Lisa Sue Hutchens before going to Raymond. Whether or not it registered consciously on the nurses, the fact was that it pleased them for Blanche to come to them first before going to see either the patient or the doctors.

This was their world. Few of the visitors ever seemed to figure it out, but the proper protocol, nevertheless, was for visitors to obtain the nurses' welcome before plunging in. Blanche seemed to know instinctively how to behave.

This was not just a job for the nurses. It was a calling. Nurse Hutchens was the only member of her family ever to have worked anywhere near hospitals or healing. She always had known, even as a child, that this was what she would do. When she was a very young girl, a little boy two years younger than she who lived next door to her family in Winston-Salem developed leukemia. The experience of watching this dear little friend struggle with the disease—childhood leukemia often was fatal at that time—became the central focusing experience of her youth and early adulthood.

Lisa Sue Hutchens became a nurse because she had seen as a very young child that nurses and doctors could step into a process in which a human life was about to end, could change the course of events, and could give life back to the sick. They could add days and weeks and years to a human life.

She went from nursing school to Baptist Hospital, where she worked first in the intermediate care unit. But she saw right away that intermediate care was not quite where she wanted to be. The other name for intermediate care, in hospital parlance, was "step-down intensive care." The place where Lisa Sue Hutchens wanted to be was the step up, intensive care itself, the ICU, the front line, the place where the technical and personal demands on doctors and nurses were greatest, the place where the battle between healers and death was hand-to-hand, urgent, uncertain, and immediate. Within six months of starting at Baptist, in June 1985, she succeeded in winning a transfer to the ICU.

Raymond Reid and Blanche came into her life the following year. On this day, Nurse Hutchens was able to impart the kind of news that was her own greatest reward in life—the news that someone was winning the battle. She told Blanche that Dr. Hamilton had pulled Raymond's GI tube and wanted him to try some food by mouth.

"Lisa Sue, can I feed him? I just know he'll do better for

me. Raymond's real funny about food, and he just loves my cooking...."

Nurse Hutchens said he had to eat a specially prepared diet.

"Oh, I know that, honey. I just think if I sit and talk to him and offer it to him, he'll relax and do better. But if there's any reason why I shouldn't..."

It would be all right for Blanche to feed him.

Blanche took the pabulum-like gruel they gave her and spooned it slowly into Raymond's mouth. He muttered appreciatively. His tongue was thick and his lips were fat and cracked. Some of the food dribbled down his chin. Blanche reached over with a damp washcloth and cleaned him.

"You'll be okay, baby. You're going to get better now."

But Raymond did not get better. In fact, that very night he suffered the first of what would become a series of sudden and hideous relapses. The effect of the arsenic dose he received that day was amplified by the general weakness of his system. His stomach and bowels churned, reversed—he vomited across the room—and then stopped working. His face turned purple, and the membranes covering his eyeballs began to blister. He moaned and twisted with pain before the night nurses could get him sedated. As soon as he was quiet, all of the tubes went back in, and glass vials of Raymond's blood went clattering down the hall on wire trays to the lab.

Chapter Eight

The danger Kroger faced in any attempt to discredit Blanche was that she would get on the stand herself, look like a million bucks, and seem like a nice lady, and all of Kroger's counterattacks would make it look as if a bunch of men were bullying her in defense of Denton—a brute, a tyrant, and a rapist.

But the noose was tightening on Blanche, too. Her money problems were growing much more severe. She had borrowed all she was going to get from Dwight. It wasn't that Dwight wouldn't help if he could, but he just didn't have the money.

Raymond probably would have helped her with some more cash, but he was too sick to arrange it. She had not worked for the better part of a year. It was all or nothing now with the lawsuit. If she won big, she wouldn't have to work again. If she lost, she would be in a bad way. With that kind of litigation and publicity on her record, and at her age, it was going to be very difficult to stay in North Carolina and survive economically.

Raymond rode the torrent of a terrible bout with arsenic for several days, and then, as his kidneys were able to get large amounts of the arsenic out in the urine, he improved again. The swelling went down. He was able to speak clearly. His sodium balanced out, his blood gases looked better, everything was improving.

Morning visiting hours in the ICU were at six-thirty and ten-thirty, and visiting hours in the afternoon were at one-thirty and four-thirty. Blanche's routine—nights and mornings with Dwight, days with Raymond—was made more difficult by the move to Baptist Hospital, since Winston-Salem was another half hour farther from Burlington than the hospital in Greensboro had been.

She showed up with brown paper grocery sacks of food— some for Raymond and some for the nurses and doctors. Raymond's favorite, she explained to the nurses, was banana pudding. She brought the food in Tupperware containers. The pudding she gave to the nurses was in clear containers, and the pudding she gave Raymond was always in an orange container. She also brought Raymond peanut butter milk shakes.

She drove from Burlington as far as Kernersville, a few miles short of Winston-Salem, where she stopped and went to Raymond's trailer in the mobile home park. There she would whip up a peanut butter milk shake for him. If she made it at her home in Burlington and took it to him, she explained to the nurses, it would be melted and runny by the time she got to the hospital.

There also was the fact that Dwight was often around at her own home, and Dwight was growing restive about Blanche's ministrations to this man in the hospital in Winston-Salem, who was supposedly only a friend.

Blanche continued to insist it was her compassionate duty to help Raymond: "He has been there for me, and I have to be there for him." As if to demonstrate there was nothing sneaky going on, she asked Dwight on one occasion to drive her to the hospital. He dropped his work for the day and took her. But when they arrived she informed him he would not be able to enter the ICU, and so Dwight waited outside in his car while Blanche went in to tend to Raymond.

One of the ways the body defends itself against a dangerous poison such as arsenic is by recognizing it quickly and then launching an immediate campaign of violent vomiting in order to get as much of it out as possible in bulk before it has a chance to enter the stomach wall. One of the most effective media in which to disguise arsenic and many other poisons is milk or any milk-based food. By the time the body recognizes the arsenic molecules in the fatty sluice of milk surrounding and buffering it, it is too late—much of the arsenic already has slipped through the stomach lining and is already marching through the blood.

In the universe of the ICU nurses, there are two tribes. There are nurses. And there are the others, the sick people and their families, the ones who come with sickness in them and do not know the rules, the ones to whom death and battles with death are shocking and foreign. The nurses must maintain a psychological fence between themselves and the other tribe in order to do what they have to do and to maintain their own composure.

Over a course of weeks, Blanche slipped through that fence. She came every morning with her bag of goodies. She came always to the nurses first and paid deference. She sat with her man and wiped vomit from his face. She even won their permission to bathe Raymond, which was not a pretty task on the days when his gastrointestinal tract was exploding.

The nurses watched closely from the corners of their eyes. She was gentle and strong with Raymond, but she did not kiss him. She never cried. She didn't behave like one of the other tribe. She behaved like a nurse.

Blanche asked questions about Raymond's care in an aggressive, persistent manner that would have annoyed the nurses, except for one thing: they were such good questions.

She used the right terms. When she spoke to them, the country accent and the bird twitter left her voice: she spoke concisely and well. She asked if the nurses had noticed that the neuropathy, which first had been noted in the hands and feet, seemed to be proceeding along the extremities toward the trunk of the body.

Yes, they had noticed.

Were Raymond's respiratory symptoms suggestive of a weakened diaphragm?

Yes, they could be.

Was the onset and progress of the neuropathy, from the extremities toward the diaphragm, not suggestive of Guillain-Barre?

Yes, it could be.

Was Guillain-Barre not an autoimmune disorder, and might it not be complicated or attended by plural infections?

They weren't sure. That would take some research.

Gradually, the nurses forgot whether Blanche was there on one visiting hour or another. While they shooed other families out the door, they allowed Blanche to stay whenever she wanted. Raymond's isolation had been modified somewhat so that the nurses did not have to suit up in order to go near him, but everyone else was supposed to wear mask and gloves. They told Blanche she didn't have to.

She held the peanut butter milk shakes up to his cracked, swollen lips and poured them slowly into his mouth. "There now, baby," she said. "That will help you get strong again."

The nurses also listened. There were some things about Blanche that never quite added up. They heard her wheedling Ray Jr. and Stevie, urging them to stay away. "You have your studies, Stevie, and Ray, you can't just leave a job and expect it to always be waiting for you. I'm here, boys. I'm here every day, all day, and I'm looking after your daddy the best anybody can. He doesn't even know you're here half the time. Just go on back, and if anything happens one way or the other, I'll let you know."

But then the nurses heard Blanche prattling away at Raymond in the high-pitched singsong voice as she spooned banana pudding into his mouth. "Them boys never come to see you, Raymond. I think that's terrible, they're your only flesh and blood, they should be here every day, it shouldn't be just me, Raymond, I'm not even your wife, I shouldn't have to be the one to tend you."

They shrugged it off. The ICU is a place where the odd little niches in everybody's personality get exposed.

It was late evening. Blanche had stayed long past the end of the afternoon visiting hour, perched over Raymond on a swiveling stool at the side of his bed, with her purse clutched in both hands. Twice she had left to go to the bathroom. The rest of the time she had sat almost motionless over Raymond, reaching once in a while to daub his face where the tubes went in, tracing her fingertips absently over his swollen wrist. "It's terrible how you're doing, Raymond. Your bowels are just terrible. The smell is real bad. They need to wash you. I can't do it now, honey, I got to go.

She rose and walked to the window, staring out. "I've got diarrhea real bad myself. I always seem to have it. I had it bad when I was a little girl."

She murmured to the window in tones almost too soft for him to hear. "They had to take me to the doctor's house one night. He saw me in his kitchen. His wife was there. She was crying. I think she was nice."

Raymond turned his face toward her. "Blanche?" he said with his thickened tongue. "Blanche, where are you? Where are we? Are we ... where are we, Blanche?"

In the middle of that night, the alarms went off on Raymond's monitors. The nurses on duty snapped to attention and moved to his side swiftly, pulling on gloves. He was a Code Blue, meaning he had stopped breathing. A tube was inserted through the mouth down into the lungs, and Raymond Reid was hooked to a Bear II ventilator. He was now alive only because the machinery around him was keeping him alive.

Dr. Hamilton suspected a massive blood infection. Dr. Troost came back to examine Raymond. Signs of growing weakness in his muscles had turned to complete paralysis in the feet and hands.

When Blanche showed up the next morning, the doctors briefed her on what had been happening over the last twelve hours. She listened attentively. They said they were planning a massive battery of tests to eliminate every possible cause until they found their way to the truth.

When they were done talking and were about to leave, Blanche said she wanted to ask them about Guillain-Barre again. In her chats with the doctors, Blanche had been campaigning for Guillain-Barre syndrome for several days now, and it actually was not a bad thought. The signs and symptoms of Guillain-Barre are very close to the gross physical signs and symptoms of arsenic poisoning, which was why Guillain-Barre probably was the single most common misdiagnosis of arsenic poisoning.

There was great debate and no definitive answer concerning the cause of Guillain-Barre. Much of the new evidence pointed to a viral agent, but there was equally strong evidence to support the thesis of an autoimmune disorder—that is, a disorder in which the body's immune system turns on and attacks its own tissues.

The principal similarity between Guillain-Barre and arsenic poisoning is in the most notable early neurological symptoms. Both arsenic and whatever causes Guillain-Barre begin at the toes and fingertips and cause the eating away of the myelin sheaths around the nerve cords. The result is a tingling, numbness, and pain in the "stocking-and-glove" configuration—affecting the areas that would be covered by a pair of stockings and a pair of gloves. Both also cause an overall weakness and mental dullness. At least for a while, they are easy to confuse.

Some of the staff believed Blanche was right—that she had come up with the solution to the puzzle. But Troost and Hamilton were not convinced. Some of Raymond's symptoms were consistent with Guillain-Barre. Some were not. The overall pattern of the disease—the severe attacks, followed by notable recoveries, followed by severe relapses—did not fit Guillain-Barre at all.

Guillain-Barre generally begins at the fingers and toes and works its way inexorably up to the diaphragm, where it can cause death by suffocation. If a patient is kept alive on a ventilator until the attack peaks and subsides, most Guillain-Barre victims recover. But the pattern is a gradual and relentless march from the fingers and toes to the center of the body, followed by a healing pattern which moves in exactly the opposite direction, beginning with the recovery of the diaphragm and working its way back out slowly to the extremities. Raymond Reid's neuropathy didn't seem to move that way, and the sequencing of the attacks was all wrong.

The other troubling thing was Raymond Reid's mental state. People suffering from severe Guillain-Barre are often depressed and preoccupied with their affliction, but they do not have the severe mental symptoms Raymond was exhibiting.

That part—the extreme mental confusion—was indicative of brain damage, which was not typical of Guillain-Barre. On June 27, 1986, Troost and Hamilton came to the conclusion that the up-and-down pattern of Raymond Reid's affliction and the brain problems could be consistent with "heavy metals intoxication"—the medical term which means poisoning by lead, mercury, manganese, thallium, or arsenic. They ordered a heavy metals scan.

A scan sampling the urine over a twenty-four-hour period would screen for all heavy metals. In Raymond Reid's case, the test would not find any of the other metals in greater than "background" or normal amounts, but it would find arsenic.

At that point, in fact, the arsenic in Raymond's urine was six and a half times the normal amount. The environmental means by which people can contract heavy metal poisoning—through the skin or lungs—could not produce levels anywhere near what his urine would show. The only explanation of the levels the test would find would be that Raymond had ingested arsenic by mouth since being admitted to Wesley Long Community Hospital in Greensboro.

There is no normal reason for arsenic to be present in a hospital. For several weeks, Raymond had been too incapacitated to dose himself with arsenic. The only conclusion that could be drawn from such a test would be that someone was attempting to murder Raymond in the hospital by putting arsenic in his food or in one or more of the tubes, through the stopcock valves.

The process by which the doctors came to the conclusion that a heavy metals scan was needed was typical of the way large teaching hospitals are run. In the grand scheme of things, Raymond was Dr. Hamilton's patient, and Dr. Troost was a consultant to Dr. Hamilton. It was Dr. Hamilton's job to order tests and prescribe treatment. It was the job of consulting physicians to offer suggestions to "the attending" concerning possible diagnoses and treatment.

The actual neurological testing of Raymond, however, was not carried out by Dr. Troost. Even though he was Dr. Hamilton's neurological consultant, he, too, had a consultant. The appropriate tests to measure neurological damage were a nerve conduction study and an electromyogram or EMG.

The EMG specialist at Bowman Gray was a colleague of Troost's—Dr. Francis O'Neill Walker. It was Walker who was responsible for the actual tests, which did not mean that he himself did the tests. Instead, Walker dispatched technicians to do the tests, watched some of the work being done, and then analyzed the results. It was Walker who suggested to Troost that there could be any of several diseases or disorders at work and that one of them could be heavy metals intoxication.

Troost's role, then, was to recommend to Hamilton that he consider ordering a scan for heavy metals. But while ordering the test was Dr. Hamilton's responsibility, it was not his job. Actually putting the order into the computer was the job of Dr. Darrell Thomas, who was a "house officer" or medical resident working under Dr. Hamilton. It was the residents—doctors in training, working for low wages on exhausting schedules—who did the actual hands-on work of the hospital.

On a typical day, Dr. Thomas, the resident, would come into the ICU to examine Raymond while Hamilton, the attending, and perhaps Troost, Walker, and other consultants waited in the hall to hear his report. Hamilton, as attending, might well go right back in behind his house officer and recheck Raymond to see how well Dr. Thomas had done, but for the most part the hands-on stuff, such as ordering the test, was the resident's responsibility.

Which did not mean that the resident himself actually ordered the test. Actually what the resident did was order the nursing staff to see to it that the test was run. And actually what the nursing staff did was contact the hospital laboratory and tell it to come do it.

Every bit of this process worked as it was supposed to work in the case of Raymond Reid's arsenic test. Walker recommended to Troost, who recommended to Hamilton, who ordered Thomas, who ordered the nurses, who ordered the lab. The lab came like clockwork at four the next afternoon and began collecting the urine precisely as instructed. The lab sent the urine off at eleven that night to the SmithKline Beecham Clinical Laboratory on the outskirts of Atlanta.

On the next day, acting on the assumption that Blanche might be right, that Raymond's problem could still be a very serious attack of Guillain-Barre and that Raymond did not have time to wait for any more test results, the ICU began performing plasmapheresis, the ultimate tube job. All of Raymond Reid's blood was drawn out of his body—not just a sample, but every drop of it. Working gradually through the day so that his body would always maintain a normal overall content of blood, the machinery attached to Raymond by tubes sucked out his blood and took it apart, cell by cell, storing the blood cells over here and the plasma or fluid over there. Then the machinery built new blood for Raymond, putting his own red and white cells back in but floating them in a man-made solution rather than in his own plasma. The process had been proved to have a salutary if less than fully understood effect on Guillain-Barre sufferers. It was ineffectual against the arsenic that was killing Raymond Reid.

While Raymond was undergoing plasmapheresis, SmithKline was subjecting the urine sample to the appropriate tests and backup tests for heavy metals. The finding was a level of 655 units per measure of fluid. A normal level is 100 units. The question was how. The answer was murder.

At two thirty-three on the morning of July 3, 1986, a computer modem at the SmithKline lab dialed the phone number of a computer modem at North Carolina Baptist Hospital. When a connection had been achieved and the two computers had agreed on each other's protocols, the computer in Georgia transmitted a stream of data to the computer in Winston-Salem. After the two computers had signed off from each other and after their modems had hung up the phone, the Winston-Salem computer sent its data package to a printer elsewhere in the hospital.

The printer cranked up instantaneously and produced a report of the findings in quadruplicate on color-coded sheets of paper with large round holes at each of the upper corners so that the reports could be added to thick prong-folders at each of the destinations where they were intended to arrive. There was an orange copy that would be sent back to SmithKline for verification that the report had been received at Baptist, a green copy that would go into the archives of the Baptist Hospital laboratory, a white copy that would be added to the prong-folder referred to as Raymond's "chart" (already almost a foot thick), and a yellow copy intended for "the physician."

At the very moment when the test result was coming in to Baptist, an event was taking place that worked a dramatic and profound effect on teaching hospitals everywhere in America— an event that took place every year at precisely this same time. Almost invisible to the lay public, it was to hospitals what a complete rotation of all front-line troops would be to a war. It was that week—that period of two days, in fact—when last-year medical students all over America graduated from school, and residents in teaching hospitals all over America went through rotation. The previous shift of young doctors who had managed to learn something from their sleepless stints departed to other posts. They were replaced by fresh young doctors, newly formed and eager, who had not yet had an opportunity to learn the routines of hospitals.

It was the responsibility and job of Dr. Darrell Thomas, the resident, to see to it that the lab results on Raymond Reid's heavy metals test were watched for, received, read, analyzed, and reported on to the attending, Dr. Hamilton. But Dr. Thomas was gone. He had that very day rotated away from Baptist Hospital and out of the life of Raymond Reid.

Before he left, however, Dr. Thomas had written an "off-service note" to the incoming resident who would be in charge of Raymond, telling him all about Raymond's case and alerting him specifically that a heavy metals test was being run at SmithKline and that the new resident should be on the lookout for the results.

The yellow copy for "the physician," then, was intended to go to the new resident. It actually was delivered to a pigeonhole filing cabinet at the nursing station in the ICU. The nurses, who had ongoing responsibility for maintaining the chart, saw the report come in. They watched while the new resident, Dr. Ron Temple, pulled the report from the pigeonhole, read it, and then scratched a notation on the chart. The nurses added their own note to their own record of the day's activity, saying, "Dr. Temple in, aware of lab work."

But the word never went back up the chain of command that the results had come in showing above normal arsenic levels in Raymond Reid's body. Something didn't click. Dr. Temple either didn't understand the report or misinterpreted the findings or simply failed to do what he should have done and surely would have done, had he comprehended what the report was really saying—that Raymond Reid's body was being devoured by arsenic.

It was Ron Temple's first night on duty.

The slip of paper from SmithKline was fastened to the top of the prong binder that held Raymond Reid's chart. In the days and weeks ahead, a blizzard of other slips of papers, notes, and clipboard pages fell on top of the arsenic report, burying it deeper and deeper in the drift of paper that made up Raymond Reid's chart. The results were always there. But the results were lost.

Raymond improved. The doctors assumed the plasmapheresis had helped. His mind cleared. The breathing tube came out. One by one, most of the other tubes were withdrawn. He could sit for short periods and almost feed himself.

Raymond was lying down and feeling weak one afternoon when Stevie appeared for a visit. Both Stevie and his brother, Ray Jr., were handsome, athletic-looking young men who attracted the attention of the younger nurses. The nurses usually kept their distance from families of patients, even handsome young male members of families, but as Raymond improved, the mood around his bed began to loosen up.

That day Stevie said, "Can I bring you some tapes, Dad? Maybe some Jimmy Swaggart tapes?"

Just able to whisper again, Raymond nodded and smiled. "I'd like that."

"I'm gonna go do it right now," Stevie said. "I'll drive out to your trailer and get them."

"Now Stevie, there's no need . . ." Blanche started to say.

"I have nothing else to do. I'm going to go get the tapes for him."

He had always accepted Blanche as a well-meaning but odd person. Even in all the pain and confusion of his parents' divorce, he never had blamed her for anything. But in the long agonizing weeks of his father's illness, Blanche had begun to grate on him as never before. Her advice to him and his brother that they should stay away from their father struck him as crazy, inexplicable, and offensive. But he kept his feelings to himself.

"You want some company?" one of the better-looking young nurses asked. "I'm off."

"Sure."

Blanche watched with sharp bird eyes while the pair left. When she turned, Raymond shrugged and managed a wink.

When Stevie returned to Raymond's bed, Raymond motioned his son to bend low. Raymond had weakened again and was unable to speak aloud. He looked up into his son's face with a twinkle in his eyes and mouthed, "Did . . . you . . . fuck . . . her?"

"Dad!" Stevie said, blushing and straightening up quickly. He laughed. "Come on!"

Raymond was smiling. Blanche closed in on Stevie, half smiling but with eyebrows raised curiously. "What'd he ask you?"

"Nothing."

"What'd he ask you?"

"Nothing, Blanche."

"What'd you ask him, Raymond?"

Raymond shook his head no.

"Looked to me like he asked you if you fucked her."

"Blanche. Forget it. Okay?"

"Well, did you fuck her?"

"No, Blanche, I did not."

"Well, why not? Growing boy your age needs some pussy once in a while. What's the last time you had some good pussy?"

Stevie turned and put his hands up. His face was twitching uncomfortably. "Hey, Blanche! Okay? Can we drop it? I didn't fuck her, okay?"

He whirled away from her and left the room.

Raymond's former wife, Linda, came that afternoon. She and Blanche left the room together at one point and went downstairs to smoke in the lobby. Another woman sharing a bench with them said, "Do y'all have somebody up there?"

"Yes," Linda said. "My ex-husband." She nodded toward Blanche. "He's her boyfriend."

The woman shook her head and smiled.

"I'm his past and she's his present," Linda said. She and the woman on the bench laughed. Blanche said nothing.

On the way back up to the ICU, Blanche hissed in Linda's ear, "Do you not think that looks bad to talk like that to people? Do you? I can't believe you said that. I'm a Christian woman, Linda, and I don't like to look like that in front of people."

"I'm sorry, Blanche. I didn't mean anything by it."

"I just cannot believe you would talk that way to a total stranger. How do you think that makes me look?"

"I'm really sorry, Blanche."

"But you did it anyway. Now it's done. I'm just so embarrassed."

"Blanche. Listen to me. I'm really sorry. I did not mean to embarrass you. I won't ever say anything like that again."

Blanche walked ahead in injured silence and resumed her post at Raymond's bedside.

Stevie drove back to the trailer at Kernersville. He had decided to stay there over the weekend and do some painting and fixing up. Getting the trailer ready for his father was a way to build hope.

He poked and fussed through some of his father's things in the trailer. He found a safe—the kind of locked, weighted, fireproof box that is sold in hardware stores. There was a key in the lock. He could not resist. He turned it and the door pulled open.

Stacked against one side were some silver bars Raymond had bought just after the Hunt brothers of Dallas had caused the price of silver to crash. There was a small metal toolbox inside the safe. Stevie pulled it out. It was heavy.

He opened the top. It was the coin collection. There in a gleaming pile were mementos of each of those moments when his father had taken him and his brother on his knees and shown them the coins he had bought for them, one for Ray, one for Stevie. Stevie closed the box and put it back, fighting back tears.

There were envelopes in the safe. He opened them. They were all insurance papers and stock certificates. He leafed through them, then put them back. He found a photograph— a blurry color photograph of a black man in a white shirt kissing a blond white woman who was wearing a Kroger uniform. There were indistinct images of other people in the back- ground, possibly holding drinks at a party.

In the very back of the safe was a minicassette tape. He pulled it out and snapped open the clear plastic case. He rose slowly, walked to his father's voice-activated tape recorder, and put it in.

His father's voice was first, angrily accusing Blanche of infidelity. On the tape, Raymond told Blanche she put the make on every man who came in the store. Blanche was coarse and shrewish in her own defense, telling him to go fuck himself if he didn't like the way things were.

Blanche said suddenly, "Are you taping me, you son of a bitch?"

Stevie heard a rustle of clothing over the microphone, and then the tape went quiet. He put everything back in the safe and closed and locked it. Then, acting on an impulse, he pulled the key out of the safe, took it across the room, and taped it to the underside of a shelf in a cabinet. He left and returned to the hospital.

Blanche left the hospital shortly after Stevie left. She drove back to Greensboro to the private office of a doctor there. The doctor told her she would need to come back for X-rays.

That night she told Dwight, "My breasts have been big and itchy and irritated till I just about couldn't stand it. And do you know what that doctor said to me? He told me my breasts were swelling up like that because I wasn't having enough sex! He said if I had sex with a man more often, it would help make that go away."

Blanche had been telling Dwight three stories—that her experience with Denton had turned her off to sex, that she felt sinful about sex outside the married state, and finally that her lawyers had warned her not to do anything to mess up her case. Dwight was relatively certain that abstinence did not cause swelling and itching of the breasts. He took Blanche's odd little lie as her way of saying that she was in the mood again.

Betsy Reamer came to see Raymond, as did some of the men he had worked with in Kroger management over the years. As he improved, Raymond began to do what he could to allay their fear and shock on seeing him.

"I've been real bad," he said. "I damn near died. But they've done real good for me here. I think they've got this thing about licked. I seem to be coming back real good."

"And Blanche has been so..." He began to choke up. "I'd be dead if it wasn't for Blanche. She's here every day, all day long. She watches these doctors like a hawk. She questions every single thing they do. And they all love her. They never get mad at her. She's my guardian angel."

Negotiations with Kroger had reached an impasse, and her lawyers were confident they were almost ready for trial.

Toward the end of her sessions with McNiel, Blanche began to stray beyond her charted course and talked about things she hadn't planned to discuss.

"A friend of mine's daughter came to me in a dream last week. She was on a beach, and there was a bunch of people chasing her. She was trying to get away from their clutches. She was all covered with blood and other, other things on her, something. She would stop and sing at them, 'Who can wash away my sin?' That would keep them away, they couldn't get her when she sang at them. It was my friend's daughter in it, not me."

Dr. Hamilton sent Raymond back across the breezeway to the intermediate care unit. Raymond continued to improve, and Blanche continued to visit him every day. As he improved and came back to his normal self, however, Raymond became more and more impatient with everything that was going on. "I don't feel like they have any idea what's wrong with me," he told Blanche.

"They think it's Guillain-Barre."

"Yeah, but Blanche, they...it keeps coming back. They can't explain that. I'm doing better now, but I was before, too. It keeps coming back. I just got to get some answers."

There were Kroger people there the next morning when Blanche bustled in, dressed to the nines, full of cheer and en-couragement, carrying her bag of goodies. "This hospital cook-ing is so terrible, Raymond can't stand it. Now that he can eat again, I'm fixing for him."

She fished out the Tupperware, and the nurses came glid-ing around like friendly sharks. "Oh, I brought some for y'all, too, don't worry," she said, handing them one of the clear con-tainers. "There's chocolate eclairs in that. I know how y'all feel about my chocolate eclairs."

There was a round of giggling and smiles. Raymond beamed. "She's the best cook there is," he said. "She's keeping me alive in here."

Blanche fished out two white pint Styrofoam containers and a third smaller one, all sealed at the top with aluminum foil. She smiled at Raymond. "Banana pudding?"

"Mmm-boy," he said, licking his chops. "My fa-vo-rite."

"Here," Blanche said, handing the two larger containers to Lisa Sue. "These are for y'all."

"Oh, Blanche."

"Y'all are the ones keeping my man alive, and I got to share my pudding with you for it."

Lisa Sue took the two containers gratefully. She bowed out and went across the hall to a break room, where she ate a small amount of pudding from one container. She had just eaten

dinner before coming on duty, so she wasn't hungry. She threw
out the rest of what was in the container she had eaten from
and put the second one in a refrigerator in the office of the
head nurse in ICU, to be shared by the other nurses.

When she peeked back in, Blanche had pulled a peanut
butter milk shake from the bag and was lifting it to Raymond's
lips. "That's his favorite," she was telling the Kroger visitors. "I
have to stop by to his trailer house and make them up or they'd
be all soupy if I tried to carry them all the way from my place.
How's things at the store?"

Lisa Sue hurried on. The Kroger people were full of gossip,
glad to be able to talk about something other than Raymond.
They asked what was going on with her lawsuit.

"They offered us twenty-five thousand dollars a long time
ago, you knew about that, and we turned that down flat. Now
it looks like they're going to go to trial on it, which my lawyers
say is stupid."

A friend from Kroger was with Raymond several hours
later when the massive dose of arsenic hit his system. He sat
upright, his eyes widened, and a jet of vomit shot out of his
mouth and splattered against the television set at the far wall.

The friend backed away from the bed trembling and began
to shout, "Blanche! Blanche! Come quick!"

When Blanche appeared moments later, Raymond's head
had dropped back to the pillow, and the friend was covering
her mouth and pointing mutely at the television set.

"That can mean a heart attack," Blanche said flatly. She
went to his side.

He clutched her hand and stared into her eyes. "Blanche,
go get them. Go get them right now. It's bad. It's real bad this
time. Go get them."

At that moment Lisa Sue was coming through the breezeway on her way somewhere else and peeked in. Blanche looked
up. "You've got to help me, Lisa Sue," she said. "This doctor
in here doesn't know what he's doing. Just look how he is."

There was not much Lisa Sue Hutchens had not seen, but
she was shocked when she saw Raymond. It was unbelievable
that his condition could have changed so grotesquely in such a
short time. Her eyes quickly inspected his face, his general skin
condition, the monitors and tubes. All of his vital signs were
bad, urine production was bad, he was gasping for air. She was

afraid he was going to have a heart attack at that moment, before her eyes.

But it was Raymond's eyes that made Lisa Sue Hutchens gasp. He was wild with panic. His eyes were huge and rolling, like the eyes of a caged animal. His voice was already thick and gurgling. With weak trembling fingers, he attempted to clutch her hand and pull her to him.

"Help me," he whispered hoarsely. "Please help me or I'm going to die."

She made sure first that a house officer was alerted. Then she returned to the bed to comfort Raymond. But her heart was not in it. His deterioration was too incredible, too devastating and sudden. Something terrible was wrong with him, something wholly unnatural, something she had never seen before, a frightening thing inside, a beast devouring him from within.

Chapter Nine

Lisa Sue was relieved when the resident showed up and Raymond was bustled back down the hall to the ICU. The tubes that had been disconnected were all reconnected. The breathing tube went down his throat, the GI tube went in his nose, the full set of IVs were put in again. Blanche stood at his side the whole time. By late that night, the arsenic blisters had reformed and broken through most of his gastrointestinal tract, sending out rivers of bloody rice-water stools. What urine he produced was full of blood and undigested carbohydrates. His blood gases were beginning to drop, the platelets and white cells in his blood were beginning to come apart, the inside of his mouth and the outer surfaces of his eyes were blistering, his face was beginning to turn a blue-purple.

His body fluids were beginning to leak through the walls of organs and blood vessels. His body also was beginning to retain fluids, so that the ghastly process of swelling began in earnest, almost before the eyes of the nurses and doctors peering down on him, like the blowing up of a balloon.

His speech began to slur and fade. He had been down this road before. The worst part now was that he knew what to expect. The last time this had happened, the nurses had taught him a system for communicating after he lost the power of speech. He hurried this time to teach it to Blanche. He motioned to Blanche with his eyes, and she bent low over him. In a gurgling whisper, he mouthed into her ear: "Like this." He made a clicking sound in his throat. "Yes."

She nodded. "One click for yes," she said.

He nodded to show she was right. "Like this," he said. He made two clicking sounds. "No."

She nodded again.

Raymond Reid slipped beneath a merciful fog of drugs.

Blanche went back to the doctor in Greensboro the next day. His nurse sent her into his private office instead of an examining room. He came in and sat at his desk.

"Mrs. Taylor, I'm very sorry, but I have hard news for you. The lump, as you know, is quite large, and the biopsy shows that it is malignant. We will have to perform a radical mastectomy."

"Which means?"

"Most of the breast."

"One breast."

"I hope so. And a good deal of the lymphatic structure in the armpit above it. You have cancer, Mrs. Taylor. Breast cancer. It's very serious."

Two days later, Blanche approached Karla Ann Ruth, one of the RNs in the ICU.

"You sure have pretty handwriting, Karla," she said. "I wonder if you could help me with something. Raymond has been dictating some things to me, and I just scratched them on this old scrap of paper. Would you recopy it for me? It's so messy, I'm just afraid nobody can read it like this."

Karla looked at the scrap Blanche was holding. There was one paragraph scrawled on a piece of paper about the size of a filing card. "Sure," Karla said. She took a blank worksheet from her clipboard. She sat down at a desk and put Blanche's scrap beside her. It began, "I, Raymond Reid, being of sound mind . . ."

She paused and looked up at Blanche. Blanche smiled back. "Thanks really a lot, Karla."

Karla continued with her task. The paragraph directed that all of Raymond Reid's real and personal property be divided in equal shares among his two sons, Stevie and Ray Jr., and "my friend, Blanche K. Taylor."

Blanche took the draft will to her attorney in the sexual harassment suit, James F. Walker of Gibsonville, who recommended she take it on to a friend of his, Robert D. Hinshaw, an attorney in Winston-Salem who would be nearer the hospital. Hinshaw rendered the crude holographic will as a legal document and then took it, accompanied by Blanche, back to the hospital.

With the nurses standing at the bedside to interpret Raymond's clicking sounds, Hinshaw asked Raymond a series of questions about his wishes. After satisfying himself that Raymond knew what he was doing in spite of his suffering, Hinshaw took the will back to his office to make some modifications. Again accompanied by Blanche, he presented himself a second time with the will.

By now, Raymond was far beyond being able to sign a document. Hinshaw held the will up before Raymond's blistered eyes, asked him more questions, and watched the nurses while they watched Raymond reply. Through the miasma of drugs, pain, confusion, and fear, it was clear to all of them—to the nurses, to Hinshaw, to some of the Kroger people who were visiting—that Raymond Reid truly wanted his will changed and wished deeply and intensely to do something to provide for Blanche after his death.

Hinshaw signed each of the seven pages of the will in Raymond Reid's name. In tiny letters after each signature, he scrawled, "by RDH."

Three evenings later, the alarms went off at the ICU nursing station. On the upper monitor line, Raymond Reid's heartbeat had gone flat. The nurses sounded the code alarm to summon the doctors. Two nurses stepped quickly to his bedside to examine the monitors and tubes. Blanche stepped back out of the way wordlessly. Two other nurses rushed to the bed with a crash cart and a defibrillator cart. They were ready with the cups in their hands to give to the doctors when the doctors burst in through the swinging doors.

Fifteen minutes later, with every marvel of medical science

working at full tilt to save him, Raymond Reid returned to life. His heart achieved a weak but fairly stable beat of its own, and his blood gases began to nudge back up toward a life-sustaining level.

The next morning, Stevie appeared with his girlfriend. He had come down from college to visit his mother, Linda, in Burlington. Blanche was there waiting, dressed in her best-looking yellow jumpsuit with her hair and makeup perfect. Blanche filled Stevie in on the details of his father's near-death the day before.

Stevie leaned over his father and gasped. Raymond's face had swollen like a beach ball. Because the arsenic had turned the walls of Raymond's blood vessels into sieves, the only way the doctors could maintain sufficient blood pressure in his veins was to keep pumping in IV fluids at greater and greater pressures. In addition to all of the other swelling, the IVs had pumped in an additional sixty pounds of fluid in a twenty-four-hour period, almost all of which was leaking out of his veins as fast as it went in. The result was what is called "third-spacing"— a form of swelling almost never seen in living bodies outside an ICU.

His face had ballooned out so hugely that the swollen flesh had engulfed all of his features. His mouth was lost in the swelling, and his nose was barely discernible. When he opened his deeply sunken eyes, they were opaque with yellow reptilian scales, ooze and blood.

But the most frightening aspect of his appearance was the skin. The swelling was so huge that the skin, normally an elastic tissue, could not stretch far enough. All over his body the skin had begun splitting. Rivers of fluid weeped from the raw fissures on his face, as his skin began to tear like water-soaked Kleenex. If this went on a few more days, he no longer would have skin.

Very few people could look at Raymond. The nurses and the doctors could, but he was a terrible sight even for them. Almost none of the family could. The boys fought bitterly with Blanche at this point to keep the Kroger people away, but Blanche continued to slip them in. The Kroger people could not look at Raymond for more than a split second without gasping and rushing away. But for some reason Blanche insisted on whisking them in to show Raymond to them, chitchatting along all the while as if Raymond had been here for his annual physical.

Blanche could sit with him. She sat for hours by the bed, whispering to Raymond and staring at the featureless splitting puffball where his face had been.

Lisa Sue Hutchens watched Blanche sitting with Raymond. Her heart went out to Blanche. Blanche could brave death, could look past the grotesque and gaze with a quiet eye on the human life within. Blanche had, Nurse Hutchens thought, the soul of a healer.

Stevie stayed with him less than a minute on this visit. Then he had to leave the ICU to regain his composure. He kept walking until he reached the elevator, rode down, and then walked out the front door of the hospital, where he finally collapsed on a bench. Someone sat beside him.

It was Blanche.

"Blanche," he gasped. "Blanche, what are we gonna do? What are we gonna do if Daddy dies?"

"We'll have to run to the bank and get his safe deposits cleared out before the state finds out about it," she said. "Then we'll clear out all his accounts."

Stevie stared at his hands, trying to absorb what he was hearing. He turned his tear-streaked face up to her. "No, Blanche. That's not what I mean. I mean, how am I gonna live without my daddy?"

Blanche stared off toward the traffic moving in front of the hospital. She drew a sighing breath. "Just be strong," she said in her bird voice. "Just be strong."

Linda came to the hospital that afternoon. Each time she came, Blanche took her aside and filled her in on what was going on. The two were friendly and warm with each other. But on this afternoon, Blanche had to leave. Stevie and his mother were standing alone at the bedside when two of the doctors appeared.

"We have a very strange set of circumstances here with Mr. Reid," one of the doctors said. "His illness is very severe for Guillain-Barre, and the overall pattern is not consistent. We are doing everything we can to determine what's going on with him."

When the doctors walked away, Stevie turned to his mother, his face twitching angrily.

"Mama, I want that bitch kept away from Daddy. I think she's trying to poison him."

"Who are you talking about?"

"Blanche."

Linda stared at her son, disbelieving, unable to speak for a moment.

"Stevie, stop that. Blanche cares for your father, she loves him, she's here every day, fighting these doctors when they need to be fought and watching every move these nurses make."

He kept shaking his head. "I don't care. I don't care. I don't trust her. I don't trust that crazy bitch. I think she's trying to kill my daddy."

"Is it . . . ?" She pointed to herself. "Is it because . . . ? Stevie, Blanche did not cause my divorce, I hope you understand that."

"It's not that. I just . . . it's . . . there is something wrong with that bitch, something bent." He collapsed in sobs and left the room. Linda rushed after him to comfort him. He apologized for what he had said.

The next morning Stevie returned to the ICU. Somehow Raymond was able to communicate that he wanted to see Linda about something, something to do with Ray Jr. Stevie called his mother and told her to come.

Linda was attempting to do the right thing by her sons and former husband and still hold on to the excellent job she had acquired recently as an environmental impact report auditor for a chemical company. It was a demanding position with a lot of responsibility, the best job she had ever had. When Stevie called, she said, "I know what your father wants to talk to me about. He wants to know if Ray is coming back from Colorado. Go back in there and tell him Ray has his tickets and is on his way."

She then got on the phone to Colorado, told Ray what was happening, told him she would arrange for his tickets and that he needed to get himself to Denver. She called the airline and reserved tickets for him. She drove straight to Winston-Salem to the hospital.

When she went in, Raymond was able to talk a little, but he could barely hear. She leaned over the swollen mass where his face had been and shouted: "Ray is coming back tonight! Do you understand, Raymond? Ray is coming back tonight!"

"What time is it?" he asked.

"Ten in the morning. I am going to work. Ray will be here tonight. I will be back."

Ray Jr. made it to the hospital that evening and saw his father alive.

The next morning, when Ray and Stevie arrived at the hospital, Blanche met them downstairs, fashionable and composed as ever. She walked to the elevator with them. When the doors closed, they were alone in the elevator.

"Now boys," she said, "if your daddy passes away today, you don't want no autopsy done on him. He's been poked and prodded enough, and it won't bring him back for them to cut him all to pieces like hamburger meat."

The boys walked in a daze with her down the long flourescent corridor. A little bearded man in a suit was standing with his shoulder touching one wall watching them approach. There was something tentative in the way the man held himself. He stepped forward when they were near and waved them to a door across the hall. They followed him and found themselves standing in a tiny chapel. The man introduced himself as the hospital chaplain.

He told the boys their father was dead.

A doctor appeared. It was Dr. Kyle Jackson, the last intern who had been responsible for Raymond. Lisa Sue Hutchens came in a moment later. After Dr. Jackson had expressed his sorrow over Raymond's death, he said, "I think we need to do an autopsy to answer some of these questions."

Blanche shook her head adamantly. "No, the boys don't want an autopsy. Their daddy's been cut on enough."

"I really think it's important, Blanche," Lisa Sue said. "There are so many unanswered questions..."

"No. No. They don't want him cut on."

"Mrs. Taylor," Dr. Jackson said, "he is beyond suffering now. We are only talking about his body."

Blanche moved in on the intern. She stuck her finger in his face. "I hope now you're sorry for what you done. Now maybe you see that you weren't giving Raymond the care he needed. Maybe you will care for your next patient. And now you want to cut on him some more. The boys don't want that. Do you, boys? Do you want that?"

The finality of the death of their father was just settling on Ray and Stevie. They were fading into a dense fog of grief, and the voices around them were blending together in tinny dissonant babble. They shook their heads no. The intern shrugged and stalked off angrily. Lisa Sue walked out.

When Linda came off the elevator a moment later, she saw them all piling out of the chapel and had no idea any discussion had taken place concerning an autopsy. She simply assumed there would be one, because there was so much they still didn't know.

There was not to be one.

Raymond's body was sent to Low's Funeral Home in Burlington that day. The next day, Blanche drove to Linda's house in Burlington to pick up the boys, so that the three of them could go to the funeral home and make arrangements.

As soon as that had been accomplished, the boys found themselves sitting in Blanche's car in front of the small bank across the street from the Burlington Kroger store. It was the bank where Blanche and Raymond had taken the store's night deposits for years. It was also the bank where Raymond had his personal checking account.

The boys, still in a fog, followed Blanche into the bank and took seats in a waiting area. The manager came over quickly when he saw Blanche and asked how she was feeling.

"I'm fine, Tom. How're you?"

He asked how Raymond was.

"Oh, not very good," she said. "And those doctor bills just keep on going. You know Raymond give me a power of attorney for his account. And he just wants us to close it out. He has a little over eight thousand dollars in it."

The manager was uncomfortable. He said he wasn't sure if the bank had enough cash on hand and would have to go check. He disappeared in the back.

It dawned on the boys that Blanche had just given the banker the impression their father was still alive. They figured she knew what she was doing.

He returned five minutes later with a thick stash of cash in various denominations. Back in the car, she said, "I'll just take this all over to Jim Walker's office, because they're lawyers and they'll know what to do with it.

"Oh boys, I know this is all hard, but you know, when it's over, what I think we should all do is take this money and buy a little business together and just go into business and be one big happy family. Wouldn't that be nice?"

It was a theme she had been sounding repeatedly in the last two days. In her other reverie about life after Raymond's death, she talked about taking the boys on a luxurious vacation, a cruise, perhaps, to Hawaii or the South Seas. They listened numbly. The image of Hawaii was pretty and merciful. Stevie smiled to himself.

She dropped the boys off at Linda's house. From there it was a quick ride by herself to the other bank where Raymond had his safe deposit box. With his key in her hand and a warm greeting for everyone, Blanche was in the vault in minutes and had emptied out the contents of Raymond's box.

Raymond Reid was laid to rest in a wooden casket with polished brass handles. He looked better than he had in the last several months of his life. His thick dark hair was neatly swept back and sprayed in place. The fluids had drained from his body and the skin had fallen back into place on a handsome face with a strong aquiline nose, broad brow, dark eyebrows, and well-formed chin. He wore a dark blue pinstriped suit, a blue shirt with button-down collar, and a dark tie with thin brown and white stripes. His hands were folded at his waist.

A few days after the funeral, Blanche called and found the boys at home alone, while their mother was at work. She said she needed to come over. When she arrived, she asked Stevie to go out to her car and bring in the safe from Raymond's trailer in Kernersville.

"I don't have no idea what's in it, I've never seen it opened," she said in the birdlike voice, "so I thought we should all open it together and see."

Stevie brought it in, wondering what she was going to do for a key. But the moment he put the safe down on the floor, Blanche produced a key. It was not the key he had taped under the shelf, which had been rusty. This key was shiny and new. She must have gone to the store where Raymond bought the safe and bought a replacement key for it, Stevie thought.

She handed the key to Ray, who knelt down on the floor and opened the safe. Stevie watched while Ray pulled things out. None of the insurance papers were there. When Ray

opened the box containing the coin collection, Stevie bit back
a grunt. At least half of the collection was missing, maybe more.
The silver bars were missing.

Stevie stared at the box on the floor and then at Blanche.
Both his mother and Ray had made it clear to Stevie that it
only added to their grief and pain for him to question Blanche.
As far as they were concerned, Blanche was an odd but good-
hearted woman who had given many years of her life to Raymond Reid. So Stevie said nothing about the safe.

Blanche handed the boys an accounting of their father's
estate, prepared by Walker and Hoy, her lawyers in the sex
suit. It was the first the boys knew of their father's new will
cutting Blanche in for a third of Raymond's estate. Her share
was $22,556 in cash immediately and a third of whatever they
raised by selling Raymond's trailer, car, and other personal
property.

The boys were under the impression that Raymond's Kroger life insurance policy for $137,392 was not included in the
will. But Blanche had a major surprise for them.

"Raymond wanted me to have a third of that, too. It is in
the will."

The truth was different. The insurance company was
bound by law to distribute the money according to the beneficiaries named in the policy, not according to the will. But
Blanche said Raymond's intent in the will was to give her a third
of everything, including the insurance money. She expected
the boys to hand over $45,797.33 to her when they received
the money.

Ray said, "If that's how Daddy laid it out, Blanche, then
that's how it's going to be."

Blanche's severe money problems suddenly were over.

A week after Raymond's death, Blanche's brother-in-law
in Washington, D.C., who had been struggling with cancer for
two years, finally succumbed. A few days later, Blanche's elderly
aunt died of old age.

Blanche saw Dr. McNiel one last time and told him, "I feel
like Job."

One month after Raymond Reid's death, Dwight and
Blanche drove to the town of Boone, a picturesque resort town
in the Blue Ridge Mountains. They spent a romantic weekend

together. It was during that weekend that they decided to become engaged.

On the way back down out of the mountains, Blanche said, "Dwight, I have something to tell you that I know you're not going to like."

"What?"

"Raymond Reid made me the executrix of his estate."

Dwight drove in silence for a while, allowing the full import of this news to settle in. Blanche had always insisted that her relationship with Raymond was platonic. Raymond Reid had sons, even a loyal ex-wife he could have named to execute his will. Naming Blanche to do it was not the act of a platonic friend. Money, like sex, is by nature not platonic. But they had finally settled on an engagement, and Dwight's dream of a healed life was about to come true.

"I think that's your business," he said.

She said nothing.

The next day they drove to Burlington and visited the Van Scoy Diamond Mine, a jewelry store. Blanche picked out a ring with a diamond in the center and a ruby on each side. It was a hefty investment for Dwight, but he was very proud of it. They left it at the store to be sized, and Dwight went back the next day to pick it up. When he slipped it over her finger, he was as happy as he had been in many years. They didn't call it an engagement ring out loud, but they both knew that it was.

Blanche impressed on Dwight that their engagement would have to be kept a strict secret between the two of them. Her lawyers were moving ahead and hoped to bring the Kroger suit to trial within the next several months. In preparation, they had asked Blanche to spend some time with more psychiatrists, including a Dr. Selwyn Rose of Winston-Salem.

After seeing Blanche, Dr. Rose was prepared to testify that Kevin Denton's persecution had ruined her life and rendered her a "nonfunctional person." Blanche pointed out to Dwight that knowledge of her engagement to him in the middle of all this would be useful to the Kroger attorneys. Dwight said he understood.

It was both an exciting period for Dwight and a difficult one. He and Blanche spent time together whenever they could, sandwiched between his duties as a pastor and her work on the lawsuit, which was becoming ever more demanding. But

Dwight, who was a determined man where major goals in his life were concerned, wanted to see the relationship consummated properly, tied up and finished with a marriage. He did not enjoy the furtive aspect their meetings sometimes assumed. When they were alone together, she sometimes wore the engagement ring for him. The rest of the time she did not wear it.

Dwight did not try to hide his relationship with Blanche from his parishioners. He might have, given the fact that Blanche's lawsuit was taking place in the next county and was beginning to attract a good deal of attention in the press. But it was the way of the small mill towns of North Carolina that people in the town of Carolina would mind their own business. What happened in Guilford County was Guilford County's concern. Dwight's parishioners knew they had landed an educated preacher who nevertheless was one of them and who obviously loved them. He was a good-looking man and a whole man, and he had found himself a widow woman who, at age fifty-three, was still good-looking. That was all they needed to know.

Even though a polite haziness was maintained concerning the precise status of their relationship, Blanche immediately began to fit in and become a part of the lives of Dwight's flock. She always asked how people were doing and always remembered what they had told her before of their personal lives. She was endlessly thoughtful and took cakes and other small comforts to people who were sick or suffering an emotional or spiritual pain.

In all of her interest in the personal affairs of the parish, Blanche was especially watchful of Dwight. On one occasion, Dwight received a phone call from a woman in the church who said she had been having an affair with a man, that the man was breaking it off, and that she was having thoughts of suicide. Dwight rushed first to counsel the woman, and then, in his typically determined and thorough fashion, he started trying to get in touch with the man involved in the affair—a man who was not a member of Dwight's church. The man finally agreed to meet with him. The man's explanation of the affair was that the woman in question, Dwight's parishioner, was "oversexed" and had initiated the affair.

Dwight made the mistake of passing on this story to Blanche, mainly because he thought it was ridiculous and adolescent of the man to excuse his own behavior that way. But Blanche became very anxious, jealous, alternately angry and tearful whenever the woman's name came up after that.

There was another occasion that aroused even greater anxiety in Blanche. One day while she was at the parsonage and Dwight was running an errand, a man came to the door. Blanche stayed back in the kitchen and did not answer. The man knocked for a while, then looked in the drive and probably saw Blanche's car but did not see Dwight's. He left.

Blanche went to the door and opened it a crack to watch him depart. A scrap of paper fell to her feet. The man's name and phone number were written on it. She lifted it up and examined it. It was the name of a man Dwight had mentioned to her. Dwight had said the man was a homosexual.

Blanche flew into a frenzy when Dwight returned. She wanted to know what the man wanted with Dwight. He told her it was a personal problem, something he couldn't discuss.

Blanche stared back blankly. It was in this kind of discussion that she and Dwight were farthest apart. Raymond had not been religious when she and he had begun their relationship, but he had come around to sharing her interest in religion, and, because he learned it from her, his religion was centered on the teachings of Jimmy Swaggart, Jim Bakker, and the other fire-and-brimstone TV preachers Blanche loved.

Dwight was another story. All of his erudition and education seemed to have watered his religion down to nothing, Blanche felt. She told him as much, and he held up his hands, smiled, and said, "Perhaps, Blanche, it would be better if we did not discuss theology."

By the summer of 1987, Blanche had other things to worry about. Kroger had decided to go to trial on the lawsuit. It was show time.

Blanche's family gathered at her side in the courtroom in Greensboro—her daughters, her sisters and brothers, the entire clan. It was much more than a gesture. It was an important statement that the jurors would weigh carefully. A person with a family—a loyal clan—was a person of substance and not a wandering opportunist.

The same principle meant that Kevin Denton's clan had to gather, too—his wife, daughters, and friends.

Kroger fielded a full table of attorneys, as did Blanche's team. When all of the experts and other witnesses were either in the court or waiting outside, and when all of the regular courthouse hangers-on had taken the early seats, there was barely room for the crowd of titillated onlookers who gathered each day. At the center of it all was Blanche, sitting at the plaintiff's table with every eye in the room upon her.

She managed to dress modestly but stylishly and had her hair and makeup perfectly done for each day of trial. She looked like a nice dignified woman who also happened to be very attractive.

Kroger's defense was complex. First, the Kroger lawyers argued that Blanche's relationship with Denton had been consensual. They argued secondly that the company had done the only thing it could, which was to fire Denton the moment it learned what was going on. The third and most perilous leg of the defense argument was left to Denton.

It was Denton's job to get on the stand in front of his family and friends, admit to a certain amount of sexual activity with his subordinates and in particular with Blanche, and then convince the jury in spite of everything else that Blanche had entrapped him in the pants incident.

For the onlookers and the media, the evidence was a delicious slice. The cartoon with the naked lady hanging from a ceiling fan was introduced, as was the "white milk" business.

Dr. Selwyn Rose testified for the defense that as a result of her treatment at the Battleground store, Blanche had become "a nonfunctional person."

"She has suicidal thoughts," he said. "Most of the time she does nothing."

In response to questions from her own lawyers, Blanche gave a toned-down but still quite candid account of Denton's advances. She also testified that she had pleaded with her supervisors in the store to protect her from Denton and that they had ignored her.

Kroger tried to make something of the fact that Blanche had said early on that she had made incriminating tape recordings of Denton and then had failed to produce them. They tried to argue that Blanche had never produced the tapes because the tapes would have incriminated her.

Kroger worked to build a body of evidence showing

Blanche had never complained or warned anyone in the company of what was going on until after the incident in question.

Then it was Denton's turn at bat. While his family and friends looked on, and while the jury sat practically hanging out of the jury box in order to hear every word, gauge every expression, and weigh each tiny inflection, Denton told his tale. He spoke in a manner which he intended to be remorseful but which, given what he had to say, came across to most observers as crocodilian.

Yes, he had engaged in sexual relationships with some of his subordinates, but nowhere near the number Blanche had suggested. Pressed on the point, he said the number was four, but that all four sexual relationships had been consensual. Pressed on that point, he said the women in question had expressed their consent by not voicing any objections.

He painted Blanche as the archetypal oversexed woman. She had approached him with dirty "ethnic jokes." She had kissed him several times. Denton admitted he had had three sexual encounters with Blanche the month of the incident. He said that Blanche had come to him in the conference room a week before the incident, embraced him, and "fondled my genitals," and then suggested they meet one night the next week in the conference room for the real thing.

Denton said he had come to the conference room on the appointed night and had found Blanche putting away women's uniforms. He said he made a joke about how big the uniforms were. And then Denton told the court that he himself had slipped out of his pants and had put on the pants of one of the female uniforms.

It was at this point that the Kroger lawyers, watching the jurors like hawks, began to grow concerned. It was as if almost anything else Denton could have told the jury might have slipped through—but not putting on women's clothing. The faces of the jurors darkened visibly, their eyes sharpened, and their bodies stiffened in a posture of extreme reproach. From beneath a lowered brow, Blanche's eyes watched the jurors' every breath.

Denton testified that while standing in the darkened conference room in a woman's uniform, he had said to Blanche, "Are you ready?" He said Blanche left the room at that point, and while she was gone, he took off the woman's pants and his own underpants, so that when she returned he would be standing there naked from the waist down and ready for sex.

The Kroger lawyers called a conference with Blanche's lawyers. The suit asked for $3.6 million in actual damages and $10.4 million in punitive damages. If Blanche won at the Superior Court level, Kroger would appeal. Blanche was ahead on emotion in this court, but she might lose on the law in the next one. At any rate, appeals would tie the case up for years. Would she take $275,000?

When the lawyers had taken their cut and when Uncle Sam had taken his lick, Blanche would have just over $100,000 to put in the bank. The settlement offer was a fraction of what it would cost Kroger to continue fighting her. It looked like a fortune to Blanche.

She and her lawyers took it. The next day the *Greensboro News & Record* published the story under a big headline, KROGER HARASSMENT SUIT SETTLED. In the story, members of the jury told the *News & Record* they were entirely on Blanche's side, had bought none of Kroger's story, and believed Denton was an ogre and Kroger knew about him all along.

They dismissed Kroger's argument of a setup out of hand. Blanche's lawyers had told her to get proof. She got it. Without the pants, one juror told the paper, Blanche would not have had a prayer. But Denton was the one who took his own pants off, of his own free will, and clothed himself instead in a lady's pants. They said they would have given Blanche a minimum of $7 million.

The amount of the settlement was a strictly held secret, but most people in Burlington wrongly assumed the settlement probably was the lion's share of the $7 million mentioned in the jury story.

Blanche's lawyers attempted to sell the settlement publicly as a tie. They might find themselves doing business with Kroger again. Blanche honored her promise to keep the amount quiet. She frankly enjoyed having people think it was much more.

All in all, it was an enormous victory for Blanche. She had gone toe-to-toe with the huge national company that had employed her for thirty years. It had thrown all its resources at her, the best lawyers, detectives, and witnesses money could buy, and she had defeated it. She had walked away with money.

* * *

A month after the settlement, Blanche checked herself into the hospital and underwent a radical mastectomy. Dwight was at her side often, as were all the members of her extended family. She was tough and dignified through the entire process.

One evening a month later, Dwight prepared a modest supper for them at the parsonage. Blanche had little to say, so he talked. He talked about his beloved scuppernong grapes. One of the first things he had done when he moved into the parsonage in Carolina was plant a vine of scuppernongs—a golden-green grape native to the South and named after the Scuppernong River in North Carolina, from an Algonquian word which means "place of the magnolia." Dwight could gobble them by the handful. Having his own tiny vineyard of them by the side of the house was his way of being rooted again, tied back to the soil of his beloved North Carolina, barely an hour's drive from the tobacco farm where he had grown up.

In the middle of his long soliloquy on scuppernong grapes, Blanche looked up and said, "Dwight, will you be horrified by my body when you see it?"

He stopped and stared at her in silence for a long moment. Then he reached across the table and gathered her hands in both of his hands.

"Oh, Blanche. You are so beautiful. And strong. And good. You mean so much to me. You can have no idea what you have meant to my whole life. Please, please, know that nothing could come between us. I see a very beautiful lady sitting across the table from me, Blanche Taylor. It's true that one small change could make you more beautiful."

She smiled in spite of herself through tear-blurred eyes. "Oh, Dwight."

"You know what I mean, don't you?"

"Yes."

"The one thing that would make you perfect in my eyes would be for you to change your name to Blanche Moore."

He came around the table to her. She hugged him hard and kissed his face, smearing her rare tears across his cheek.

"Dwight," she said softly, smiling. "Dwight. Do you know what is funny? Do you know something really funny that I have never told anybody else but you in my life?"

Dwight paused and looked at her. Blanche was not big on funny things. This was a moment to mark.

"What, Blanche?"

"I have always hated that name."

"My name?"

"No, no, no, no. Oh, I'm sorry, Dwight. No, not at all. I love your name. My name! I hate my name. I have always hated my name."

"Your name?"

"Yes. Blanche. I hate that name. I just hate it. I always have. Isn't that strange?"

Two days later a letter arrived at Blanche's trailer house with Dwight's return address at the top. She took it inside, sat at her kitchen table, and opened it.

"Dear Blanche,

"Blanche, Blanche.

"P.S. You are the most kind, caring, giving, thoughtful, considerate, gentle, tender-hearted, selfless, loving, generous, responsible, honest, thankful, concerned, charitable, benevolent, merciful, patient, just, virtuous, sincere, faithful, trustworthy and decent person I have ever known. You are also quite attractive, and I like you."

In the months ahead, Blanche underwent extensive reconstructive surgery. She was proud of the fact that her own breasts were sufficiently large that the surgery could be accomplished without the use of any synthetic implant or tissue substitute. She had often talked about having a breast-reduction operation, and she treated the mastectomy in some conversations as if it had been a breast reduction.

Dwight had been introducing Blanche more and more into his own family circle, bringing her along for family gatherings and encouraging his siblings to get to know her. Nola, Dwight's sister in Reidsville, North Carolina, was neither a naive woman nor a prude, but she found Blanche's behavior about the reconstructive surgery odd.

Confronted with a room of relative strangers, Blanche

would shove her breasts up and forward and say, "That's all me in there, I swear it's true."

But the family also saw how dearly Dwight loved Blanche and how attentive to Dwight Blanche seemed to be. Dwight's other sister, Nellie Hayes, who lived in Pittsburgh, got to know Blanche on visits home to the family farm. She came to like her very much. As her brother did, she chalked up the breast remarks to a harmless and even winning eccentricity.

Just as Blanche had completely cut herself off from the Taylor family following James's death, so she cut herself off from the Reids. From the moment the last penny of the estate fell on her palm, she never called or wrote or contacted the Reid boys again. Months went by.

Finally the Reid boys called Blanche. They had been stewing, especially Stevie. At the time of his father's death, he had been too overwhelmed by the pain of the experience and by grief to know what to do. He and his older brother had followed Blanche around Burlington like zombies for a week while she collected all of their father's accounts. They had agreed to pay her the third of the life insurance money she had told them Raymond wanted them to give her. But the money had been a long time in coming to them from the insurance company.

As time had passed and they had begun to recover from their loss, the boys thought back through all of their transactions with Blanche. It was as if a thick haze of grief finally began to part, and instead of seeing a welcome dawn in its place, they saw a great deal that was ugly and disquieting in the way Blanche had handled herself. In the first place, a good deal of their father's estate was in Kroger stock or pension fund money that had to be wrested from the Kroger bureaucracy. Kroger was not recalcitrant, but the process was arduous and took place on a business and legal terrain that was foreign to the boys.

Blanche, who was supposed to be the executrix, was of no help. She called them almost every day, however, to check on their progress in securing the Kroger money, and she often made mention of the fact that she was reporting everything to her lawyers, who also had somehow more or less become the boys' lawyers in the deal.

As soon as Kroger paid off on their father's life insurance, the boys paid Blanche her third of it—nearly $46,000. Months later, the estate had been fully liquidated, and there was $52,000 in cash left to be disbursed among the three of them.

But by then, their attitude toward Blanche had changed. They realized she had lied to them about things during the process and that she had pushed them around generally in an effort to get more money out of them than she had coming.

Ray and Stevie decided to go see the lawyers. They asked to see their father's will for the first time. The lawyers showed them the will, but the boys' visit to the lawyers came close on the heels of the Kroger settlement, and the lawyers were still feeling very protective of Blanche and her award.

Ray was the one who finally put a point to things: "Did the will say we legally had to give Blanche a third of the insurance money or not?"

"No."

"Well, should we have given it to her?"

The lawyers were no help. They said they wanted the boys to settle that question with Blanche, not with them. The boys left with the distinct impression the lawyers thought they were a couple of ungrateful young money-grubbers looking for a way to find fault with a kind woman who had done everything in her power for them and for their father, before and after his death.

It was not a good feeling. In fact, they felt worse and worse the more they thought about the whole business with the money.

Stevie had never mentioned the missing contents of the safe to Ray. He was embarrassed about having snooped, and in the back of his mind he had kept thinking, "Well, just around the corner here, something is going to happen and Blanche is going to pull all of the missing stuff out of a drawer."

That did not happen. When Stevie did tell his brother about the safe, Ray decided it was time they called Blanche and asked her to explain the whole situation. Both boys were visiting their mother in Burlington. Ray called Blanche and tried to initiate a conversation about the remaining money, but she hurried him off the phone.

The next day, when Ray was in the shower and Linda was at work, Blanche called back. Stevie took the call.

Ray had received a new answering machine as a Christmas gift. As soon as Stevie realized it was Blanche on the other end, he reached down and pushed a button on the machine to record the call.

Blanche was midway through the reconstructive surgery at the time. She began by trilling a long apparently delighted hello and then launching into a long soliloquy on her condition.

"I'm just standing here looking at this bosom that I don't have anymore. I am lopsided! I had that diarrhea, and here I wind up withering my bosom. I'll just have to have another one put on.

"You know, Stevie, when I was a kid, I used to put tissue paper in my bra because my boobs weren't big enough to fill it up."

Stevie was beginning to grow irritated. He finally cut in and told her they needed to talk about money. Blanche went quiet. Stevie then launched into his own speech about dividing the money—that he and his brother wanted her to have anything and everything their father wanted her to get. Their only concern, he said, was the insurance.

But the word was barely out of his mouth before she cut back in. "It's in the will, Steven, if you read the will, it says the insurance and the assets were to be split three ways. So what is your question?"

The problem was that Stevie and Ray had seen the will by then, and they knew that the life insurance was not mentioned in it.

He started: "Your lawyer says it doesn't have to—"

"Yes it does," she said, cutting back in sharply. "It says it in the will. If you read the will. It's in the will. It's what your dad had stated."

Blanche departed onto a long digression about the Kroger settlement and how much less she really got out of it than people thought.

"I have a letter here," Blanche said, "that your dad had written that says if anything happened to him that his insurance and his assets were to be split three ways, and I . . . I'm not trying to take anything from you all, really I'm not. I don't feel that I have taken anything from you all really."

She paused.

Stevie, his voice trembling slightly, said, "You know, Blanche, me and Ray are a lot younger, and we're his kids, and

I just feel like that, it just don't seem right, something's not right."

"All right," she said angrily. "All right. Keep the damn money. I don't want your money, Ray. I never wanted a thing from you boys. Never! Not a damn thing!"

After Ray's phone call, the Reid brothers never spoke to or heard from Blanche again.

A few weeks after the Reid estate had been settled, Blanche and Dwight took one of their short getaway trips to the mountains. On that trip, they spoke about getting married more seriously than they ever had before. On the way home, Dwight decided it was time to start putting a fuller personal history on the table.

"You've never asked why I was divorced," he said.

"No. I figured you would tell me when the time came."

He laughed. "Is this time okay?"

"Surely, Dwight," she said amiably. "Whatever you feel you want to tell me, you just go ahead on and say it. Feel free."

He drove a few moments more in silence. Telling it was extremely uncomfortable for Dwight. He had no idea how Blanche would take it.

"My wife and I were divorced as the result of a long relationship ... an affair ... that I had with another woman."

Blanche peered at him. "Who was she?"

"She was my secretary. I was very much in love with her, and I had hoped that she and I might one day be married. It was her choice that it was not to end that way."

Blanche had not moved her eyes from his face or blinked since he had started talking. "Have you ever seen her again?"

"My wife?"

"The woman."

"Yes. Yes I have. She came down and stayed at a local motel for a couple of weeks over a year ago, because she had some things she needed to work out. We talked a great deal, but that was the extent of our contact."

Blanche stiffened. She turned and stared at his hands on the wheel. "Go ahead," she mumbled softly.

"I am not proud of this fact, and I suppose there is a side of me that wishes it had never happened, although I would

have to say in the very next breath that I was deeply in love
with her for a very long time. But of course I regretted losing
my church and very nearly losing my ministry altogether and
losing a very happy life with my family."

While he told her the entire long story, from beginning to
end, Blanche did not speak or display any emotion at all. She
stared through the windshield, her eyes dull and unblinking.

For a long while after he had finished, she was silent.

"Blanche, can you share some of your feelings with me at
this moment?"

"Sinner," she muttered in a low hiss, with her eyes on his
hands.

"Did you say 'sinner'? I certainly am aware that what I did
was sinful, but..."

"Preacher," she muttered.

"What?"

She finally turned to face him. Her eyes were huge and
black. "You are a preacher," she said, voice high up in her
lurching, keening singsong. "You are a vessel of the Lord, but
you sinned, you sinned a vile sin against the Lord and against
your wife. You betrayed your holy trust."

"Blanche, I know that..."

She was shaking her head, looking away, speaking in a low
guttural curse. "Oh no, oh no, oh no. Oh no, you must not,
you must never."

"Blanche."

"Take me home. Take me home this minute. Don't talk to
me until you get me home."

Blanche began to sob. She dropped her face into her hands
and sobbed harder and harder until her entire body was shaking. Dwight pulled over onto the icy siding and stopped the
car. Very hesitantly, he extended the fingers of one hand to
her shoulder, then his whole hand, then slipped his arm around
her to comfort her. She put her forehead on his shoulder,
reached up with both hands, and took his shirt front.

"Oh Dwight," she said. "My daddy was a preacher. He was
a very wicked man. A cruel and wicked man. He did things so
wicked. So wicked."

"What things, Blanche? What did he do?"

She looked into his eyes. Her own eyes were wide with

terror and her lips trembled. "He did things... things. To me. I was just..." Her entire face began to quiver, and then it collapsed inward on itself in sobs. As she gave way to violent sobbing, he held her and rocked her on the front seat of the car on the shoulder of a rural North Carolina road.

Chapter Ten

After his revelation to Blanche of the adulterous affair in his past, Dwight began to press his suit for marriage harder than ever. Blanche seemed to have recovered from her initial shock and anxiety. In fact, she never mentioned the affair again. But the relationship was altered. It felt different. There was a pebble in the shoe, and Dwight's compulsion to get it out and to render things smooth and blissful again propelled him toward a public and official recognition of their relationship.

His daughter, Deborah, twenty-six, came down to visit the parsonage at Carolina at least once a month. She was an attractive young woman with a pixie sense of humor and an uncanny resemblance to actress Debra Winger. She had graduated from Radford College in Radford, Virginia, but the going had not been easy for her. Her way in life was often to find a way around obstacles rather than go through them. Her infectious laugh and quick wit were her most useful survival tools. She was working as a management trainee at a car rental franchise in Hampton, Virginia, in 1988 when Dwight began to encourage her to spend time with Blanche on her visits.

Blanche was not an easy piece of work for Debbie to figure out, but she decided to do her best. It was clear from every word her father said and in every breath he drew that he was deeply in love with this woman.

During one visit, Dwight said, "Blanche, why don't you take Debbie down to the outlet mall. Burlington has the largest outlet mall in the South, Debbie. You should go."

"I really don't need anything, Dad."

"Go on. It will give you girls a chance to talk."

They climbed into Blanche's car and headed for the outlet mall, a huge modern shopping center on the interstate at the southern edge of Burlington. All the way there, Blanche chittered and pecked at Debbie in her friendly little sparrow voice.

"The outlet mall has had the best deals lately, because none of that stuff they've been ordering from New York has been selling up there. I mean, you don't know if that's good or that's bad. You can buy those coats and dresses down here now for twenty dollars that they've been making to sell up there for two hundred, but it's because the fashion's just not working, so should you buy them or not, I don't know. I go for clothes that I like, I never pay attention to all the trends, I've got beautiful clothes I wear every day that I bought ten years ago and they don't look a bit out of style.

"You know what, Debbie, you know what I've always wondered, and now we're in the car I guess I'll just go ahead and ask. Your brother Doug, is he still bitter toward your father?"

"About what?"

"Are you?"

"About what, Blanche?"

"The divorce."

Debbie was taken aback.

"No. No. Neither one of us is bitter. I accepted all that long ago. I have no problems with it. I was sad when it happened. I was in college, I was nineteen, it was kind of rough on me. But my mother and father are adults. Why?"

"I just wondered. My parents got divorced. My daddy was a preacher like Dwight. He was a very wicked man. He wanted my mama to take him back, but she wouldn't do it. He left her for a young girl. My brothers were very bitter toward him for it. Very bitter. That's why I wondered about Doug."

"Doug? No. No, he's not bitter about anything, Blanche."

They parked the car and started across the huge parking lot. It was late spring and already muggy hot in North Carolina. Blanche continued to chatter as they walked.

"Your mother must have been very bitter toward him, though, leaving her like that for another woman."

Debbie looked up and paused. Dwight's affair had never been spoken of by Debbie and her father.

"She is not bitter, Blanche."

They walked into one of the larger outlet stores. Miles of spring raincoats on racks were lined up ahead of them in neat rows. Blanche began to walk quickly down the rows, her eye flying over the fabric, taking in the general cut of the coats without ever slowing until she saw one she liked, and then she would stop and pinch and hold and smooth and even sniff the garment to see how it was made.

"What kind of woman was this woman, anyway?"

"What woman, Blanche? My mother?"

"Lord no. This woman your father had the affair with. She must have been a slut. A very wicked slut and a whore. Do you know she came down here and shacked up in a motel with him?"

"Listen, Blanche, I really don't care to hear anything at all—"

"Well, it was after she had went back to her husband up there in Virginia! And she came down here and shacked up. I think that just tells the story about that. Only a whore would do something like that."

"No, you're wrong, she's not like that, she's a very nice person. Just as my mother is a very nice person, and my father is a very nice person."

Blanche's glance shot up into Debbie's eye. Blanche stood stooped over the extended sleeve of a coat and leered up into Debbie's face.

"Your father is what?"

"My father is a good man."

Blanche dropped the sleeve and straightened herself. She lifted a long finger and held it under Debbie's nose. She was angry.

"Your father is a wicked man. He is an evil man. He deserves whatever he gets."

Debbie stared back at Blanche, trying to figure out what she was talking about. Dwight had made some embarrassed references to Blanche's fundamentalist religious beliefs, trying to prepare Debbie, perhaps, for this sort of outburst. Debbie tried to chalk it up to that. All Debbie knew for sure was that she had had enough of the outlet mall.

"I want to go home now, Blanche."

"We just got here, honey."

"I said I want to go home. Right now."

They drove back to the parsonage in silence. Debbie departed for Hampton that afternoon in her own car. She tried to put the entire business out of her mind, but during the entire trip through the mountains and back into Virginia, Blanche's words kept replaying in her mind.

That week, Dwight finally persuaded Blanche to agree that they would be married after Thanksgiving. He talked her out of an even later date by arguing that anything after Thanksgiving would push them into Christmas, which was always a minister's busiest season, and that would effectively put them off until 1989.

Cautiously, he began to make plans, and Blanche seemed to come along nicely. They would be married in the church at the close of a regular Sunday worship service. For Dwight, the marriage ceremony would be a ceremonial cleansing and healing of all the wounds of time. There, in his regained capacity as a minister, in the company of his beloved new flock, he would be joined in holy matrimony with the woman he so dearly loved, and his life would be whole and bright again.

Blanche announced that her daughters had hired a caterer to provide a reception in the church hall following the ceremony. Dwight assumed it was in fact Blanche herself who would be paying for the reception, but he saw how important it was to her that it be publicly perceived that her daughters were footing the bill.

Blanche had always been completely close-mouthed with Dwight about her money. She had never told him what she actually received in the settlement or what her net worth was. Dwight had done just the opposite. He had described to her in detail his savings, which were minimal, his retirement plan, which was adequate, and his insurance and death benefit package. She had listened carefully to everything he had told her about himself, but she had told him nothing about her own money, and he had not pried.

He relished the planning for the wedding. On the night before, there would be a dinner in the church hall. The ladies would cook, and the men and the children would come and eat, and they would all sit at long folding tables with white paper tablecloths. The parish would hum and buzz with the same excited teasing and giggling there had been at the Easter breakfast when Dwight had first met her. He was a very happy man again, and he believed he was about to become even happier, if that was possible.

Blanche was busy with a new business venture—a tanning salon on the edge of Burlington she had bought for her daughters, Vanessa and Cindi. She told Dwight on one occasion she was "only an investor" in the business, but she admitted on another that she was the only investor.

It was a good investment. The tanning salon proved popular in Burlington. After a long chilly winter, people in the Piedmont all headed for the coast. Lots of people were eager to get a head start on a tan before going to the beach or to nurture a tan long after a visit to the beach. Cindi and Vanessa did a good job of running the salon.

One of their regular customers was Sharon Wolfe. She and her husband, Rick, owned a convenience store in Haw River, the little mill community just south of Deep Creek Church Road where Blanche's trailer park was located. Sharon visited the tanning salon one morning and noticed to her distaste that there were flies buzzing around the tanning beds, attracted there by the smears of tanning oil left behind by other users.

That afternoon when she came into the store to relieve her husband, Rick said, "Have the girls got ants up there in the tanning salon?"

"No," she said, laughing. "I was just up there this morning, and all I saw was a bunch of flies around the beds. Why?"

"Blanche came in this morning looking for some kind of ant poison. Anti-Ant. She said did I have any, and I said no. She said, 'Well, you ought to get it, it's good stuff.'"

"Ha!" She laughed. "Blanche is so weird."

* * *

Dwight's attack began with severe diarrhea, nausea, and vomiting. He had never suffered from stomach problems before or from any real health problem to speak of. He tried to ascribe it to his intense excitement in anticipation of the wedding now only a month away. But when he developed pain and tingling in his arms and legs and a bad skin rash, he went to see a doctor. His doctor told him he was suffering from a mild attack of a disease called shingles.

Three weeks before Thanksgiving, Dwight and Blanche went out to dinner at Mayberry's. That night, Dwight sat up straight as a board in bed and vomited across the room. He collapsed on his back in an agonizing nausea. At that point, Dwight's body already held in it what would normally be considered in medical texts a lethal dose of arsenic. But Dwight's body was not normal. The normal body excretes most of an arsenic dose within four days of ingestion and then takes six more days to get rid of the rest. It is during that six-day period that the kidneys convert small amounts of the dose to the much less excretable and much more toxic arsenite form.

But Dwight's body was able to process and get rid of the arsenic much faster and more efficiently than a typical body, creating and retaining much less arsenite. Whether it was a vigorous youth and a relatively abstemious adulthood or just an accident of chromosomal pairing, the fact was that Dwight Moore was a man who could ingest several times the normally fatal arsenic dose and live to tell about it.

The next day, still feeling terrible and a little shocked by the night's dramatic vomiting incident, Dwight arose, dressed himself, and prepared to make house calls on sick parishioners.

"What did you eat at Mayberry's last night?" Blanche asked.

"What do you mean, what did I eat? I ate the bean-and-bacon soup and I had the chicken sandwich."

"What did you drink?"

"Blanche, I drank tea."

"That's right. The bean-and-bacon soup and a chicken sandwich and tea. And that's just what I had. I had the same as you. And I feel sick as a dog, too."

Dwight looked her over. She didn't look sick at all. She certainly had not experienced any incidents of projectile vomiting he was aware of. But he took her word for it. They both ate at Mayberry's, they both ate the same thing, and they were both sick.

"It must have been the food," he said.

"Yes. It must have been."

There was a sweet metallic taste in his mouth, and his breath smelled like garlic.

Dwight continued to feel very sick through the next forty-eight hours and to experience diarrhea and vomiting, but he persisted in carrying out his daily rounds and duties. Blanche prepared him bowl after bowl of starchy potato soup and glass after glass of iced tea, things she said were good for a distressed gastrointestinal tract.

On Tuesday, he drove Blanche to a small clinic in Burlington. For weeks she had failed to go get the routine physical examination she needed in order for the marriage license to be issued, so Dwight insisted that morning that he would run her over to the clinic and they would get it taken care of.

"Blanche is fine," the doctor said afterward, "but you could look better, Reverend Moore."

"I've been experiencing a severe cold or something, with a lot of diarrhea and vomiting. I've started today having some severe nasal congestion," Dwight said.

"Take some Tylenol," the doctor suggested.

Driving home from the clinic, Dwight was suddenly hit by a massive attack of nausea. He wheeled his car clumsily up on the shoulder, stopped, forced the door open, and let his head drop. He vomited and vomited onto the gravel beneath him. He saw that there were burgundy strands of blood in the vomit.

He heard Blanche laughing behind him. It was her trilling, silly, little-girl bird-laugh. "Oh, Dwight," she laughed, "here we are on our way home from getting my test for a marriage license, and you're vomiting."

Dwight was beginning to have trouble understanding what Blanche was saying. At that point, the bulk of the most recent dose had left his bloodstream. Most of it had been excreted in his urine, but a dangerous amount was being absorbed into his body through the mucous membranes even while he vomited.

The leaching of fluids through damaged organ and vessel walls into areas where they were not supposed to be was already causing swelling throughout his body, some of it visible from the outside and some of it hidden within the bone structure of the body. In particular, fluid shift and swelling inside Dwight's skull were beginning to squeeze his brain and he was already beginning to suffer the early symptoms of encephalopathy, like a very painful, very unpleasant form of drunkenness.

Blanche told him to slide over. She came around and took the wheel, still laughing. Dwight pushed himself away from the wheel and got himself over to the passenger side. He looked up grinning, sheepish and confused, wiped a strand of vomit from his chin, and then shouted and writhed as a bolt of pain struck him in the stomach.

"We just have to get you home, baby," she said.

Blanche pulled the car into the driveway next to the parsonage. Dwight sat still on the car seat, staring straight ahead through unfocused eyes.

"Come on now, Dwight. Get out."

He pushed open the car door jerkily, then stumbled slightly as he stepped down from the car. He was staggering toward the door. She came around, took his elbow, and steered him. "People see you, Dwight Moore, they gonna think you're drunk." She helped him into the house. He staggered to the bedroom and collapsed prostrate on the bed, moaning dully.

Soon cooking smells came from the kitchen. Blanche was brewing up a pot of potato soup and some iced tea.

She helped him up from the bed and led him to the small kitchen table.

"Here, baby, this will help settle your stomach."

She blew on the spoon for him and lifted it gently to his lips. "Go on now. It will cure what ails you."

He sipped down the soup and drank some tea. He rose slowly, waving her away, and staggered to the bathroom, where his body gave way to a violent storm of vomiting and diarrhea. His eyes drooped closed and he began to fall asleep between the waves, only to be violently reawakened by another attack.

She looked in on him through the cracked door. He was on his knees, with his elbows resting on the toilet seat and his head slumped against the wall.

"You've got that twenty-four-hour flu," she said.

The next day when he woke he said, "Take me to the hospital."

Blanche put him in the car and took him to the emergency

Blanche Taylor Moore on trial

Blanche and James Taylor with their daughter Vanessa, 1954

Dwight and Blanche Moore on their honeymoon trip to visit his family just before his last and near-fatal arsenic attack

Raymond Reid

Left to right: Steve Reid, Linda Reid-Sykes, and Ray Reid, Jr., 1991

Dwight Moore takes a sip of water while testifying against his wife, Blanche, during the fourth day of testimony

In the autopsy photograph, Mees lines on Raymond Reid's fingernails show the results of severe arsenic poisoning.

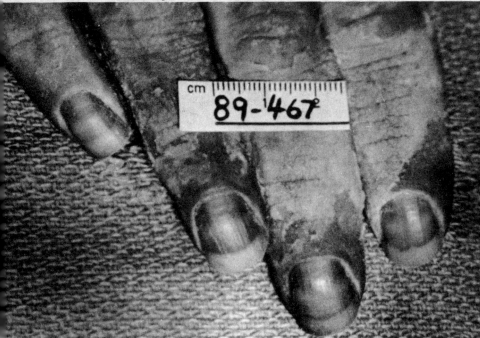

Blanche listens to the testimony during her trial.

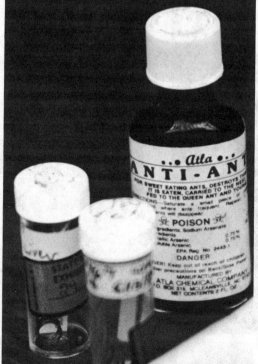

The bottle of ant poison found at the home of Blanche and Dwight Moore

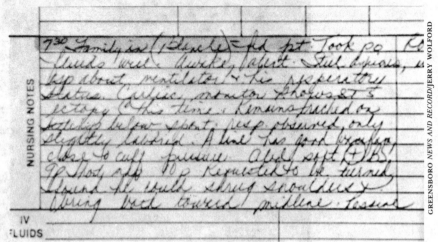

Nurses' notes showing an entry: "7:30 Family in (Blanche)—fed" patient

Nurse Wanda Moss points out to prosecutor Janet Branch the white lines on the fingernails of Raymond Reid in a photograph during testimony.

Forsyth County Superior Court Judge William Freeman listens to arguments during the trial.

Nurse Lisa Hutchins during her testimony

Left to right: Steve Reid, Linda Reid-Sykes, and Ray Reid, Jr.

room of Alamance County Hospital in Burlington. He stayed in the emergency room all day, wracked by diarrhea and vomiting, with Blanche always at his side. Toward the end of the day, a doctor came to the litter where he lay and told Dwight he was suffering from a "bowel obstruction." He told him to go home and eat only a liquid diet called Enrich.

An orderly wheeled Dwight to the door in a chair. In order to get from the emergency room to the front door, they had to go by the cashier's window. A ragged, dirty little man in an unlined raincoat was standing at the window as they passed. He turned and eyed them intently.

That night was hell. Dwight lay kicking and moaning loudly on the bathroom floor, soaked in his own offal and wracked with pain. He asked Blanche to take him back to Alamance County the next morning. After several more hours in emergency, a doctor noticed that Dwight's stomach was distending at an alarming rate. The distension was very unusual from the perspective of the ER doctors at Alamance. So sudden and extreme was the bloating in Dwight's stomach and bowel area, in fact, that an observer might have been reminded of a scene in the movie *Alien*. An X-ray was quickly ordered.

Arsenic, which is often called a heavy metal, is not actually a true heavy metal in molecular structure. It is more accurately described as a close cousin of the heavy metals. But in X-rays it is exactly like a heavy metal. It is radiopaque, meaning it is impenetrable to X-rays, just as the true heavy metals are. It shows up as if it were a puddle of molten steel.

When he was X-rayed at Alamance County Hospital, Dwight's body was in the process of achieving another of its heroic victories over a series of truly massive doses. Already having excreted most of the arsenic in his urine, he was moving another bulk of the substance out through the small upper intestine, which leads from the stomach to the large intestine. That pool or mass of arsenic showed up as a black sharp-edged mass midway down the small intestine.

An oncologist—that is, a cancer specialist—was called to look at the X-ray. It was possible the mass was an extremely fast-growing, unusually dense cancer, he said. The doctors did not use the word "cancer" with Dwight. Instead, they told Dwight and Blanche that his bowel was obstructed by a physical mass.

But Blanche read their faces. She rushed to the telephone, called Dwight's sister, Nola, in Reidsville, and said, "Now Nola, listen close. I can only say this once. The doctors have told me they have found a mass in his stomach, it has spread into the bowel, and it is cancer."

Nola collapsed into a chair after hanging up the phone and wept into her hands.

The doctors came back to see Dwight.

"We need to operate as soon as possible, Reverend Moore, but unfortunately your heart is starting to act up on us."

"My heart?" Dwight asked. He was barely able to follow what they were telling him, but he did understand they were saying he was having heart trouble. He was amazed. His heart had always been robust.

"Never had trouble before," he said.

The doctors looked at each other. The profile the heart showed to the doctors was that of an aging, long-diseased, and rapidly failing organ. It was difficult to believe that Dwight Moore had never had any heart trouble before.

The doctors waited two more days for Dwight's heart to straighten out. Finally it did indeed begin to recover as his body began to achieve another stunning comeback from another huge dose. As soon as the heart came back into a roughly manageable profile, the doctors showed up again at his bedside. Blanche stood off just to one side and behind them, listening intently.

"Reverend Moore, you have cancer. We have got to operate right away. You need to know that when you come out from under the anesthetic, you may very well have a colostomy. Do you know what that is?"

He nodded his head dully. The encephalopathy was still affecting his thinking so severely that he was unable to assign any importance to what they were saying. He knew he was inches from death.

The scalpel slid across the smooth white skin of his shaved belly, cutting down through layers of tissue until the surgeon reached the inner sac of muscle and membrane containing the bowel. Pushing deeper, the knife parted these darker tissues. Skilled hands laid the tissues aside.

Measuring his way carefully along the bowel, referring to the X-ray and a page of densely scrawled notes, the surgeon found the exact spot where the mass would be found. The knife plunged into the bowel itself and laid it open.

Nothing. There was absolutely nothing there. The inner lining of the bowel was severely inflamed. But there was no mass. Working together, the doctors lifted the entire snaking length of Dwight's intestine, small and large, up out of his body, feeling each inch of it with their hands as they went.

Nothing. No lump. No mass. There it was on the X-ray, plain as day, big as a fist, dark as a cannonball. But here was the bowel itself in their hands. And there was nothing. It was one of those moments when years of training turn to mist and blow away, and the doctors are left gaping and baffled. There was no explanation. They laid the bowel back down inside Dwight's body as if carefully packing a fragile Christmas gift. They sewed together the muscles and membranes, sewed up the skin, and sent him to the recovery room.

When he came out from under the anesthetic, the doctors were there again. They told him he did not have a colostomy. They told him he did not have cancer.

Dwight, who could now think again, said, "What did I have?"

"You had a kink in your intestines. We pulled the entire intestine out and straightened it and put it back in."

Blanche listened intently, switching a glinting bird-eyed stare from the face of one doctor to the next while they spoke. She seemed especially riveted by the description of the removal and straightening of Dwight's bowel, as if this conversation were the most important she had ever heard in her life.

For the next several weeks, Dwight's major challenge was to recover from abdominal surgery—always a severe shock for any human body—followed by a long and tricky recovery. His unusual constitution served him well, however, and he began to pull back more quickly than do most abdominal surgery patients.

He and Blanche were able to converse again. The first thing Dwight said, when his head had cleared sufficiently, was: "Blanche, what about our wedding plans?"

"I think you're too ill, Dwight."

"I don't. I'll get over this. I want to go right ahead on schedule and do it the way we planned."

She stared at him. "You're too sick."

"I will recover," he said. "We will proceed as planned."

The doctors sent Dwight home to continue his recovery. Blanche told Nola, "Dwight and I are going to have to live in sin for a while, because I'm going to have to move in with him to care for him."

The doctors brought Dwight back in for a set of barium X-rays to see if they could discover exactly what had happened to the mass they had X-rayed the last time. They expected to find it or traces of it somewhere lower down in the tract.

Instead, they found a new mass, twelve inches higher than the old one. The new mass was another dose of arsenic Dwight had ingested while attempting to recover from the abdominal surgery. The doctors simply had no explanation for what was going on. The mass they saw the first time could not have moved backward up the bowel. The anomaly this time was that Dwight seemed to be doing much better. He was clear-headed, he was walking, the abdominal distension had left him. They told Dwight they did not advise another surgery right away.

Shortly before the wedding date, Dwight was struck down by a severe, hammering attack. Blanche told people in the church there would be no wedding and they should think about hiring a substitute minister.

He stayed at home in agony for some weeks. The little house he had loved so dearly became a torture chamber, its walls folding and changing colors before his nauseated eyes, every corner and every window offering a new river of vomit and torment. Finally on December 1, 1988, Blanche took him back to Alamance County.

He was shaking, trembling, clammy white, incoherent, passing bloody rice-water stools, vomiting a milky foam, horribly swollen and distended. They hooked him up to an IV in order to pump him full of fluids. They put him on a monitor: his pulse was high and jagged but his blood pressure was low. They listened to his lungs and heard the telltale "crackles" that mean the lungs are filling with fluid. He was not producing urine. They took X-rays. His bowel was a patchwork of masses. They decided to operate immediately.

Dwight's sister Nellie flew down from Pittsburgh and stayed in Reidsville with Nola. On the day of the surgery, Nola and Nellie drove to Deep Creek Church Road to pick up Blanche and then drove on down to the hospital in Burlington.

Blanche brought a cassette tape with her. It was a rehearsal tape Dwight had made of himself singing his own favorite hymn, "Master of the Wind." Dwight had a handsome singing voice. He took singing seriously in the church and often worked at home on certain hymns in which he planned to lead the congregation.

Blanche slipped the cassette into the player in the dash of Nola's car. As Dwight's voice filled the car—strong, melodic, brimming with the deep happiness that had been in his heart the day he had been rehearsing—Nellie's eyes filled. She dropped her head and began to sob quietly to herself in the backseat.

Blanche was in front with Nola. She turned, looked at Nellie for a moment, and then began giggling. "Look, Nola," she said, in the bird voice. "Nellie's bawlin'."

Blanche continued to snicker and laugh. Nellie continued to cry. Nola drove on, her normally large blue eyes narrowed to slits. Nola didn't have any idea what was wrong with Blanche. But she knew something was wrong, and she did not like whatever it was.

Chapter Eleven

Again the knife slid through the skin of his belly like a snake swimming through water, dodging this way and that to avoid the knotty red-purple ridge of his last scar. Again the knife dove into the bowel itself, and again the bowel came up, handful by handful. The operation took three hours.

Again there was nothing.

Dwight recovered with incredible speed. His body was still able to pump out the arsenic doses quickly. Weakened as he was, he was still able to mend rapidly from the massive surgeries he was undergoing. Two weeks after the operation, the doctors told him he could complete his recovery at home.

During this second surgery, Blanche had spent much less time at the hospital than she had during the first one. As soon as Dwight became coherent again, his powers of acuity and insight returned to him in full. This second time, he could see that there was something wrong in his relationship with Blanche. She was pulling back. Something about him seemed to irritate her or make her angry.

He had been through savage bouts of illness that had brought him low. He was a man very conscious of his own physical dignity. He had spent weeks crawling and writhing on the floor before this woman, soaked in his own filth and sweat. Perhaps something in that experience had caused her to find him repulsive.

Until that point, Dwight had read all of Blanche's reluctance as a defense mechanism that he intended to overcome and penetrate. He knew by then there was something wrong in her life and heart. The only uncontrolled and unposed emotion he had seen from her had appeared in that moment on the road on the way back down from the mountains, when she had tried to tell him something about her father and her childhood. In the offhand, sometimes coarse remarks she made about sex and even in her strange religious notions, Dwight heard echoes of an injury. She dwelled high up in a tower of mystery, and Dwight Moore meant to scale that tower, free her, carry her back to his own castle, and live happily forever.

But after the second surgery, he saw sadly that there was some other darkness between them. She was pushing him away in a manner that could not be overcome by diligent love. In the meantime, Nola had been urging him to come convalesce at her house instead of going home to the parsonage to be tended again by Blanche.

"Blanche," he said, when they were getting ready to discharge him, "I think I'll go to my sister Nola's house in Reidsville and recover there."

Her reaction was not what he had anticipated.

"Why do you want to go and bother Nola?" she said. "You just come on home and I'll take care of you again."

"No, Blanche, I don't think that would be good."

"Why not? What wouldn't be good about it? Is this Nola's idea?"

"No."

"Didn't I take good care of you?"

"Blanche, you know that's not what I'm saying. But I have already spoken with Nola, and she has made room for me in the house, and that's what I am going to do."

"Fine, Dwight," she said, rising, obviously angry. "Do what in the hell you want to do."

Nola and her husband, Howard, drove down and picked

Dwight up. He was unable to walk under his own power. His arms and legs were palsied and his hands and feet tingled and were numb at the same time. He was haggard and looked as if he had aged ten years in the last month.

But the Halbrook house in Reidsville was a good place to be. It was a low brick ranch-style home on a road just outside the old town of Reidsville, built on a hill that sloped steeply behind the house. At the bottom of the hill was a little woods and a steel outbuilding where Howard, a furniture-quality carpenter, kept his shop. Out in front of the shop were a couple of stands of bees, stacks of white wooden boxes in which Howard kept swarms of bees whose honey he harvested every year.

Dwight was also a hobbyist beekeeper. He couldn't join Howard in the "bee yard," as the area was called in beekeeper parlance, but he could watch him doing his winter work from the window: scraping old honey frames clean, repairing damaged bee boxes, and generally getting ready for spring, when the bees would swarm out over the countryside again.

Tens of thousands of bees would come roaring out of the hives, flying over an area of several square miles to gather nectar from spring blossoms. Every evening they would return to the hive, where their queen awaited them and where they would work the long night turning nectar into honey. In the quiet of Nola's home, watching Howard from the window, Dwight allowed the strength of the land and the cycle of the seasons to flow back into his veins. His body began another of its miraculous recoveries from near-death to vigor.

Blanche did not call. He called her on a few occasions, but she was cool and dismissive. Nola called Blanche, because Nellie was coming to visit, as were Dwight's brothers, David, who lived in Titusville, Florida, and Dennis, who lived near Reidsville in Rockingham County. Nola was planning a get-together and wanted Blanche to join the family.

"Oh, Nola, I'm sorry," Blanche said, "but I'm having to help the girls out working in the tanning salon and I'm tied up every night until real late. Maybe some other time."

Nola counted the days Blanche had not seen Dwight since his brush with death in the hospital and was not pleased with the number.

But Dwight seemed unfazed by Blanche's distance from him. He had long ago come to accept that Blanche could be peculiar in the way she chose either to express or not express affection and empathy. She could be incredibly close, caring, and concerned, almost obsessively concerned about another person's very personal and inward condition. And then a cloud would come over her, and Blanche would disappear into herself. She would step inside and close the door after herself, and she might as well have stepped off the face of the earth.

Dwight knew he had been very ill. He knew something of what illness did to the people who cared for the ill as well as to the ones who were sick themselves. He was a minister, after all, with years of experience sitting at the sickbed, sitting at the deathbed, standing by the grave. He knew that serious illness and the proximity of death evoked responses in people that simply overpowered their normal sense of decorum and manners. Death, dying, great pain of the heart—these were coins in the currency of his daily work. He was surprised by little. He knew Nola disapproved of the way Blanche behaved toward him. But he believed Blanche had nursed and served him far beyond the call of romance. And he loved Blanche.

On New Year's Eve, 1988, Dwight asked Howard to drive him back to the parsonage in Carolina. He could walk. He was still numb in the hands and feet, but the palsy had left him, and he was getting stronger every day. The first thing he did when he was alone in the parsonage was pick up the phone and call her. She told him she could not come and be with him.

Blanche took part that night in a "Watch Night Service" from nine to midnight in a little house-church in Burlington. That night a strange little preacher with a shock of greasy hair standing straight out from one side of his head beckoned for the demons to swirl up out of her throat. Blanche shrieked and roared as she felt them leave her.

When the new year arrived, Dwight was alone in his bed in the parsonage, thrashing, held just on the tantalizing edge of sleep by the tingle in his hands and feet. He wondered where she was and what she was doing.

Dwight continued to improve dramatically in the weeks after New Year's Day. The last symptom to leave him was the glove-and-stocking peripheral neuropathy that caused his hands and feet to tingle and go numb. The doctors at Alamance told him they thought it might be a temporary side effect of the anesthetic used during his operations. By the end of January, even the neuropathy was gone.

At this point, Dwight had ingested enormous doses of arsenic—enough to have killed most men, certainly enough to have left permanent damage to the nervous system in the vast majority of individuals. It was a quirk and virtue of his own constitution that Dwight Moore was exceptionally resistant to arsenic poisoning.

As he improved, Dwight began calling Blanche more and more often. He was convinced that her distance from him was only an obstacle that he, as her lover, was duty-bound to overcome. There was also a certain amount of urgency born of the fact that he, as a preacher, was either going to have to break the relationship off for good and forget it, make the union legitimate in marriage, or face the prospect of another parish scandal in his career. He worked hard at wooing Blanche back, and gradually Blanche began to warm again. She returned to the parsonage, and he returned to her bed in the trailer home on occasion. Dwight aggressively pressed Blanche for a new date for their marriage.

On March 22, Dwight's thirty-year-old son, Doug, a chemist living in Montclair, New Jersey, became the father of a baby boy. Dwight wanted badly to get up to New Jersey to see his first grandchild.

"I would like you to go with me, Blanche," he said. "As my wife."

Blanche was in a corner. She had been sleeping with Dwight for the better part of three years, off and on. She had often professed her deep and exclusive love for him. She and Dwight already had publicly announced one wedding date, canceled only at the last minute because of his illness.

It would seem that now there were only two things she could do—agree to marry him, or tell him she had changed her mind and did not want to marry him after all.

She agreed to marry him. Both she and Dwight thought that after the last fiasco in which everyone in the parish practically had been left standing at the altar waiting for them, this ceremony should be quick and simple. On a Wednesday evening, April 21, 1989, with Dwight's old friend and colleague the Rev. Jim Rosser officiating and two elderly women of the church as witnesses, Dwight Moore and Blanche Kiser Taylor were married, and Blanche became Blanche Taylor Moore.

Blanche, Dwight, the two ladies, and Jim Rosser all went to the Western Steak House and had dinner. Afterward, Dwight and Blanche returned to the Carolina church, where Dwight conducted an evening prayer meeting. In spite of the serious tone of the meeting, there was a great deal of glancing and smirking among the parishioners, most of whom had been on the telephone all afternoon before the meeting reporting to each other every detail of what had been seen at the church earlier, who had come and who had gone, who had been wearing what, where they all had eaten dinner and what remarks had been overheard.

At the conclusion of the prayer meeting, they all stood somberly and allowed Dwight to make his own official announcement of the marriage. The moment he finished, the little group exploded in cheers and shouts, hugs and kisses and slaps on the back. The people of the little church had come to see Dwight's healing and the restoration of his happiness as their own collective fate, incarnate in one person. They were proud of their educated preacher. They were happy that he had found Blanche, and now they were elated that he and Blanche had married.

Dwight and Blanche already had packed their things in Dwight's Plymouth Horizon. They didn't even go back to the parsonage after the meeting. They climbed into the car and drove several hours through the night to the Holiday Inn in Henderson, North Carolina. On the way they snacked on fruit they had bought for the trip at Stan's Fruit Market in Burlington. The next morning they ate in the Holiday Inn dining room and had pancakes and link sausage for breakfast. They put in a long day on the road the next day, stopping only once to eat a meal at a Hardee's in Virginia. Blanche snacked on the fruit. That night they stayed at a Howard Johnson Motor Lodge in Baltimore. They were too tired by the drive to be hungry. Later that evening, before turning in, Dwight went to the motel restaurant and ate some ice cream and apple pie.

They arrived in Montclair at Doug's house on Friday afternoon. Dwight's daughter, Debbie, and her boyfriend, Andy, had been on the road, too, coming up from Hampton, Virginia. They arrived at Doug's house Friday evening. Dwight, restless as usual, went out for a newspaper while the women cooked a spaghetti dinner.

The next morning, as people awakened, they found their way to the kitchen and fixed breakfast for themselves. Doug and his wife, Barbara, had an infant to care for, after all. Dwight ate cereal and grapefruit and drank coffee. The house filled up with people in robes and pajamas, all awaiting the morning presentation of the young prince.

At last his mother brought the baby out to a chorus of oohs and ahs. Doug found his way around the room, genially inquiring after everyone's sleep. Both Doug and Debbie had acquired their father's smooth easy manners.

Doug and Blanche had met before. Doug liked Blanche. The high-pitched bird chatter and the seemingly innocent but always deeply probing questions amused him. She seemed to him like a typical specimen of a certain Southern type—the hyper fast-talking woman who is as dizzy as a fox.

Blanche took the baby from Barbara and held him in her arms while the rest of the family gathered around cooing and grinning.

"You see what you've missed, Dwight," Blanche said. "By getting divorced from Lorene and losing your family like you have. You should be enjoying all these moments like this, but you can't on account of what you did."

Dwight laughed it off. Barbara rolled her eyes at Doug, but Doug shrugged it off, too. Blanche was weird, that was part of the deal. But Blanche was nice, and his father loved her.

Blanche followed Doug into the kitchen and cornered him.

"I guess you know that Elaine Vinson came down to Burlington to see your daddy once and stayed in a motel."

"Blanche," he said, banging a coffeemaker around busily, "that's my dad's business, and I'm not really interested."

"You know they had to have sex together."

"Blanche," he said, trying to laugh it off, "give me a break, will you? I don't want to talk to you about my dad's sex life."

"Why not? You should. Look at what he's done to you and your sister."

"He hasn't done anything to us," Doug said, now serious. "He has always been a wonderful father and a good man."

"Well, that Elaine Vinson is a slut."

"No, no she isn't, Blanche," he said, laughing again. "She's a really nice person, too. It was just one of those things. Hey. Let's talk about something else."

"Let me tell you something, Doug."

Blanche drew up so close to Doug that he unconsciously pulled himself back from her. Her eyes were black, and there was not a hint of humor anywhere on her face.

"She better never cross my path, because if she does, I might just have to put her lights out."

That night they all took the baby out to dinner. The next morning they fended for themselves again in the kitchen and then went to church together. They came back to Doug's house, delicious with the scent of a roast Barbara had been cooking slowly all morning. Debbie fixed creamed potatoes, and they enjoyed a long warm meal together, filled with the kind of rich, quiet, deep-running happiness that only babies can bring into a house.

And then all of a sudden this wonderful interlude of family togetherness was at an end. Debbie and Andy had to be back at work in Virginia the next morning. Dwight and Blanche had to be on their way. They all took a heart-aching leave of the baby, thanked Doug and Barbara for a wonderful weekend, piled into their separate cars, and went their separate ways.

Dwight and Blanche had planned to take the scenic coastal route down the seaboard, down the Garden State Parkway through Atlantic City, across Delaware Bay on the Cape May ferry, down through Cape Charles, across the Chesapeake Bay on the toll bridge to Norfolk, and then back west through North Carolina to Burlington.

Dwight ate a pastry on the Cape May ferry. He stood at the rail, watching the whitecaps roll out to sea. At first he tried to tell himself was just a little seasick. When he finally had to admit to himself what was happening, his neck broke out in a sweat of pure fear.

It was back. He slumped to a bench, sitting at first, and then fell to his side. The arsenic was making blisters on the surface of his stomach that swelled up and burst in a matter of minutes. The nausea that swept over him was insane, roiling, green, sharply painful.

When they got off the boat, Dwight collapsed in the backseat. He raised his head once, to tell Blanche to turn off their planned route, drive straight across Delaware to Washington,

and from there to go by the straightest route possible to
Burlington.

They drove into Burlington just after dawn. Dwight was
still weak but was already feeling better than he had. Blanche
wanted to stop off and see her daughters, so they did. When
they walked into the parsonage at nine in the morning, the
phone was ringing. It was one of Dwight's parishioners, a cancer
victim who had been taken to the hospital during Dwight's brief
absence. The woman had learned that she did not have long
to live.

He was still weak and nauseous, but he was much better
than he had been in the car the day before. There was nothing
in the house to eat except Rice Crispies, so each had a bowl of
cereal. Then Dwight told Blanche he had to leave. He drove
to the hospital, where he spent two hours at the side of his
parishioner.

Blanche was distressed about the masculine bleakness of
the parsonage. For one thing, there were no curtains in the
house at all. If she was going to live there, she said, there would
have to be curtains. She drove into Burlington to shop for some
while Dwight tended to his dying parishioner.

When Dwight got back from the hospital, he changed into
his yard clothes and went out to the garage. The yard was
already getting dandelions, and Dwight was far too fastidious
about his yard to allow that sort of thing to go on, even for a
day, if he could help it. To a man who had grown up raising
tobacco plants by hand, there were few antagonists on earth
more detestable than weeds. He mixed up a batch of Spectracide
and went out to spray the cursed intruders.

Blanche came back around noon with a carload of blinds
and curtains and a paper sack from Hardee's. She and Dwight
sat down in the little kitchen and ate chicken sandwiches and
drank iced tea. She chitchatted noisily about the window
treatments.

"I got blinds for all those windows right out there in the
front, but I didn't measure. These are the Sears kind you can
make bigger or smaller, least that's what the man said, but I've
never done it, I don't have no idea how to do it, do you? Then
I got these curtains on sale..."

"Blanche..." he said. He had finished half of his sandwich.

"I think they'll be nice, they're just cheap little things, but

I can make nicer ones later, we just need to have something up in the meantime, I don't understand how you stayed in here all this time with no curtains and all these people just lookin' in at you every time they walk by into that church..."

"Blanche..." He had half risen from his chair.

"It's just a little old house, but it's all right for now, and with you helping me I think we can get the curtains and the blinds up today, then of course I have to decide how much of my stuff I'm going to move in here and how much to give to Cindi and Vanessa and all that..."

Dwight opened his mouth and a stream of vomit shot out and splatted against the far wall. He fell to his knees, groaned, collapsed flat on his belly and face, and vomited again. Blanche took him by one arm and began dragging him toward the bathroom.

"I'm gonna go ahead and start on the curtains first," she said, pulling him along while he scrabbled with palsied feet, a flailing arm and lolling head, "but later on I'll need your help with the blinds. He showed me, but I don't have no idea what he was saying about how to size these things."

Dwight lay in bed, moaning with pain and nausea, all that afternoon while Blanche puttered around the house, working on the curtains, examining the condition of the cabinet shelves, and cleaning. He passed a ghastly night. Blanche slept on the sofa in the living room as she had the night James Taylor died.

He was still very sick all day Tuesday, but he was already beginning to regain some of his incredible vigor. Blanche fed him potato soup that evening, and he became violently ill again. The next morning he was still very sick. That afternoon he asked Blanche to drive him back to the emergency room at Alamance County Hospital.

When she brought him in, the ER doctor got on the phone and called the same doctor who had treated Dwight before for his "bowel obstruction." The doctor looked him over, listened to his complaints, and then ruled that his old bowel problem was kicking up again. He prescribed a shot of Phenergan, and he sent Dwight home.

That night Blanche fed Dwight soup again. Soon after eating, he became so sick that the nausea swept past the Phenergan as if it were not even present in his system. Begging and barely able to speak, he pleaded with Blanche to drive him back to the Alamance County ER again. There the doctor gave him another shot of Phenergan and said he was going to send him home.

"Please, Doctor," Dwight said, "send me to another hospital. I'm so sick. Maybe someone else can figure out what's doing this to me."

But the doctor was at the end of his shift and said he did not have time to gather Dwight's chart together in order to refer him to another hospital. He told Dwight to go home.

Blanche fed Dwight again. This time when the wave of pain and nausea began to crest, Dwight begged her to drive him the forty miles to North Carolina Memorial Hospital in Chapel Hill. She agreed and helped him into the backseat of the car.

The ER doctors at North Carolina Memorial examined Dwight and took a history. But they refused to admit him to the hospital without a referral from his doctor at Alamance County. They gave him another shot of Phenergan and sent him back forty miles in the backseat of his car to the parsonage. He felt some relief for a brief time, and Blanche was able to get a few spoonfuls of potato soup down him.

By Friday morning, Dwight was near death. Up until that point, his body had been able somehow to resist the arsenic very effectively at the molecular/enzymatic level. But finally on Friday morning, the walls of his internal organs and the tubes of his blood vessels began to turn to a leaky mush. His kidneys were largely shut down. He had retained thirty to forty pounds of fluid in the last twenty-four hours. He was almost incoherent with pain and brain swelling.

Debbie called.

"How is my father doing?" she asked.

"Oh, he's going to be all right," Blanche said. "It's this bowel thing acting up again. He's been real sick, but they've been giving him Phenergan, and that seems to help. Don't you worry now, Deb, I'm taking care of him."

Blanche hung up the phone and went to Dwight.

"That was Deborah. She said she's too busy to come see you. I just was so hurt, I couldn't believe it."

In the miasma of pain and disintegration he was experiencing, Dwight could understand almost none of what she was saying to him. He kept repeating numbly, "Hospital . . . hospital . . . hospital."

She took him back to the Alamance County ER again. This time, as soon as the doctors saw him, they sent Dwight to the ICU and hooked him up to tubes and a monitor. They saw that his kidneys were almost gone, that he was suffering brain damage or brain distress of some kind, that his breathing pattern was ragged and distressed, and that his heart was going haywire. It was clear that Dwight Moore was about to die. They agreed to ship him to North Carolina Memorial.

On the long ambulance ride to North Carolina Memorial, Dwight was alone with a paramedic while Blanche followed in his car. The brain swelling had subsided slightly, and his ability to think returned. He asked where they were taking him, and the paramedic told him. He said he was pleased. Now, he thought, we'll get to the bottom of this. Never once that night did he think of the possibility he might die.

This time, North Carolina Memorial admitted him. As soon as Dwight was in, he became the charge of Dr. David Wohns, a third-year fellow in the cardiology department at the University of North Carolina at Chapel Hill.

Wohns sat down and took a careful history. Blanche was eager to provide all the details of Dwight's many visits to the hospital and what had been prescribed and which operations had been performed. Wohns listened but continued politely to hew to his own course. His first thought was that Dwight might be suffering from a massive generalized infection, and he ordered the blood work that would give him an answer. But even while that was being done, he continued to press for a full history.

He wanted to know what all of Dwight's symptoms had been. He wanted to know where Dwight had been. He wanted to know what Dwight had eaten. He wanted to know what Dwight had done.

"When?" Blanche asked.

"Right before the attack that took place when you got back from your trip."

"He did work. He went to see somebody. Then he came home and worked in the yard."

"What work in the yard?"

"Dandelions. Getting rid of dandelions."

"How?"

"Spraying."

"With what?"

"With, you know, pesticide, or whatever it is you call it."

"Herbicide."

"Yes. For weeds."

"Poison."

"Yes."

"Then he could have been poisoned."

"I don't know."

"Well, we need to check for poison. You need to go to your home tomorrow, Mrs. Moore, and gather up all of the pesticides and herbicides and anything else that's out there in his garage or in the house and bring it all in here."

"Yes, Doctor. I will."

Wohns picked up a pad and scrawled an order to the ICU nurses: "Toxic Screen."

Chapter Twelve

Debbie called the parsonage and received no answer, so she called Alamance County Hospital to see if her father had been taken back there. Alamance informed her he had been transferred to North Carolina Memorial in Chapel Hill. She called there and eventually got Blanche on the phone.

"How is he?"

"He's fine."

"But why is he there?"

"Just to do tests. Dwight was not satisfied with the doctors at Alamance, so he asked to come over here and have some tests made. He's going to be just fine, honey. I'm with him."

Debbie hung up. She sat and stared at the phone. Her father's new wife had just assured her that her father was all right. But all of a sudden nothing in the entire situation added up. How could he be all right? If he was all right, why was he in and out of the hospital, why was he in a new hospital? Why was Blanche always so odd, so not quite there? What in the hell was going on?

Debbie had a friend in Hampton who was an ICU nurse. She picked up the phone and called her.

"I just need someone who knows the right questions to ask to call down there for me and find out what on earth is going on with my father. I don't know about his wife. She's . . . there's something just missing."

The friend called and eventually found her way through the switchboard to Wohns. She explained who she was and why she was calling. The friend hung up from her conversation with Wohns and called Debbie back immediately.

"You need to pack your bags, Debbie, and tell them at work you won't be in, and you need to call your brother and tell him to do the same thing, call your mom, and you all need to go right down there on the next plane you can get on."

When Dwight had come into North Carolina Memorial, the medical staff had assumed he would not live long. While Debbie was getting the word from her friend, the hospital was in the process of calling Nellie in Reidsville to tell her the family needed to gather.

Within twenty-four hours, all of Dwight's family had come together at North Carolina Memorial. Debbie was there, with Andy, her boyfriend, and Doug and his wife, Barbara, were there. Nola and Howard came. Dwight's brother David and his wife, Evelyn, had come from Florida. Dwight's aging father had come with his wife, Elizabeth. Nellie had come from Pittsburgh, and Dwight's brother Dennis, who lived three miles from their birthplace in Rockingham County, had come.

Blanche and Debbie stayed with Dwight that night after visiting hours had ended in the ICU. Blanche stood on one side of the bed, and Debbie stood on the other. The nerve damage from the arsenic caused a generalized shaking and palsy at times, so that his entire body would flail and twitch. When it started, Blanche would rub his arm on one side, Debbie would rub the other arm, and together they would talk to him softly in a chorus of comforting sounds. After a while, sheer exhaustion would prove to be more powerful than the palsy, and, while they rubbed him and cooed and spoke softly to him, Dwight would collapse into a fitful sleep. Even his sleep was hard to look at: he was grotesquely swollen, his eyes were oozing and blistered, and his breathing was wet and ragged.

Dawn was still two hours away. Debbie was suddenly overcome by a wave of physical and emotional exhaustion. "I've got to go down in that stairway where they can't see me and smoke a cigarette," she told Blanche. "I need a break."

"You go on, honey. I'm okay here with him. It's all under control."

Minutes after Debbie had left, Dwight's bowels erupted in a volley of bloody diarrhea, soiling the bed and floor. Blanche called the nurses, who cleaned him up quickly and efficiently.

Blanche bent over and looked at his face. His eyes were closed. She walked to the small window and looked out. She spoke softly to the window. "Oh, poor Dwight. That's such a terrible diarrhea you have, honey. I just hate diarrhea. I seem to have it all the time myself."

She whispered in the little-girl voice, so the nurses wouldn't know she was talking. "I've had bad diarrhea ever since I was a little girl. Real bad. I've always had it. You know what happened to me once when I was a little girl, Dwight? Real little, so little I don't hardly remember it, just sort of.

"My intestines fell right out of my anus. Can you believe it? It really happened, Dwight. My daddy took me to a doctor's house in the middle of the night. Everybody was in a panic. I smelled terrible. I was so embarrassed, and it hurt so bad. I still remember a lady standing there and crying over me. She looked at me, and she vomited. It must have been the doctor's wife.

"I was a mess. My skin was flapping on my bones. My bowels was hanging out from my bottom, dragging right on the ground. That doctor had to take and shove them back up in me. He sewed me up. That's why I've always had such bad diarrhea, I'm sure, because he never got them back up in there right."

Dwight was not asleep. He drifted off a few minutes later.

Debbie stayed away for a couple of cigarettes. It was difficult for her to go back. When she did get back, Dwight was still asleep. Less than half an hour later he woke and was suddenly in much worse condition than ever before. He started to flail on the bed, and his heart monitor went Code Blue. The nurses came running with the red crash cart. Doctors came running, tubes went into his nose and down his throat. Dwight was hooked up to a Puritan-Bennett 7200 computerized ventilator. Debbie realized she needed finally to prepare herself for her father's death.

Blanche watched the process of intubation with a distracted gaze. "He's just not gonna make it," she said in the little-girl voice. "He can't get no better, he's just too weak. Poor Dwight. He's gonna die."

The results of the heavy metals scan came back to North Carolina Memorial by automatic computer link just as they had come back to Baptist Hospital for Raymond Reid. But this time when the results came back the system worked. An intern saw the results, understood them immediately, and alerted Dr. Wohns early on the morning of May 13, 1989. Wohns read the results several times and placed a call to the lab to check to see if there might have been some mistake.

There was no mistake. The lab had triple-checked. The test results showed that Dwight Moore's system contained twenty times the lethal dose of arsenic—the most arsenic that had ever been found in any living human being in the history of the hospital, enough to kill a large mammal, enough to require that the medical literature be amended on the question of how large a dose of arsenic a human being can survive.

In all three of the most recent arsenic poisonings in North Carolina—Raymond Reid, Sandra Coulthard, and Dwight Moore—there had been positive results on a laboratory test for arsenic. In each case, the lab had sent back a result that could have meant only one thing: someone was trying to murder this patient. Only in Dwight Moore's case was the result heeded.

At nine-fifteen in the morning, Wohns notified the resident, who went directly to the ICU, where Dwight's family already was gathering. He asked them to leave the room and the corridor outside the ICU and return to the small waiting area, where they were to wait for him and for Dr. Wohns.

Then Wohns and the other doctors went in to see Dwight. They expected to find a man moments from death. Miraculously, Dwight was already pulling back, if ever so slightly. He was in great pain, he passed in and out of lucidity, but while lucid he could talk and think. He could even answer questions.

Wohns told him he had ingested a massive quantity of arsenic.

"Maybe when I sprayed," Dwight said.

Wohns didn't think so. But at the moment, saving his life was more urgent than solving the puzzle of his poisoning. There was a therapy that could save him—chelation. But it could be quite painful.

Dwight grasped the idea they were presenting to him and examined it intently. They could make him well. It would hurt. He couldn't possibly hurt worse than he did now. He managed a shrug. "Well, let's get started."

Wohns stayed for a while and talked to Dwight, carefully gauging his responses. Through all of the agony and disintegration Dwight was suffering, a bright clear light shone in his eyes—a willingness to face anything in order to live. In the corridor after he had finished talking to Dwight, Dr. Wohns made the last determination he needed in order for his diagnosis to be complete. This man, he decided, was not suicidal.

The family stayed close by in the ICU waiting area. It was a small shelter carved out of an open corridor, with only three walls, open to the hall on the fourth side. The walls were a yellowed institutional off-white. There were eight molded steel seats with uncomfortable vinyl padding. They were a large crowd when they gathered, some sitting, most of them standing and leaning against the wall. They avoided each other's eyes. They assumed they were about to be told that Dwight was dying or already dead.

The time dragged. It was close to ten o'clock in the morning. A few picked magazines out of a magazine rack. Doug stood in the arched opening to the area surveying the rest of them. Grandpa Moore was sitting. Blanche sat alone at one wall. Nellie and Dwight's brothers sat together against the third wall. Dwight's first wife, Lorene, had flown down from Virginia and was there with her husband, Richard Culotta. The Rev. Jim Rosser, who had married Dwight and Blanche, was there as well.

Finally three doctors arrived. Wohns started off. He told the family the medical staff had been concerned about a generalized buildup of poisons in Dwight's system. The good news was that his system had been rebounding forcefully from the time of his admission to North Carolina Memorial until the previous night's reversal. The bad news was that the most recent attack had been a dramatic one.

Then the head of toxicology spoke to them. He said the hospital had been able to carry out thorough research and testing on the toxins Blanche had brought in from the parsonage, but none of them had been capable of causing Dwight's condition.

Then he said: "Reverend Moore has ingested a massive quantity of arsenic."

There was silence.

"From where?" Nola asked.

"We don't know that. It is such a huge amount that it had to be ingested orally or introduced intravenously."

"Introduced?" Doug said. His question went unanswered.

"It must have been an accident," Debbie said.

Dwight's father had used arsenic for years as a pesticide on tobacco plants. "I thought they took arsenic off the market," he said. "I thought you couldn't get it anymore."

The resident spoke. He said Dwight obviously had an unusually strong constitution, that he was in for a rough time in the next twenty-four hours especially, but that if he survived the initial treatment for arsenic poisoning there was reason to hope his constitution would pull him through. He might well live.

Those words, that he might live, were what everyone heard. The business about arsenic was too arcane, too weird, for the family to absorb all at once. They had been preparing themselves for Dwight's death. Now he might live. They fell into each other's arms in hugs and tearful embraces.

Over the hubbub of sobbing and exclamation, Dr. Wohns uttered the final part of the presentation. "I have ordered that Reverend Moore be moved to a separate enclosed area normally used for patients who require sterile air, and I have ordered that a sitter be present with Reverend Moore at all times, and that no one, neither medical personnel nor family, be allowed in Reverend Moore's presence unless the sitter is there."

On that note, the doctors excused themselves and left.

The term "sitter" was another word from the language of hospitals. No one was quite sure what it meant. The group began to break up and drift apart into smaller clutches.

But Doug went off down the hall to be by himself. He was a chemist. He understood exactly what the doctors were saying. The arsenic had to have been ingested or introduced. They were putting a sitter in his father's room—a guard, in other words.

Someone was trying to murder his father.

He found a place in a staircase where he could be alone. He needed to stand quietly, get his breath, and bring his heartbeat under control.

This was deliberate. What his father had been going through had been done to him. Someone was trying to murder his father.

His mind raced through the possible suspects. It had to be Elaine Vinson. Blanche had tried to tell him Elaine was coming down to North Carolina to see his father, that she had not given up on the relationship. She was probably jealous of Blanche. She had to be the one. He hurried back down the hall and just caught Dr. Wohns before he got on the elevator. Doug followed him onto the elevator.

"I think I know who it is," he said, as the elevator doors closed.

Doug was only the first to figure out what the doctors were really saying. Back in the waiting area, a small group huddled around Dwight's father. Debbie was not among them. It could be Debbie, they decided. It might have something to do with Dwight's leaving the family after the affair with Elaine was discovered.

On the other side of the room, another knot had gathered. It could be Doug, they said. He's a chemist.

Down the corridor in the other direction, Blanche stood talking with Jim Rosser. "I sure hope they don't start asking questions about Raymond Reid," she said.

Dwight immediately began receiving chelation therapy— the same treatment that could have saved Sandra Coulthard and Raymond Reid, if only their arsenic test results had reached someone who realized the results spelled murder.

The doctors introduced a metal ion into Dwight's system. In some ways, his body took the ion for a poison like arsenic. The side effects were tough, especially given Dwight's body's tendency to fight back hard. In the meantime, however, the molecules of the ion were hunting down all of the arsenic molecules in his body and binding with them in a new nontoxic substance, which was either excreted or bound harmlessly with the bone. The substance used for the chelation was dimercaprol—basically the same thing the British had formulated in the early years of World War II as British anti-lewisite or BAL.

As soon as the doctors and nurses had set the therapy in motion, Dr. Wohns sat down with Dr. Robert Edward Cross, director of the North Carolina Memorial Hospital Toxicology Laboratory. Their shared mission normally was to cure people of disease and to preserve life. They reviewed the evidence carefully. The amount of arsenic Dwight Moore had ingested could not have been absorbed by his body through either the skin or lungs. That was totally impossible, given the levels.

Wohns and Cross looked into each other's eyes and saw the same unavoidable conclusion: the diagnosis was attempted murder.

At midday on the day they began chelation, Wohns and Cross called the Chapel Hill Police Department and relayed their findings to a detective. The detective said he would call back. By late that day, he had not called.

All of the family members were in and out of Dwight's room, concerned about whether he would make it through chelation. A nurse's aide was there watching them like a hawk at every moment, but it was still an extremely disturbing circumstance for Wohns and Cross. One of those people in the room with their patient probably was the murderer.

They called back to the Chapel Hill PD. The detective said there was some concern at management levels in the police department that North Carolina Memorial was a state facility, that this sounded like a long and difficult kind of investigation, and that the Chapel Hill PD was not entirely certain it was obligated to take on a case that involved a crime on state property. He said he would get back to the doctors on it in the morning.

By late the next morning, the doctors had received no call. Dwight was weathering the chelation well. That raised another chilling possibility: whoever was trying to kill him might be motivated to try again.

As physicians, they were on totally foreign ground. How could any of this be happening? How was it that they could call the police, alert them to an ongoing attempted murder by arsenic, and get back a long bureaucratic answer about jurisdictions and investigative costs?

They didn't have time to figure it out. If the Chapel Hill PD wasn't coming, then they would have to try something else.

They called the North Carolina State Bureau of Investigation.

In some ways, the SBI is the state-level equivalent of the FBI, a centralized and prestigious investigative agency with access to techniques and personnel that are beyond the reach of many local police agencies. In some ways, however, the SBI is unlike the FBI. Its jurisdiction is less clear, and in most cases it must be invited into a case by a local police agency.

The doctors' call was taken by a criminal agent at SBI headquarters in Raleigh, the state capital. The SBI campus, on the grounds of the old Governor Morehead School for the Blind, looked like a genteel, slightly tatty old Southern college.

The agent who took the doctors' call was calm, patient, and totally unsurprised that two highly placed physicians had called him with an allegation of poisoning. He interviewed the doctors carefully, worrying over questions that seemed almost irrelevant and at least far less urgent than the fact of attempted murder itself. He was especially interested in when the symptoms they described had first appeared. Where and when, he asked them, did Dwight Moore get the first dose?

The problem the doctors did not see but the agent did see was still the first one the doctors had encountered when they tried to get some police help: turf. The agent in Raleigh figured that Dwight's murderer had started trying to kill him in an unincorporated area in Alamance County. The crime may have continued in Orange County, but it started in Alamance. Therefore it was an Alamance County crime.

There were two minuses in that situation and one possible plus. Minus Number One: The SBI agent whose district normally covered Alamance County was on vacation. Minus Two: The SBI suspected Alamance County Sheriff Richard L. Frye might be mad at the SBI, ever since an SBI agent had run against him unsuccessfully for sheriff and during the campaign had made allegations about his effectiveness. (As it turned out, Frye was satisfied with having defeated his challenger and carried no grudge.)

Plus Number One and Only was this: SBI agent David McDougall, whose district adjoined the district of the vacationing agent, had turned down the Sandra Coulthard case the year before. Headquarters had called and asked him to take it, but he was on a much-delayed vacation with his family when the case broke. He had refused to leave his family to take the case.

During the entire ensuing year, McDougall had shared an office with the agent who did wind up taking the Coulthard case, and it was clear that having to forfeit the case had pained McDougall greatly. All in all, McDougall ought to be ripe for this new arsenic case in Alamance, and if anybody could smooth out the Alamance sheriff, it would be McDougall.

At thirty-nine, David McDougall was Hollywood-handsome, dark-haired, fine-featured, with an intelligent, even scholarly face and a certain gravity of manner. He wore dark suits and white shirts and kept his hair cut neatly. When he talked, particularly about a case, a streak of case-hardened swagger appeared in the body language. He could come across like a young high-profile executive, a professor, or a tough guy.

This case would involve lots of forensics, lots of chemistry, and then none of the evidence might mean a thing in the end. Poisoning was a proof that sent shivers down the spines of experienced law enforcement people. There was never anybody who had seen the poisoner do the deed. You could spend years and tons of money proving scientifically that somebody had been poisoned. All the defense had to do was stand up, present some evidence about how people could ingest poison accidentally, and then make the defendant out to be Mother Teresa.

Law enforcement had to stitch up every inch of the story. It had to be airtight, unassailable. The prosecutor would have to show that the accused was capable, had a motive, and had lots of opportunity and that no other conceivable suspect had the same motive or opportunity. This case would involve lots of cross-jurisdictional coordination and work with medical people, who are always so terrified of civil suits that they never want to say anything to anybody.

Eventually they would figure out who had done it. But that certainly did not mean they would succeed in making a prosecutable case, let alone get a conviction. Then the agency would be in worse shape than ever. Poison is always big news. The SBI criminal agent in Raleigh already knew enough about the victim and the people around him to know that these were respectable people. This was not a case of Joe Criminal blowing away his worthless dope-dealing brother-in-law. The people in this case might even be prominent in their own community. That and the poison angle would make this case very high-profile, very sexy news.

If the SBI traipsed into the middle of it, pointed to a suspect, and then failed to make the case, it would be very bad news for the agency. Now that Wohns and Cross had called, of course, there was no way the agency could walk away anyway, even if it had been inclined to, which it was not. But it was all very tricky. A case like this was immediately a front-burner deal, a career-maker or a career-breaker.

This case was ideal for David McDougall. SBI headquarters reached him on his car phone. They gave him the basic layout. He hung up and called Dr. Wohns from the car.

Debbie had returned to Hampton, Virginia, and Doug had gone back to Montclair, New Jersey, both having left instructions that they were to be called at least twice a day with updates and both prepared to jump back on a plane at a moment's notice.

Blanche, Nola, and Nellie maintained the watch. Dwight was recovering, but the effects of the last dose had been so massive and the chelation was so hard on him that he was still going through unmitigated hell. Utter exhaustion put him to sleep and pain awakened him. While conscious, he was still slipping in and out of lucidity.

Alone in the room with Dwight and the sitter, Blanche said to the sitter: "I have things I need to say to my husband. Could we not be alone for just a minute?"

"No, ma'am. You cannot be in here with him alone."

Blanche complained about it to the other two women. Her face was contorted with anger. Then, taking a seat primly on one of the metal chairs in the ICU waiting area, she turned her face away from Nola and Nellie for a moment. She turned back to face them with the open, sweet visage of a perplexed girl.

"Right after Dwight sprayed the yard that day," she said in the girl voice, "he came in the house and wiped his hands on a towel that was hanging there by the sink, and then after, I dried my face on that towel, and my face just swole up terrible. I had to go the doctor, and he gave me a shot for it."

Nola stared back at her.

"Blanche," Nola said, "Dwight didn't spray his yard with arsenic."

"Well," she said with a flip little shrug, "I don't know what he sprayed with, but my face swole all up and I had to get a shot."

Nola leaned forward on her own metal chair and frowned into Blanche's face. "Blanche, it had to be ingested. They said it couldn't be through the skin or the lungs. It had to be ingested."

"Well, I don't know about those chemicals," she said.

Later that afternoon, Blanche approached the doctors with the story of the tainted towel. They took notes and politely excused themselves from her presence.

That evening, Blanche approached the doctors again. "I just thought of something that totally slipped my mind before. Dwight is a fanatic about eating grapes, and we bought some fruit that had grapes in it for our trip to New Jersey. It was just a week or two before our trip when they found those poisoned grapes from Chile with cyanide in them and everybody all over the country was scared of grapes. You know, it was after that trip when he started feeling so poorly."

It was after dusk when David McDougall called Dr. Wohns from the car. They talked for an hour while McDougall worked his way toward home down the crowded freeway through the Raleigh, Durham, Chapel Hill Triangle area. The Triangle, dotted with universities and research laboratories, is just at the eastern edge of the long central flats of North Carolina, where the land begins to plunge and climb. On a dark evening shiny with rain, the roads are a tangle of BMWs and redneck pickup trucks, carrying people home to sleek condo towers, big new neo-Georgian homes, tumbledown farms, and trailer parks. All the way home, grilling Dr. Wohns over the hollow snapping circuit of the cellular phone, McDougall was already figuring the complexities of the case, the science and the boondocks politics. It would not be easy. He allowed himself to be a little bit excited. He and the doctors talked again by phone that evening.

For his first task the next morning, Agent McDougall addressed his most important strategic agenda item. He called Sheriff Frye in Alamance County and told him he needed to talk about an Alamance case that had come up. But first McDougall went through the necessary Southern ritual of inquiring after family and exchanging a few wry remarks about recent events in professional sports.

Sheriff Frye was no ogre. He was terse. He looked out for his own people and his own territory. He didn't appreciate some SBI guy running against him for office and using things he knew from the SBI to try to make him look bad in front of his own county. But Sheriff Frye could work with a good man like McDougall.

"Sheriff, we wanted you to know what we were doing, because, as we see it, it's really your case."

"Yessir."

"We have already invested some effort in it, and I would think you would want us to stay on it with you, in an assisting role."

"Yessir."

"I'm headed out to the hospital this afternoon after I make some more calls to interview the victim, and I thought you might want to send someone along with me."

"Yessir."

"Anybody you could spare would sure be great, but on a case like this the ideal from my point of view would be to work with one of your best."

There was a long pause. Frye said he would assign Phil Ayers. Ayers was the best Frye had to offer. He wondered if that would be satisfactory.

McDougall said, "Yessir."

By early afternoon, McDougall had finished briefing Detective Ayers and they were on their way together to North Carolina Memorial.

Ayers and McDougall were the same age and had come to the same general temperament from different directions. McDougall was a college cop; Ayers was a high school graduate who had worked his way up from patrol. They were both smart, skeptical, and very self-controlled.

On the way, McDougall told Ayers some of what he remembered about the case his officemate had made the year before on Robert F. Coulthard, Jr.

Ayers said he wondered what the doctors had thought Sandra Coulthard was suffering from, if not from arsenic poisoning.

"Guillain-Barre syndrome. You ever hear of that?"

"I'm not sure."

"I had a relative who died of it," McDougall said.

"It's fatal?"

"No, no, it's almost never fatal. That was what was so unusual about my relative's case. Every once in a while it can be, and in her case it was. But my ears kind of pricked up when I heard the agent on the Coulthard case say the docs had diagnosed her as suffering from Guillain-Barre."

"Why is it so similar?"

"It progresses the same way, starts in the hands and feet as a numbness or a tingling, and it has a lot of the same symptoms, paralysis especially. But it's really not similar. Arsenic has so many more symptoms, and it's so much more extreme, if a doctor knew to look for arsenic he would never be confused. But nobody ever thinks of arsenic."

"Because nobody ever thinks of murder."

"Right. Especially not nice people like these are going to be."

Before Dr. Wohns introduced the two detectives to Dwight, he made it plain to them that an overly stressful interview could seriously endanger Dwight. Dwight was off the ventilator, but he still had tubes running in and out of his nose and veins, he was still on a heart monitor, and he was still a very sick and very fragile man. It was clear from what he said in his lucid moments that Dwight believed he had somehow poisoned himself accidentally. It was a stunning miracle that he was still alive. It was very much in the realm of possibility that in presenting the specter of murder to him, McDougall and Ayers could kill him.

On that note, Dr. Wohns took them in. Dwight was awake and seemed to be able to understand what was being said to him. He lay motionless on the bed but turned his eyes quickly as each person spoke to him. McDougall sat close to his face.

They talked very generally for a while about his illness and the prognosis for his recovery. Dwight knew what this was. It was bedside manner. He did it for a living. He went along with it as graciously as he could. But through the fog of pain and drugs, it came clear to him that these were police officers. They were detectives, in suits. They were talking to him about his illness. He tuned himself up a notch and listened as hard as he could to their questions.

Phil Ayers was asking him about his son.

"How often does he come to see you, Reverend Moore?"

"Oh, several times a year. They have a baby now. So less."
He smiled.

Ayers smiled back. McDougall smiled. McDougall and Ayers stole quick little glances at the heart monitor.

"What about your daughter, Reverend Moore?" McDougall asked. "About how often does she get home, then?"

"Ah, I would say, more often than my son. Perhaps once a month. We're very close. I'm very close to my son, too, but he's farther away, and he has a family to look after."

The heart monitor was still looking all right, but Dwight was not. Another wave of nausea was cresting. The detectives excused themselves, to let him rest and to use the time doing some interviewing in the corridor. The corridor, in fact, was a busy place: Blanche was engaged in a histrionic argument with one of the ICU nurses.

"For all I know, you gave him the arsenic! You won't let me in to see my own sick husband who may be dying, and you're the one who feeds him, you could be the one that did it!"

"Mrs. Moore," the nurse said, "no one can be with him alone without the sitter. Those are just the rules. And now the police are here."

Blanche looked up appreciatively. "Well, I need to talk to you men," she said.

The detectives took dutiful notes while Blanche gave them the story of the towel and the swollen face. Late in the afternoon, they went back in to see Dwight.

"Reverend Moore, can you tell us anything about your estate?"

"My worth?"

"Yes."

"It's not much. I've always been a poor clergyman."

"Do you have any life insurance?"

"Yes, I have some. I have three policies. I forget exactly how much each one is. I believe the three policies total fifty-eight thousand dollars."

People back at SBI headquarters had already done the homework on Dwight's worth. In combined insurance and lump-sum pension benefits, he was worth a quarter of a million dollars. Dead. The beneficiaries would be his son, his daughter, and his wife.

Watching the heart monitor closely, McDougall said, "Reverend Moore, can you tell us the names of any people you know or any people close to you who have died in the last few years?"

Dwight's eyes opened a degree. The line on the monitor barely flickered.

"I'm a minister," he said. "It's my job, my calling..." his voice trailed off.

They waited.

"I had a parishioner who died of cancer recently."

They took the name of the parishioner. They waited patiently while Dwight dredged his memory for the names of other parishioners, of distant friends and acquaintances who had died in recent years.

"Do you know if any people close to either your son or your daughter have died in recent years?"

"I don't know of anyone."

"Mr. Moore, I want you to understand that we are here to protect you and to see that the law is upheld. In doing that, we have to ask some things that we wish we didn't have to. If at any moment you want us to haul out of here and leave you alone, just say the word, and we're gone."

"Yes?" Dwight was watching very carefully now. The monitor was steady.

"Reverend Moore, you have an ex-wife in Virginia, is that right?"

"Yes."

"And is there anyone else there to whom you are close or with whom you may have been close in the past?"

There it was.

Out.

Dwight was ruined.

Whatever had happened to put him in this position, whatever would happen from now on, he was ruined. The affair with Elaine was part of this. The affair would become known to his beloved new parishioners in the town of Carolina. They might have suspected there was a shadow over his past, but they had been spared the graphic details. His minister's instincts told him that this would not work. It was over—the dream he had almost rebuilt. Gone. The parish in Carolina was gone. Strike two. He stopped for a moment and watched it evaporate before his very eyes.

Speaking more clearly than he had all day, Dwight said: "I

had an affair with my church secretary in Virginia for sixteen years. The affair became known to our spouses. My marriage was destroyed, and my ministry very nearly was, too."

Dwight ground out the details, Elaine's name and address and when she had last been in North Carolina. The dates obviously put her out of the picture. The detectives pressed on.

"Your wife, Blanche," McDougall said. "She was married before, was she not?"

"Yes."

"Widowed."

"Yes."

"And how did her husband die?"

"I'm not sure. Of a heart attack, I believe. Natural causes."

"Has anyone else near her died?"

Dwight was silent, staring straight ahead. "You will find this out anyway," he said. "She had a close friend named Raymond Reid who was a coworker at Kroger. He was very ill and died, and Blanche tended him and did a lot for him."

This was a new name. McDougall and Ayers both scratched notes.

"When was this, Reverend Moore?" Ayers asked.

"It's been about three years, I think."

"And do you know what he died of?"

"Yes. It was Guillain-Barre syndrome."

McDougall and Ayers exchanged involuntary glances. They looked at the heart monitor. Dwight was doing fine, but they both needed a break. They excused themselves and retired from the room. Once outside, they went for coffee and a conference.

Chapter Thirteen

Now McDougall and Ayers had real work to do. Here was Dwight Moore, loaded with enough arsenic to kill a horse. Here was his wife, running around the hospital accusing nurses one minute, blaming Chilean grapes the next, and then buttonholing doctors with her story about the towel and the swollen face.

And now here was some guy named Raymond Reid, the wife's close male friend (had Reverend Moore been slightly awkward in describing that relationship?), who supposedly died of Guillain-Barre—something that people almost never die of but that is frequently misdiagnosed in cases of arsenic poisoning.

McDougall got on the phone to Dr. John Butts, chief medical examiner of North Carolina. Butts and McDougall were a good match. They were about the same age. Like McDougall, Butts was a specimen of the new look in law enforcement—a serious, straight-on, Brooks Brothers kind of man.

The actual structure of the medical examiner's office in North Carolina had been put in place by Butts's predecessor,

Dr. Page Hudson, who was much more the sort of romantic figure typical of the older generation of coroners. Hudson was a disarming gray cloud of a man, shambling and disheveled in his way, but always with a deductive rapier in hand, stalking a corpse for evidence the way Sherlock Holmes stalked London.

Butts wore starched white shirts and red ties. He was an athletic-looking man, kept his auburn hair cut short, and made only one small gesture in the direction of flamboyance—a pair of half-moon reading glasses, which he allowed to slip down toward the end of his nose in an affectation of owlish wisdom. Otherwise, walking down the streets of Chapel Hill where the headquarters of the medical examiner's office were located, John Butts could be taken for a sober young banker.

He was very bright. Forensic pathology was a life calling for him. He had graduated in chemistry from Duke in 1968, got his medical degree from Duke in 1972, and took three years of special training at Duke in anatomic and clinical pathology. As soon as he had finished his long academic training, Butts came directly to the state medical examiner's office in Chapel Hill for a year-long internship in forensic pathology. Then he did a year of residency at North Carolina Memorial in clinical pathology, after which he returned directly to the medical examiner's office as an assistant.

In 1986, the year Raymond Reid had died, Page Hudson had retired from office and taken a position as a professor of clinical pathology and laboratory medicine at East Carolina University, where Steven Reid went to school. In semiretirement, Dr. Hudson made himself available to criminal defense lawyers as an expert witness. Given the criminal traditions of the region, Dr. Hudson was especially expert in the matter of arsenic poisoning, having worked on almost two dozen arsenic cases in his career.

And so was John Butts. He had been in charge on only two cases—Coulthard and one other—but he had been at Dr. Hudson's side for many more. He had another advantage that might not show immediately through the smooth shell of his businesslike exterior: John Butts had been around state government and bureaucrats a lot—his whole career—and he knew exactly how much screwing up to expect in the average person's performance of duty.

As soon as he got on the phone with McDougall, Butts

started asking questions. When did Moore's problems start? What were the early symptoms? What were the late symptoms? What was the rate of progression? Did the man up there in North Carolina Memorial seem to get better and then have sudden relapses? How much did McDougall know about this Raymond Reid?

McDougall and Ayers already knew a lot. They had been on the phone to the medical people in Winston-Salem, and they had a fairly good oral description of the progress of Reid's disease and death.

At the end of the conversation, there was a long silence. Finally Butts said the Raymond Reid case sounded very much like an arsenic poisoning and that he would put his staff on it full-blast.

Butts gave McDougall a quick explanation of the sort of evidence he would need to make a case. Obviously they would meet later and plan a strategy. Much of the evidence was going to be locked inside Dwight Moore's body, as it might still be locked inside Raymond Reid's, and it wasn't going anywhere. The two important things that could be lost, Butts said, were hair and fingernails.

There are two common folk beliefs about arsenic in North Carolina, both totally untrue. One is that arsenic is used in embalming fluid, so that once a person has been embalmed, the poison used to kill him can never be found. In truth, it has been illegal throughout most of this century to use any amount of arsenic in embalming fluid.

The second is that arsenic is hard to trace in the unembalmed human body. In truth, arsenic stays in the dead body almost forever. In the living and the dead, the hair and fingernails are perfect maps and calendars of the doses. After each dose, when the body has excreted all it can and is trying to find a place to bind up the remaining arsenite, it sends it in a wave to the skin, trying to sweat it out. The hair and nails, which are horny outgrowths of the skin, hold it. In the nails it appears at "Mees lines"—little white waves that grow slowly out with the nail. In the hair it is invisible but can be detected accurately by laboratory methods.

Before leaving the hospital, McDougall asked if anyone had cut Dwight Moore's hair or nails since he had been admitted. No one had. The question, however, found its

way down to the ICU waiting area where the family was gathered.

Linda Reid came home from work that night and played
the messages on her machine. For the third time in two days,
there was a message from a Phil Ayers at the Alamance County
Sheriff's Department. The first two times she had assumed it
was a call about barbecue tickets or something and she hadn't
returned the call. But this was the third call.

She called Stevie at school and called Ray, where he was
working on a Christmas-tree farm near Boone, up in the mountains. They were both such good boys that she really didn't
suspect them. And she knew she hadn't done anything wrong
herself.

"Look, I hope you guys don't have any surprises waiting
for me out there," she told the boys.

"No, Mama, not at all," Ray said, laughing. "You don't have
any for us, do you?"

"I'll let you know."

Dr. Modesto Scharyj, the regional medical examiner over
the Winston-Salem district, had a message on his machine, too.
His boss back in Chapel Hill wanted him to examine the chart
on a man named Raymond Reid, who had died at Baptist Hospital three years earlier. In particular, Dr. Butts wanted him to
check to see if anyone had ever run an arsenic test on Reid. It
was already a very full day.

That night when he got home, David McDougall had a
message waiting for him. It was from Dwight Moore. Moore
wanted to see him. Immediately.

Dinner was on the table. McDougall's family looked up
expectantly at him. He walked back out the door, got in the
car, and drove back to Chapel Hill.

At night, when the rest of the hospital is half asleep, the
ICU glows from a distance down the long white corridor, like
a green humming space station. It is the one place that cannot
afford to sleep. Dwight was awake and waiting. His face was
even more drawn and pained than it had been during the earlier
interviews. He was beginning to be able to raise his hands off
the bed, but they shook and flailed if he tried to keep them
aloft too long. His voice occasionally quavered and failed him.
But his eyes were strong, clear, and determined.

"I have been thinking about the questions you have been asking me, Detective."

"Yes."

"It's quite clear to me where your thinking is taking you."

McDougall said nothing.

"You think my wife is trying to murder me."

McDougall paused before answering. "We have to go through a certain process of elimination with anyone who could be a suspect—"

"You think Blanche is the main suspect," Dwight interrupted.

"We think she is a strong suspect, sir."

Dwight lay back on the bed, his mouth working silently in the shadows. He was fighting off a wave of nausea. All of the high-tech equipment in the room created a continual blanket of humming in the air, under which McDougall could just barely hear him sucking for breath.

"Call it off."

"What, Reverend Moore?"

"I want it called off. I won't press charges. Call it off. Now."

McDougall looked at the heart monitor. Dwight was fairly strong. McDougall dropped his head and stared at the floor for a while.

It's police work, he thought. A calling, a profession, a thing men and women learn to do, take pride in, enjoy in spite of the tough picture. But sometimes it is all overwhelmed by sadness. Sometimes it is so sad.

"Look, Dwight," he said at last, "I know that you are trying to come to grips with some very difficult things, at a time when you are still a very sick man. But I have to tell you something. I've got doctors here who are ready to go into court and testify that you are full of arsenic and somebody put it in you.

"If we decide that the somebody is your wife, then this thing goes forward. With you or without you. Naturally I want you on our side. But if we have this much evidence of an attempted murder and perhaps an actual murder—"

"Who are you talking about?"

"Raymond Reid."

"No, no, that's wrong. You will find that this is all a big misunderstanding. It's an accident. My wife is guilty of nothing. She's a fine person."

"Reverend Moore, we have got to do what we have got to do."

"I understand that." Dwight was silent for a long moment, obviously turning something over in his mind. "I appreciate your coming to see me on such short notice," he said. "I'm sorry to have bothered you."

"Not at all. I want you to call me at any time."

McDougall got up and took his coat in his hand. "By the way, have you seen Blanche much lately?"

"No, not a lot. I would say things have been strained. She's coming in tomorrow with her brother, P.D. He's a barber."

McDougall stopped, walked back to the bedside, and sat back down.

"He's a barber?"

"Yes."

"Why are they coming?"

"Blanche has it in her mind that I need a haircut."

McDougall slumped. He looked over at the sitter and said, "I may need your help here."

He explained as well as he could to Dwight what Dr. Butts had told him earlier that day concerning the importance of hair and nails as a physical record of the doses. Then he gave Dwight the bad news:

"I really need to pluck thirty or forty hairs from your scalp right now."

Dwight looked back at him in alarm for a moment and then smiled. "Really?"

"Yessir."

Dwight shrugged. "This is all very unusual, isn't it?"

"Yes."

"Well, you might as well get started."

McDougall found sterile plastic bags and small forceps in the room. The hair had to be plucked, Butts had said, not cut, in order for the tests to be accurate.

McDougall first made careful labels and notes to identify the bags and to describe the exact manner in which he was going to remove the hair and place it in the plastic bags, so it would be clear which end of the hair was root and which was tip. And then he set about yanking hairs from Dwight Moore's scalp.

When he was done, McDougall said, "Dwight, I want you

to understand, I really know very little about this kind of laboratory analysis they're going to do with your hair, so I'm not
necessarily sure I have taken these specimens correctly. The
other thing is, the last thing you need right now is a haircut.
Would you mind just telling her you're not in the mood?"

Dwight was noncommittal.

The next day, when Blanche and her brother appeared,
Dwight allowed them to give him a haircut—quite a close haircut, in fact. McDougall was down in the waiting area talking to
family when he heard about it. He was furious. He started off
down the hall to put a stop to it, but Blanche was already leaving
the ICU and coming toward him, and her brother was already
gone.

"Hello, Mrs. Moore," he said evenly.

"Oh, hello, Detective."

"You've been in to see Reverend Moore, then?"

"Yes. My brother, P.D., was kind enough to agree to come
up here and give poor Dwight a haircut. I felt so awful, he just
looked so bad all shaggy like that, and I think he needed it for his
spirits. You know, that's very important to them when they're in
the hospital a long time and sick and all like that—"

"Well, that's great," he said, cutting her off. "Of course, it
won't interfere with my work at all, Blanche, because I went in
last night and pulled these out of his scalp."

He held up one of the plastic bags.

The little chitchat look vanished. She looked at the bag.
Her face hardened, and she stared at McDougall. "Well, good,"
she said through a lipless sneer. "Good for you."

At that moment, Dr. Butts was taking the report of Dr.
Scharyj over the phone. Reading from notes, Scharyj gave a
general overview of what he had found while going through
the voluminous file on Raymond Reid the day before at Baptist
Hospital. There had been no autopsy. The cause of death on
the certificate was listed as cardiac arrest due to hypoxia, due
to ARDS sepsis.

The terms Scharyj had just read meant that the doctors at
Baptist had decided Raymond's death was caused by a heart
attack, which was caused by suffocation, which was caused by
pus in the lungs related to adult respiratory disease syndrome.
In other words, he got sick, his lungs filled up until he couldn't
breathe effectively, and eventually his heart stopped.

Butts was grateful for Scharyj's work but was unimpressed by the diagnosis on the death certificate. Typical of cause-of-death determinations when there has been no autopsy, it basically said, in very fancy terms, "Got sick and died." But what are you going to do without an autopsy? It would be important for the police to find out why no autopsy was done.

Butts wanted to know exactly what the record said about what Raymond Reid himself said he had been doing immediately before getting sick. Scharyj said the records showed Reid had reported that he had just finished eating a meal when the first attack struck.

Butts asked about a heavy metals test. Scharyj said he had not found one but the chart had been almost a foot thick. Butts made a note to himself to recheck for a heavy metals screen. Then he told Scharyj to send him copies of the admission and discharge summaries right away.

"Will do."

"Thank you very much. Goodbye."

He hung up the phone. Finally it was time for the basic go-or-no conversation between Butts and McDougall. Butts placed the call. First he told McDougall about the absence of an autopsy and the cause of death given on the certificate.

Butts told McDougall they definitely were going to have to go for an exhumation order.

"We are?" McDougall said.

"Yes."

"What did you find? Did they test him for arsenic?"

Butts told him his people had not found a heavy metals screen but he himself found it hard to believe someone would not have ordered such a lab at some point. He recommended that the SBI send its own people to recheck the chart.

"If they did order a lab and it came back positive, why would the diagnosis have been heart attack?"

"I don't know. But if they did order a lab and it came back negative, whoever winds up being the prosecutor on this will need to know about it sooner rather than later."

The question of who would be prosecutor was not destined to be a simple matter. McDougall had assumed the case would go straight to Steve Balog, the boyish, brown-haired thirty-one-year-old prosecutor in the 15A Prosecutorial District in Graham, seat of Alamance County. It was an Alamance case. He was the Alamance DA.

But as soon as Balog got wind that the state medical examiner's office was coming to town, looking to dig up a body in Pine Hill Cemetery, he started backpedaling. By the time the authorities were actually in touch with him about the exhumation, Balog had a very definite theory about one important aspect of the case: if the poisoning of Raymond Reid took place in Winston-Salem, then it would not be an Alamance County case, and he would not have to sign an order for one of his own dead constituents to be raised up out of the eternal repose.

It would make no difference in the end, McDougall told himself. Raymond Reid's body was in Pine Hill Cemetery, which was in Alamance County, which meant that Steve Balog would have to sign the order, as would a local judge. But it would take a few days to overcome Balog's reluctance and get the exhumation order squared away.

Linda Reid had Friday off before the start of the long Memorial Day weekend. She spent most of the day lying around the swimming pool at a girlfriend's apartment. As unhappy as her divorce from Raymond had been, Linda had come out of it a more independent woman and a fairly happy person. She had remarried briefly after the divorce from Raymond. It hadn't worked out. She kept the name—Sykes—and some good memories. There was no bitterness in her.

She was happy. It didn't hurt that at age forty-seven, she looked as if she could be a trim thirty-five. Raymond's death had been unexpected and incredibly ugly. But she had weathered it. She had her life in order. She liked her life.

By now she had spoken several times on the telephone with the detective from the Alamance County Sheriff's Department and with SBI agent David McDougall. The conversations had been brief. She really had no idea what they were after—something to do with Kroger, probably, maybe with Blanche's lawsuit again. The policemen were tight-lipped, which was fine with Linda. She had absolutely no desire to get into it.

At the end of the day, she drove back to her comfortable new ranch-style home in a pine-shaded subdivision near Elon College. She had not been home long when her phone rang. It was Agent McDougall.

"How are you doing, Mrs. Sykes?"

"I'm fine. How are you?"

"Good. Look, I need to take a few minutes of your time, and I have something to tell you that will be very stressful. Are you okay?"

"Yes, I'm fine, Mr. McDougall. What can I do for you?" She had answered the call on a phone with a long cord that sat on the divider/bar in the dining area between her small kitchen and the large living room. While McDougall spoke, she gathered up the cord in one hand and found her way to one of the chairs by the dining table.

"At my request, Dr. John Butts, who is the state medical examiner of North Carolina, has carried out a review of the chart or medical file on your ex-husband leading up to his death. As a result of that examination, he thinks there is a problem with the cause of death as given on your ex-husband's death certificate."

Her mind was whirling. What on earth was this man talking about? Was it some kind of form or license that hadn't been completed or tax that hadn't been paid?

"Dr. Butts is very strongly of the opinion," McDougall went on, "that Raymond Reid actually died of arsenic poisoning."

There was a pause.

Linda's mind was silent. "Arsenic," she said.

"Yes."

"How would he get arsenic?"

"Dr. Butts and I believe that your husband was the victim of murder by deliberate arsenic poisoning."

She was outwardly calm or numb, but her hand, which was holding the telephone, was suddenly terribly weak. Her hand was exhausted. It could barely hold the telephone. Suddenly she felt a green nausea welling up in the pit of her stomach.

"Go ahead," she muttered.

"The only way we can make this determination for sure is to seek an exhumation order so that Dr. Butts can carry out the kind of forensic work that's needed."

"You are going to dig Raymond up," she said.

"Yes. We need to."

"And do an autopsy."

"Yes."

"Oh. Listen. Oh my God. Listen to me. Do my boys know about this?"

"No."

"Well, I've got to tell them. I've got to tell them right now. Stevie's at school, Ray is up in Boone, I've... What are they going to do?"

"They're going to exhume him and carry out tests."

"Who did this? Who did it? Who would do this? You are telling me you think the reason Raymond Reid was sick and died is because someone murdered him with poison?"

"Yes."

"Who? Who?"

"We don't know yet."

"I have got to call my boys."

"Linda, Mrs. Sykes, stop! Listen to me. Yes, you need to tell your sons. But you need to understand something very important. We do know pretty much for sure that this was murder, but we do not know who did it. It is very important, so that we can continue to carry out our investigation, that you not speak to the press or tell your neighbors or even your family other than your sons about this. We have to insist on strict, absolute secrecy."

"Yes."

She stopped talking. There was a long pause.

"Mr. McDougall," she said, "you asked me two days ago what I knew about Blanche's new husband, Dwight Moore. Dwight's been real sick."

"Yes."

"What is he sick from?"

"I really do not want you to start speculating or trying to do police work."

"I said, what is he sick from?"

"Tests have determined Dwight Moore is suffering from arsenic poisoning."

Her entire face began to tingle. She felt sweat down on the pocket of her back where the shoulder blades met. Now the nausea hardened into a full-blown stomach pain.

"You think it's Blanche."

"I think it could be."

"Oh my God."

"Are you all right? I can come out there."

"I am all right. I need to hang up and call my sons right now. I will tell them what you said about not talking to the press or to anyone else."

"You gonna be okay?"

She hadn't thought about that yet. She stopped and thought it over. "Yes," she said. "I am going to be all right."

She decided she could tell Stevie on the phone. She had to call and leave a message, but he called back in a few minutes. She told him in the most calm and collected way she could that she had just been informed by an agent of the North Carolina Bureau of Investigation that his father was to be dug up and autopsied, three years after his death, and that Blanche was suspected of murdering him with arsenic.

Stevie listened without saying a word. When she had finished telling him, Stevie said, "God. I wonder who Blanche has done hoo-dooed now. Are you going to call Ray?"

"I think I need to tell Ray face-to-face."

"Yeah. You do. Just call him and tell him to get in his truck and start driving."

Ray's truck came grinding up her narrow gravel drive in the early-morning hours. Linda had been sitting at her dining table for hours, waiting. As soon as Ray walked in through the door, he said, "Mama, now don't beat around the bush with me. Tell me what this is about right now."

She went through the story for him. Ray stared at her, eyes squinting in intense disbelief and surprise the whole while. When she had finished, he continued to stare at her. Suddenly his eyes brimmed with tears.

"She put Daddy through that?"

"That's what they are saying may have happened."

"Daddy didn't have to die? He could be alive right now? He doesn't have to be dead?"

Linda said nothing. Her eyes were full of tears, and her lip was trembling. She stood by the room divider watching Ray.

His mouth dropped open, stretched open wide, and a roar erupted. He lifted his fists and waved them at the air, nodding his head violently forward and backward. "*No! No! No no no no no!* NO!"

He caught his breath and stopped nodding. He put his

hands on the table, clutched together. "They think Blanche killed Daddy? Oh, Mama, I . . ."

He stood up suddenly.

"Mama, I'm sorry, I can't . . ." His body was suddenly jerked and wracked by sobs. She rushed forward to catch him. He dropped to his knees and sobbed into her arms.

He struggled back to his feet.

"I've gotta go take a walk," he said.

"Please be careful, Ray."

"I will."

He pushed open the door.

"Are you all right, Ray?"

He turned back around. "I don't know, Mama. I don't know anything. I can't believe this is real. I . . . I've just got to go take a walk."

Chapter Fourteen

Alamance County DA Steve Balog finally agreed to take the next official step, which was for him to see Superior Court Judge J. B. Allen in Graham and seek an exhumation order. Balog's office placed some calls to the court to find out exactly how the request should be framed and what sorts of proofs would have to be provided with it. The word came back from the judge, indirectly, that the main thing Balog would need was a report from John Butts providing evidence that Reid could have been murdered by an arsenic poisoner.

Graham was the county seat, the courthouse town, accustomed for the better part of two centuries to processing the day-to-day troubles of the district.

Steve Balog's offices were in the corner of a new building across the street from the Alamance County sheriff's office and the jail. West Elm Street ran from that area to the side door of the courthouse. On one side of West Elm was a plain weathered brick building with a narrow white Chippendale door in the center, housing the law office of Mitchell McEntire, a local criminal lawyer who worked the county and state courts. On the other side, under a blue-and-white awning, was Chadwick's Restaurant, an establishment dear to the local legal profession.

Here at Chadwick's, during the long middle of a day in this Southern county seat, the judges and the prosecutors and the defense attorneys and all of their clerks and trainees and various apprentices gathered at a long table like eager rabbits to sample the offerings of the salad bar and to hear what was rustling out there in the great green garden of the law. The word "**exhumation**" alone would have set the noses at that table to twitching and sniffing at such a spirited pace that a stranger in the restaurant, watching from a corner booth, might have feared fire.

But exhumation, arsenic, and murder, all mentioned together in the self-same rumor, were almost beyond what the table at Chadwick's could absorb in a single sitting. The long table erupted in an absolute frenzy when one of the local courthouse wisemen dropped a rumor that the DA was about to ask a Superior Court judge for an order allowing him to dig up the body of a local citizen, buried three years ago in Burlington's most respectable cemetery, on the suspicion that the man's girlfriend, now married to a local preacher, had killed the man with arsenic and had come close to doing in the preacher the same way.

Mitch McEntire sat at the end of the table and listened silently, occasionally dipping his head in an appreciative grin when one of the other lawyers made an especially salient remark or asked a good question. He was a huge man—called "Bear" by his colleagues, and "Sir" or "Mr. McEntire, Sir" by most of the local miscreants. He toyed with his salad, the little fork almost lost in his large hand, and he pretended to be mildly amused by the brouhaha around him. He was making careful mental notes.

When Steve Balog and his people came to the table with their little brown bowls of salad, they were hit with a broadside of inquiries from lawyers and judges trying to find out what sort of criminal angle this exhumation would have, what sort of civil side there might be, what kind of political fallout could be expected, what hay could be made. Balog, who was by nature a taciturn young man, kept his own counsel, but enough had been said and enough overheard that the matter of the pending exhumation had already escaped for good beyond the bounds of the salad bar. The *Alamance Times-News,* after all, was only a few doors down Elm Street.

By the time Balog got back to his office, there were messages from reporters. This was not at all the kind of action Steve Balog savored. He had a reelection campaign less than a year ahead of him. Things were going smoothly for him so far. He would only have trouble if he made trouble for himself. Digging people up in the cemetery was one of those activities the political consequences of which were difficult to predict or control, especially if it turned out no crime had been committed, or, worse, a crime had been committed but no conviction could be won.

He returned some of the calls he simply could not ignore, but he tried to keep his remarks to a flat and unexcited minimum. The newspapers responded with the kind of halfway coverage—not a dismissive short item in the back but not a front-page banner story, either, something right in the middle with lots of good detail—that gives readers in a small community the impression something very big and deliciously secret is being covered up.

Linda Reid read the first stories in a kind of altered state, as if she were reading about other people in another universe. They called Raymond "a former boyfriend of the minister's wife." They called Blanche by her former name, Blanche Taylor.

There was something odd, almost cartoonlike, in the way the facts were laid out: "Reid, 50, died at N.C. Baptist Hospital in Winston-Salem one month after signing a will that left a third of his roughly $68,000 estate and executor's powers to Taylor," one story said.

She was startled. She picked it up and read it again. How did they know that? How did they already know personal things about Raymond? There was a reference to her sons.

The phone rang. It was Stevie. There were reporters calling him. He had talked to Ray. They were trying to talk to him, too. Linda reiterated what Agent McDougall had said: if they divulged any details of the case, it might make it more difficult for the police to catch . . . to catch . . .

To catch Blanche.

"You boys need to come home again for a bit."

"Yes, Mama. We do."

* * *

In Virginia, Debbie Moore was sitting alone in her apartment, staring at the phone. It had been forty-five minutes since she had hung up after talking to McDougall. For a while after the call, it had all spun around in her head so fast she couldn't focus on any one element of it. She had been a suspect. Doug had been a suspect. It sounded as if now the one they really thought did it was Blanche.

Now all of the things McDougall had been saying began to fall into place. She could see the center of it, and it made her want to throw up. Someone had tried to murder her father. She picked up the phone to call Doug in Montclair.

McDougall had many more calls to make before he would sleep. He finally reached fellow SBI agent Tom Raven and asked him whether he had been able yet to get a subpoena and go over to Winston to recheck Raymond Reid's chart for an arsenic test, as Butts had suggested. The answer was that Raven did have the subpoena in hand but had not yet been able to go look at the chart. It was an unusually busy week in North Carolina as far as court-ordered searches for arsenic tests were concerned.

Sandra Lyn Coulthard's brother, Steve Coles, was a successful North Carolina lawyer who usually defended doctors in malpractice suits. In asking questions about his sister's death in High Point Regional Hospital, Coles became convinced there had been serious flaws in the hospital's handling of her case. At that point, no one in the family had any idea that an arsenic test had been run on Sandra Coulthard and that the lab had discovered she was being murdered weeks before her husband later finished her off in another hospital. No one realized she could have been saved if the results simply had been forwarded to her second hospital.

But Steve Coles knew enough about doctors and hospitals to smell something wrong somewhere. When he expressed his suspicions to the rest of his family, his father decided he wanted to bring suit against the hospital and the doctors, if for no other reason than to find out exactly how and why it was his daughter could have been murdered under the noses of doctors.

Coles told his family he was not the man to handle the case.

Instead, he referred his father to the offices of Grover McCain, a young medical malpractice lawyer in Chapel Hill whose small firm was quickly making a name for itself.

McCain's firm was housed in a new neo-Georgian low-rise office complex just off the highway that runs down the center of the Raleigh, Durham, Chapel Hill triangle. The dozen or so lawyers in the firm, both men and women, were all relatively young and had unique, unorthodox training and backgrounds.

Bill Hamilton was typical of Grover McCain's recruits. Bright, suave, handsome, not yet forty when Sandra Lyn Coulthard died, Bill Hamilton had left Duke undergraduate school with great grades and a bad case of boredom. He talked his way into a job as the research assistant to the chairman of the pathology department at Duke.

For several years Hamilton lived the life of a research scientist, taking graduate courses and working on the chairman's projects in cardiovascular pathology. During that time he struck up a friendship with John Butts, then assistant state medical examiner.

Hungry for new action, Hamilton decided to go to law school in 1983. By 1985, he had completed his law degree and passed the bar and had been plucked off the vine by Grover McCain. When the Coles family came to McCain with the Sandra Coulthard case, McCain came to Hamilton to confer.

McCain asked Hamilton if he thought it was a good case. Hamilton said, "I would at least like to go far enough to be able to get hold of the chart and see what the hospital knew."

It was precisely the same thought that had come to Butts in the Raymond Reid case, and for exactly the same reason. Because both Butts and Bill Hamilton knew how hospitals worked, both of them knew there was a good chance the lab tests had been done for arsenic and the results lost or flubbed or misread. And so, on the same week when David McDougall was prodding his associate to get over to Winston and look back through Raymond Reid's chart, Grover McCain and Bill Hamilton were gearing up to do the same thing with Sandra Coulthard's chart in High Point.

At dawn on the morning of June 13, McDougall, Ayers, Balog, and half a dozen other law enforcement people gathered at the Pine Hill Cemetery in Burlington. The cemetery company had moved its large automated grave-digging machine to the site the previous evening.

The hydraulic pistons of the machine squeaked and hissed, its dirt-and-rust-stained claw reaching down, gouging out deep cuts in the earth with each pass. In minutes the concrete vault had been exposed. An assistant state medical examiner took pictures of the excavation and the vault and took soil samples around the vault.

There was a long wait while the cemetery workers got down in the grave with shovels and spades, cleaning clods of clay off the ends of the vault. The only sounds were the clinking of their tools against the cold gritty surface of the concrete and the low purring of the grave-digging machine in the background. Finally, when they had arranged loops of steel cable over the ends of the vault, the workers clambered out. The operator lifted the arm, and Raymond Reid rose back up out of the earth.

Three hours later, when the casket was delivered to the state medical examiner's laboratory in Chapel Hill, Dr. Butts was waiting. A technician stood by while Butts took some notes on the exterior condition of the casket. As soon as Butts had finished, the technician stepped forward and began to lift the lid of the coffin, which had already been unfastened and opened briefly that morning at the funeral home where Raymond Reid had been embalmed originally.

Here in the medical examiner's autopsy theater, a photographer stood at the ready. There was a barely perceptible drawing in of breath among the people in the room as the lid began to open. People who have witnessed exhumations before know what to prepare themselves for. It's usually shock theater—skin falling away from the face, eyeballs hanging out, florid bouquets of mold erupting from rot holes in the neck.

Raymond Reid was shocking, all right, but in a very different way. There was a slight film of mold across his face, but he was otherwise perfectly preserved. His dark blue pinstripe suit was still neat, his blue button-down shirt still smooth. There was an uncanny darkness in the hue of his skin, like a fake suntan, but his skin was otherwise smooth and completely undegraded. His hair lay neatly combed across the top of his head. He looked like Dracula—the living dead.

* * *

By this time Debbie Moore had returned to Burlington and was staying by herself in her father's house. Blanche had been staying in her trailer home. They met outside the ICU on the morning of the fourteenth and talked before going in.

"Do you know if they've found out anything, Blanche?"

"No, they won't tell me nothing. I'm so mad about all this. I'm so sick of those sitters in there. I can't even get in to see my own husband."

"Blanche, I think you can understand. I mean, they think somebody tried to kill Dad. They have to carry out a few precautions."

"Debbie," Blanche said, shaking her head somberly, "I haven't wanted ever to have to tell you this, but now I think it's time you knew. Your father has been very suicidal and depressed."

"Dad? Suicidal? No, he has not been, Blanche. He's been the happiest I've ever seen him, except for being half dead from being sick."

"It's something terrible we've been keeping from both you and Doug."

Debbie was on the verge of lashing out, but she looked over Blanche's shoulder and saw Phil Ayers and David McDougall approaching. McDougall nodded and pointed with one finger at Blanche's back.

Debbie said: "I think you have visitors, Blanche."

Blanche turned and saw them. Her face was frozen for an instant and then it broke open in a beaming smile. "Hi, boys," she said flirtatiously. "Are you all looking for me?"

"Yes, Miz Moore," Phil Ayers said. "We need to talk to you if that's all right."

"Well, sure."

"The hospital's been letting us use their little security trailer outside in the back," McDougall said. "Why don't we go down there. We've got our tape recorder all set up down there so it'll be easier."

Blanche rode down on the elevator with them, perfectly composed and inscrutable. They shepherded her out a side entrance and through a tangled construction area to the small trailer serving as the hospital's security office. At one point, McDougall took her elbow in his hand to help her over some

electrical cables on the ground. Within minutes after they had
hunkered down around a metal desk inside the cramped trailer
office, Blanche had signed a form agreeing to be interviewed,
agreeing to be taped, and waiving her right to have an attorney
present.

As soon as the tape machine was turned on, she launched
into a long shrill narration of Dwight's medical history, their
vacation to New Jersey, stops along the way, and everything
that had happened to Dwight since. She finally came to her
theories of what might have happened.

"There's a lot of bitterness in Dwight's family because of
what he did to them," Blanche said. "His son, Doug, is very
bitter. He's a chemist, you know. He would know all about
things like arsenic."

"Yes," McDougall said. "That's a good point. We're making
a note of that. But we need to ask you about some other things."

Over the course of the next hour, in response to specific
questions, Blanche told the two detectives she had returned all
of Raymond Reid's money to his sons except for $40,000 she
said he had specifically bequeathed to her.

Based on interviews he already had conducted with Steve
and Ray Reid, Jr., McDougall knew Blanche was lying about
the money, but he said nothing.

Blanche said she knew nothing about Dwight Moore's pension fund. McDougall already had interviewed a United Church
of Christ official whom Blanche had approached about getting
Dwight's pension papers changed so that she could become the
principal beneficiary. But he made no mention of it.

Blanche told the two detectives she had asked permission
from the nursing staff first before cutting Dwight's hair. Ayers
had already interviewed the nurses and knew this was another
lie. He said nothing.

McDougall allowed Ayers to ask most of the questions. He
could tell from her eyes that Blanche was more hostile toward
him than toward Ayers, and there was some crucial ground
they needed to cover before she blew up, clammed up, or called
a lawyer.

Already the focus of the investigation was beginning to shift
away slightly from Dwight to Raymond. Dwight, after all, was
an attempted-murder charge. Raymond was a potential capital
murder case.

Dwight himself was acting very iffy about things. He continued to show a marked tendency to defend Blanche. McDougall by now had carried out his preliminary interviews with the Reid boys. They would not be iffy. And Raymond Reid was not coming back to life.

Butts was convinced the lab work would show that Reid had died of arsenic poisoning and that he had ingested the fatal dose or doses after he had entered the hospital. The pattern of recoveries and relapses was too marked. There had to have been doses administered in the hospital in his case, as in Dwight's.

But certain difficulties were beginning to dawn on all of them. A fair amount of interviewing had been done already and a good deal of information gathered. It was unlikely they would come up with accomplices. It was very unlikely they would find a witness who had seen Blanche put arsenic in food or in a tube.

Blanche herself, whom everyone else saw as a sweet Christian lady and the world's favorite grandma, was beginning to look to the seasoned eyes of the two detectives more and more like a typical criminal hard case—cunning, with a good act and a bloody streak of mean in her. She was unlikely to crack and confess. The one route inside her psyche might be through her fundamentalist Christian beliefs. Otherwise, they were not going to get in, and she was not going to come out.

Getting a conviction would be grueling. What they were beginning to realize was that this case could be just what a career detective dreads: a great big, flamboyant, high-profile failure. A career-breaker. They could assemble tons of circumstantial evidence against Blanche—enough to convince the public that Blanche did it—and then they could fail to nail her.

The better shot was Reid. The doctors at North Carolina Memorial in Chapel Hill had gotten onto the trail of the arsenic and had isolated Dwight too fast for Blanche to have been able to get to him while he was in the hospital. The case in which they might be able to show her spooning poisoned pudding to her victim was Reid at Baptist Hospital.

McDougall and Ayers had carried out careful interviews with the nursing staff at North Carolina Baptist to establish objective third-party witnesses who would say that Blanche often fed Raymond Reid in their presence in the hospital. It was this ground that McDougall wanted to make sure he covered with Blanche before they arrested her, before she got a lawyer and stopped talking altogether.

Ayers put on a casual, almost bored voice, as if going through routine matters that he had almost forgotten to bring up:

"When Raymond started getting real sick when he was in the hospital, did you ever carry him food or anything?"

"No," Blanche said, without even a split-second pause. "You couldn't carry him no food."

"You never carried Raymond no food while he was in the hospital?"

"No sir, I didn't."

"Did, uh . . ."

"I don't remember taking anything into his room."

"When were . . . uh, did Raymond have a will?"

"No. Until, uh . . . not until he was in intensive care, and he kept bugging us to death about getting a lawyer to do a will for him. And I don't remember the date that the will was done, but a guy from Winston-Salem came out to the hospital and did a will, and the nurses, uh . . . they were the witnesses."

McDougall put both feet on the floor and leaned forward with his hands on his knees. "You have been very honest and straightforward and given us a lot of information, and just so you know I appreciate the fact that you came forward and volunteered all this information, what I am going to do now, just to get you out of the picture, is to ask you if you would submit to a polygraph test, to eliminate yourself.

"There is no hocus-pocus about them," he said. "I have a lot of faith in them. . . . As I said earlier, people want to look at those around Dwight that have the opportunity—those are the first people they suspect. At this point we are not ruling out anything. That is why we have asked you all this about where you were at, who he was with and where he stayed, and I know people bring him food and so forth, but our bosses are going to say that there are a lot of people who are going to take it for us, and we wonder if you will take one for us."

Blanche looked him in the eye for a long silent moment. "Well, I have no problem with it," she said at last. "Do you think I should ask my lawyer about it?"

"That's up to you."

McDougall and Ayers tried hard not to look as if they were holding their breath.

"I mean, I have no problem with it," she said at last. "David, I tried to tell you the truth, you know. I'll tell you how ignorant I am to this stuff. I don't even know how to file his insurance for health."

"You are kidding."

McDougall said it in a tone that fell exactly midway between observation, accusation, and derision. They eyed each other across the small office.

"Now like I said, I am not trying to defend myself because I have nothing to defend. I'll go in there and let you look at this stuff and do whatever you feel like you need to do."

McDougall sat up straight and was absolutely sober and solemn again. He asked if it would be all right for him to schedule a lie detector test for her the next afternoon.

She agreed immediately. But then she said: "I want y'all to understand that I did not have anything to do with the will. The lawyer came and another person was with him, and a nurse was present. Raymond didn't want Linda to be around."

Phil Ayers put his hands on his face in a praying posture and started talking with his face still covered. "Blanche, you need to tell us everything you can. Now's the time." He took his hands down and stared at her.

"I hope it don't get so far out of hand," he said, "that it can't be reeled back in, you know what I mean. I want you to understand that this is not going to be like your Kroger's lawsuit. This is not going to be Blanche against the Sheriff's Department and the SBI. This is going to be the State of North Carolina against Blanche, and it's going to be for a twenty-year felony, maybe even murder, and that's what we, when I, when I started telling you at first you've got a problem with Dwight, or you've got a problem with anything that would cause this situation with Dwight, we need for you to tell us now, don't let this thing get so far out of hand that it can't be reeled back in and something done about it, without you going to prison over it, and the..."

"Well, Phil."

"...and the reason I am saying that to you, Blanche, is this..."

"Well, I appreciate you saying that to me, Phil, but I have not...I did not give Dwight poison. I married...I didn't have to marry Dwight, as a matter of fact. I hadn't planned to get married until later this summer."

McDougall stepped in. "Let's just see how the polygraph goes," he said. "Then maybe we can talk and clear all this up."

Blanche showed up at the appointed hour the next day and took the polygraph test.

That same afternoon, John Butts issued his finding on Raymond Reid. The cause of death was arsenic poisoning. Later test results would show the exact pattern and dates of dosages, but the levels in the body tissues taken during the autopsy showed that Raymond Reid had definitely died from arsenic poisoning. Butts informed McDougall, who asked him to keep the results secret until he and Ayers had had a chance to do their wrap interview with Blanche the following day, after they had analyzed the polygraph results.

Blanche found her own way to the security trailer the next day, showing up exactly on time for the interview. McDougall waited until they were all seated, and then he rose and began speaking with his back to Blanche.

"Blanche, you need to know that the state medical examiner has ruled that Raymond Reid died of arsenic poisoning."

"Oh my goodness," she said in an even tone. "Well, now that is incredible."

"Blanche, what is your explanation . . . how do you think all that arsenic got in Dwight?"

"Well, I don't know. I told Debbie, what people don't realize is, Dwight has been very depressed and very suicidal for a long time."

Still not facing her, McDougall said: "You know, a lot of crimes are committed, and the motive is never known. But you don't need a motive. Nobody does. And the reason they don't is because the person who did it has got a reason of their own, not something somebody else has given them. It may not be something Dwight has done or Raymond did. It may be reasons of your own."

He turned and faced her. "Those are your reasons, and whatever they may be . . . but I can tell you, Blanche, and you know, we can't think of any motive, but there are just a lot of things that we've looked into that just haven't panned out, like . . . like you say . . ."

"All right, what are they?" Blanche asked sharply.

"Well..."

"I mean, for instance, what?" she said in a slightly sarcastic voice.

"Well, you know we're not, we're not going to tell all, what we know."

"Well okay then, why should I sit here and spill my guts?" Her voice had in it just the tone of tough-guy confrontation that the detectives wanted to avoid as long as possible. They still hoped they might get somewhere with the outwardly Christian Southern belle. They knew exactly how far they would get if she flipped over into her hard-case personality.

"Blanche," McDougall said, "how do you explain, what do you think is, uh, the reason Raymond would have had enough arsenic in him to kill him?"

"Oh, David, I just...this is a real shock. You know, Raymond was afraid for his job during the whole time I had my suit against Kroger, and he was just very eaten up about it and had a lot of anxiety and depression. He was suicidal at times."

McDougall shoved his chair up close to Blanche and sat down with his face inches from her face. Ayers inched himself back away from her.

"Blanche," McDougall said, so softly he was almost whispering, "I need for you to listen real close to me now. You have told us the same thing with Dwight, that he may have been depressed and taking it. I just want you to think, what are the chances, in one person's lifetime, having a boyfriend or a relationship with Raymond Reid like you did, and someone else, two separate people..."

He looked closely into her eyes. "Dwight would not have known anything about any poisoning. If Raymond Reid had been poisoned, what is the likelihood of that happening? One woman having two men in her life, and both of them dying from arsenic poisoning? We want you to see our point of view, why we are alarmed."

Blanche looked them both over carefully. She had sucked her mouth in between her teeth so that she had no lips. "I didn't do it. Even if there's arsenic in everybody I know, I'm not going to sit here and say that I did something that I did not do."

In a clinical voice, with just a hint of muttering purr beneath it, McDougall said: "I was going to say, Blanche, that on a polygraph examination, the best you can score is plus twenty-seven, and the worst is minus twenty-seven, and you were at like a minus sixteen." He smiled at her, allowing that news to sink in for a bit.

Blanche's eyes were darting around the room. She was beginning to turn her head and look in far corners, as if for something she had misplaced.

"Thank you, Blanche," Ayers said. "That's all for now."

"Bye, Blanche," McDougall said.

As soon as she was out of the room, McDougall returned a phone call from headquarters. Big news. Finally Agent Raven had gone to Winston and had examined Raymond Reid's file with a fine-toothed comb. There it was—the heavy-metals intoxication report. Just as Butts had said it would be. Stuck right in the middle of the huge stack of orders and processing paperwork, the results of an arsenic test from SmithKline. Reid was full of the stuff, right there in the hospital.

McDougall himself had pinned down another significant detail: Blanche's coworkers at Kroger had told him Blanche Moore had been sleeping with Raymond Reid while she was dating Dwight Moore and telling Dwight that Raymond was just an old work buddy.

When McDougall and Ayers showed up at dawn the next morning at Pine Hill Cemetery, the grave-digging machine was waiting again, poised this time over the grave of James Taylor. McDougall was only halfway out of his car when his eye caught the civilians standing by the grave. McDougall walked over to a lieutenant from the Burlington City Police Department.

"Good morning," he said.

"Hi there, Agent McDougall, how y'all this fine morning?"

"I'm good. Who are they?"

The lieutenant shrugged and looked puzzled. "Why, that's the Taylor clan, Agent McDougall. This is their kin we're about to dig up."

McDougall looked them over carefully. They looked like a tough old family. You never knew what was going to happen at an exhumation. Raymond Reid's had been an easy one, because of the way the arsenic had preserved him. This one had been in the ground sixteen years. It could be gruesome.

"I don't really think an exhumation needs to be a family affair, does it, Lieutenant?"

The lieutenant stepped around in front of McDougall and put his face inches from McDougall's. "These are my people here, Mr. SBI, and after you're gone out of here, I got to live with them. Now, they say they want to be here when this old boy comes up out of the dirt, and I say they are going to be here if they want to."

McDougall said nothing. The exhumation of James Taylor went smoothly, except that just as they were loading the coffin onto a truck, McDougall looked around and saw news crews filming from the cemetery fence. The lieutenant, who had gone over to the fence to hold the reporters and photographers at bay, appeared to be giving them a lengthy interview. Farther back, lurking at the edge of a shed, was a gaggle of winos who had spent the night drinking in the cemetery. One in particular, a small man wrapped in an unlined raincoat, watched the disinterment with what appeared to be fascination.

Chapter Fifteen

McDougall was back in the trailer office behind North Carolina Memorial by afternoon. Dwight still didn't know Butts had found arsenic in Raymond Reid. McDougall knew it was time to tell him. But before McDougall could get out of the little office, the phone rang again. It was Linda Reid.

"David, I have been told something that I find very disturbing. An investigator from Forsyth County has been asking me questions about Raymond's relationship with Blanche."

"Yes?"

"Well, he called me back today to check on some details of what I'd told him, and in the course of talking, he told me they'd found a test that showed that the doctors in Winston tested Raymond and they knew he was getting arsenic even when he was still alive over there in the hospital."

McDougall's blood ran cold. They were only halfway into the interviewing of the doctors and nurses at Baptist Hospital, and they still had a lot of case to make. He saw what was about to happen: Linda Reid would figure out the hospital had botched the arsenic test, Linda Reid would find her way to one of those gunslingers sitting around the salad bar at Chadwick's, a suit would be filed, and the hospital would slam its door like a nunnery at Mardi Gras.

McDougall had a tough choice to make and had to make it instantly. He was not a man who enjoyed lying. But if Linda Reid and her sons went to court with any kind of a civil suit for damages now—if the hospital even got wind of their thinking about it—then McDougall's whole case would go down the drain, and Blanche would go free.

"Nope, that's not true," he said. "I just checked with headquarters. There was a rumor of one, but we sent an agent over there just to check out that very thing, and he found there was no test run at all."

"Oh," she said. "All right. Well, I thought it sounded strange."

Before McDougall went up to see Dwight, he placed calls to the Forsyth County Sheriff's Department, the Alamance County Sheriff's Department, and the Burlington City Police Department, expressing in the strongest terms he could politely muster how important it was at this point in the investigation for the investigators to watch what they said. Now that it was clear Blanche would play hardball to the end, McDougall was beginning to get the sweats. It would be easy for Blanche to slip through the net.

At every police agency he called, the word went up and down the chain of command. All of the officers and investigators involved made up their minds to be more careful, with the exception of one, who made up his mind to teach the smart aleck from the SBI a little lesson.

The newspaper competition over the Blanche Moore story was just beginning to heat up in earnest. North Carolina is dotted with fine, very competitive daily newspapers, and the Winston-Salem, Greensboro, Burlington area is an especially closely fought journalistic battleground.

The very early stories on the arsenic investigation had been done by the *Alamance Times-News,* the weekly just down the block from Chadwick's. Once it was plain that an unusual murder story was unfolding on the community doorstep, the *Burlington Daily Times-News,* a much larger daily paper, stepped in and began doing a lot of tough reporting, easily outstripping the

Alamance Times-News. As soon as the investigation reached Raymond Reid's medical file in Winston-Salem, the *Winston-Salem Journal* reached into the pot and began beating both the *Alamance Times-News* and the *Burlington Daily Times-News.*

This was all a matter of considerable embarrassment to the *Greensboro News & Record,* which was right in the middle of the circulation areas of all the others and considered itself their superior. Early on, when the story began to break, the Greensboro paper's Alamance County bureau was in transition—one correspondent was leaving and his replacement had not been named—and, as a result, the paper blew it.

Like most newspapers that get trounced by their competitors on a story, the *Greensboro News & Record* spent a few weeks hunkered down, ignoring the story in the hope it would blow away and all of the other papers would be embarrassed for having paid so much attention to it. After a few weeks of that, it was plain it was time for Plan B: assign a team of reporters the size of the Allied landing force and crush all of the opposition with a series of brilliantly comprehensive stories.

The *Greensboro News & Record* sent Ed Williams and Taft Wireback, two of its senior aces, over to Alamance County and called in reporters from all the other beats and bureaus where there was a man to spare. In Winston the bureau was manned by Justin Catanoso, a twenty-nine-year-old reporter with a smooth outward manner and a fire in his gut. Catanoso had grown up in a small affluent community on the New Jersey beach. Every visit back to the Northeast seemed to involve at least one dinner in Manhattan at which he had to listen to old school friends from Penn bragging about their jobs at places like *Newsday* and *Spy.* They always looked up at some point in the meal and said, "Well, Justin, what is your newspaper's circulation down there in Greenville?"

He was the kind of reporter who hated sophisticated journalism, loved being out on the land digging stories out of the "true folk," and fully intended at some point in his life to go back and burn New York to the ground. In the meantime, he never missed a lick. When the word came from Greensboro that they were going to have to pull him off his regular beat and pitch in on this weird murder story, Catanoso's hands started making clawing motions and his huge brown eyes stopped blinking for several days. He could not wait.

* * *

David McDougall felt he had established a relationship with
Dwight. He needed Dwight for this investigation. He had to
use him. But he had also come to care about him. He eased
into Dwight's room and sat for a while with him before starting.
Dwight looked much better already.

Knowing the doses Dwight had endured, McDougall was
awed by his resilience. He admired Dwight for fighting back so
hard physically and keeping his personal composure and his
dignity intact in the process.

He told Dwight that today was going to be a bad-news day.

"Is it about Blanche and Raymond?" Dwight asked immediately. Dwight was lying flat on his back.

"Yes. Yes, it is."

"She was more than his friend, wasn't she?"

"Yes, Dwight. She was sleeping with him while she was
sleeping with you. Did she never admit that?"

"No," Dwight said very quietly. "No, she did not. She told
me she had never slept with another man after her husband
died. Except for me."

They were both quiet for a while. Dwight had been disconnected from most of the tubes and monitors, so the electronic buzzing had left his room. The two men could hear birds
squabbling outside the window.

"There is more," McDougall said.

"Go ahead, David."

"Raymond Reid died of arsenic poisoning. He received the
final fatal doses while he was in the hospital."

McDougall did not look at Dwight's face, but he could hear
Dwight breathing. Dwight suddenly pushed himself up, so that
he was sitting straight up in his bed. It was the first time
McDougall had ever seen him in any position but on his back.

"I want her out of my house," Dwight said solemnly. "I
want an attorney. I want her out of my financial affairs."

"I will notify your family of your wishes. You are worth a
quarter of a million dollars. Dead. Did you know that?"

"No. No, I never did. I never added it up."

"Are you all right, Dwight?"

"Oh, I'll tell you, I am all right. But I feel . . . I feel utter
defeat. I had felt that this was really a new beginning in my
life, that we were set for a good life together, that all of the

anxieties and the depression, the bad things that had happened
in my life as a result of the divorce, that all of that was finally
behind me.

"Now, to suddenly be confronted with the fact that my wife
did this to me . . . I just feel as if I'm in worse shape now than
I ever was before."

McDougall looked up at Dwight. "That's not true, Dwight.
At your worst, you were almost dead. You made it. It's a miracle.
You had enough arsenic in you to kill a horse. I think somebody
had a reason to keep you around."

Neither one of them spoke for a while. Dwight seemed to
be mulling over what McDougall had just said. Finally Dwight
said goodbye. As McDougall shut the door and left, he caught
a glimpse of Dwight sitting straight up in his bed, staring out
the window.

That afternoon Dwight sent word down to the waiting area
that he wanted to see Blanche.

She came into his room smiling.

Dwight stared at her without smiling or speaking.

"What's the matter, honey?" she said.

"Blanche, I don't want to see you again. Knowing what I
know about you and Raymond Reid, well, the marriage is over.
No matter how these other matters turn out, I could never trust
you again."

She watched him for a moment.

"Very well, Dwight. Goodbye then."

She stepped out of the room, walked down the hall to the
elevator, left the hospital, and never returned.

Bill Hamilton, the young hotshot lawyer Grover McCain
had picked for the Coulthard case, searched through stacks of
hospital records for days, and eventually he found the results
of the arsenic test that had been run on Sandra Coulthard. He
had known the test had to be there somewhere.

He also obtained samples of her hair and other tissues with
which to prove she had died of arsenic poisoning and to establish when she had received the doses. The only thing that bothered him was that her nails did not have the characteristic white
horizontal Mees lines associated with arsenic poisoning. He
wondered if he just didn't know what to look for. He had never
seen Mees lines before. Hamilton decided to gather up his evi-

dence and pay a visit to his old buddy state medical examiner John Butts.

Hamilton enjoyed the kind of relationship with Butts that allowed him to drop in unannounced. He showed Butts what he had, and Butts assured him he had the right proofs. Hamilton said he was worried about the absence of Mees lines, but Butts told him that was common. Some victims have them, some don't. It means little. If the lines are present, it's obvious.

"Here," Butts said, picking up a photograph sitting right in front of him on the desk. "Now here is a classic case of Mees lines. These are from a gentleman we just dug up named Raymond Reid, who was murdered with arsenic in his hospital room, while he was a patient at Baptist."

Ed Williams and Taft Wireback were the kind of reporters who covered a town by sifting every grain of it through a fine mesh. They worked the Blanche Moore story in Burlington until eventually they came upon the one law enforcement official who was still smarting from David McDougall's urgent call for security.

"I can tell you things about that case," the policeman said. "But it has to be off the record. Some of the people in the Reid family here were told the hospital over there in Winston run an arsenic test on Raymond Reid and then lost it. He wouldn'ta been killed if the hospital hadn't screwed up, in other words. They asked Mr. SBI Agent David McDougall about it, and he lied straight in their faces, said there had been no such test. But the truth is . . . there was."

Now the bodies seemed to be coming up out of the ground at the rate of one a week. They brought the old preacher up out of the earth—Blanche's father, P. D. Kiser—and finally McDougall saw the horror show he had been anticipating. Blanche's father had been in the ground twenty-three years. Mold, decay, insects, and worms had turned the body into something more gruesome than any Hollywood special-effects artist could ever imagine.

They dug up James Taylor's mother—poor old Isla, who had died in 1970, staring at her daughters with eyes that looked like blue marbles.

By now the exhumations were leading every local newscast

and were even being picked up by the national wire services, distant newspapers, and the television networks. Dan Rather opened with the story one night on the evening news, calling it "the unfolding of a gothic horror tale."

With each additional exhumation, more witnesses rushed to the various police agencies involved to tell them of someone else who might have been poisoned by Blanche Moore. They dug up a man named Joseph C. Mitchell, a butcher at Kroger who happened to die of a legitimate heart attack while working in the same store with Blanche.

By now Dr. Butts's findings from each additional exhumation were being published in the newspapers the morning after he completed his tests. After he had finished with the autopsy and lab work on James Taylor, Butts told a waiting crowd of reporters that he had found arsenic in Taylor's brain, kidneys, muscles, and bones. He said he also had found evidence of severe long-term heart disease.

Reading from a prepared statement, Butts said: "Given the historical circumstances, the autopsy findings, and the toxicological results, it is my opinion that Mr. Taylor died as the result of an episode of arsenic poisoning."

The reporters rushed to telephones and mobile units.

McDougall had visited Dwight several times to ask him to wear a hidden recording device and then call Blanche for a final meeting in the hospital room. They were very close to arresting her, he said, and Dwight was close to being discharged from the hospital to a convalescent home. Now was the moment. Finally Dwight agreed.

With McDougall sitting nearby, Dwight called her.

"This is Dwight," he said.

"Hello, Dwight. How are you?"

"I'm much better, thank you. I called because it was kind of abrupt the way we left things, and I wondered if there was any chance you could come back and we could try to talk things over a little better."

She snickered.

"No, Dwight, I don't think I'll be coming back to talk things over with you. You asked me not to come back, and I'm going to honor that wish."

"Very well. Well, this is goodbye then."

"Goodbye, Dwight."

He hung up and shrugged at McDougall. "No way," he said.

"Thanks for trying."

On the evening of July 18, Blanche, her daughters, and several of her brothers and sisters gathered for dinner at her daughter Cindi's mobile home off Roney-Lineberry Road outside Burlington. The last family member had arrived and the trailer door had just closed behind him when the first police car came jouncing in over the ridge at the entry to the trailer park and drove slowly down the little lane to the trailer, gravel crunching beneath its wheels. Another police car followed close behind it, and another, and another, and another, and another.

They parked their cars in a half-circle around the trailer home. By now all of the neighbors were standing on their little metal stoops or peering through parted curtains to watch.

Two officers went to the door and knocked softly. The door opened and they went in. Only a few minutes later, they emerged with Blanche between them, her hands cuffed before her. They helped her down the steps and into the backseat of a police car. Then one after another, the police cars all went prowling back up the little gravel lane and out onto the county road again. The Kiser clan stood gathered in a knot in front of Cindi's trailer, weeping and waving goodbye.

The next day, Bill Hamilton walked into Grover McCain's office with great news. The lawyers for the hospital in the Sandra Coulthard case had taken a good hard look at Hamilton's evidence, especially the blown arsenic test results, and had advised the hospital to make a substantial settlement.

McCain immediately got on the phone to Christie O'Conner, one of the local television reporters who had been calling him about the case. He told her he had big news. She said she would grab a crew and be right over. Anything related to arsenic was very hot news in North Carolina that week.

Ed Williams and Taft Wireback were in the last phases of pulling together a gargantuan series of stories on what was now called by everyone "the Blanche Moore story." They and the other members of the team had interviewed everyone who could be found who knew anything about Blanche or any of her family or any of the poisoning victims. But one last detail had been allowed to slip between the cracks and needed to be cleared up before the series began running.

Wireback called Justin Catanoso in Winston. "I have a source in Alamance who told me that the docs at Baptist Hospital actually did run an arsenic test on Reid and that it came back positive. My source says nobody could find it for a while, but now they have it."

Ever since the Blanche Moore project had gotten underway, Catanoso had been spending hours with the Forsyth County sheriff's detectives and the Winston-Salem PD investigators who had been working the Raymond Reid end at Baptist Hospital. He had been able to glean lots of useful detail from them about how the investigation had proceeded, but they had not given him anything really new or breaking.

The minute he hung up from Wireback, Catanoso got on the phone to his police sources. He needed to get it from at least two sources before he felt comfortable going to the hospital. "We've been told there was an arsenic test on Raymond Reid," he said to the first detective he reached.

"I think you're on to something," the detective said. "I wouldn't say you were wrong on that."

He called the second one and repeated his story.

"Goddammit," the second detective said. "Son of a bitch, Catanoso. We promised the damn hospital that wouldn't get out."

Catanoso called the hospital next. By now it was late on a Friday afternoon. All of the people who could speak for the hospital had left for weekend trips to the mountains or the beach.

When Catanoso hung up from calling the hospital, his fingers were literally itching to hit the keys of the Coyote computer terminal in his office. All he had to do was write what he had, hit a button, and the editors back in the newsroom in Greensboro would come bouncing out of their seats.

Sure, the series on the Blanche Moore case, which was to start running that Sunday, was already going to be exhaustive and comprehensive. But the angle about the blown arsenic test was hot. It was new. Nobody else had it. The general reader would be shocked to find out a hospital can send out a test for arsenic poisoning, get back a result that spells murder in capital letters, and then not have anybody look at it carefully enough to figure out what it means.

His hands were hovering over the computer. But way in the back of his mind, Justin Catanoso was suffering a doubt. His father-in-law was a pediatrician and medical professor. He had listened many times while his father-in-law had complained at length about how complex things are in a real medical situation and about how much harm a sloppy reporter can do if he misses the complexity.

It was a tough call. He decided he had to wait until Monday and give the hospital a chance to respond in full. That weekend, Catanoso called his father-in-law and asked him to theorize about how a hospital could miss a positive arsenic result. His father-in-law offered several plausible theories.

In this day and age, given the new technology of testing and of data retrieval, a doctor's ballpoint pen is a wand that can summon a snowstorm of information. The doctor scratches some requests on a pad, and by that night the information is pouring in by modem from the labs and the data bases, by E-mail and fax and voice message and overnight letter.

A monastic and fastidious researcher, with all the time in the world and no distractions, would be sorely challenged to organize and evaluate all of this information. Far from monastic or serene, the life of the hospital is a crisis-driven hurly-burly, an endless fire drill.

So they miss it. The doctors miss a lot of it. It comes in: they don't see it. Or they see it, but they don't read it carefully. They don't have time.

The series began to run that weekend, and it was a smashing success. Catanoso had seen most of it already, had written a fair chunk of it himself, but he pored over the copy anyway. Something about this story fascinated him as almost no other story ever had.

The next Monday, Justin Catanoso called the spokesman for North Carolina Baptist Hospital and told him he knew there had been an arsenic test for Raymond Reid. The spokesman said he would call back.

He called an hour later. "We will have no comment on it."

"Look, I'm not trying to screw you guys," Catanoso said.

"We are just not going to comment on it, Justin, one way or the other."

"Do you deny it?"

"We just do not intend to comment on it."

The day was young. Catanoso got into his car and drove to Burlington, where he intended to spend the morning poking around the courthouse.

On his way to the courthouse, however, he spotted two young men who looked very much like the pictures he had seen in his own newspaper that weekend of Ray Reid, Jr., and Steven Reid.

Ray and Stevie were on their way to the courthouse too, to see what could be done about getting Blanche removed as executrix of their father's will.

Catanoso tried to buttonhole them, but the Reid sons politely demurred from answering any questions.

Catanoso asked: "Did you know there was an arsenic test done on your father while he was in the hospital, and it came back positive?"

The boys declined to comment and ducked out of the reporter's path.

That evening Ray and Stevie gathered with their mother, Linda, at the little table between the kitchen and the living room. They were all silent together for a long time.

"Why would McDougall have lied to us?" Ray said.

"I have no idea," Linda said. "He must have had some reason at the time. We have to take all this a day at a time."

"I try, Mama," Ray said. "I try to figure out what all of this is. But none of it is real. I just keep thinking, 'This can't be happening to us.' Half the time I feel like I'm going to walk around a corner and there Daddy will be, fine as ever, and this will all be just a terrible dream."

All three were fighting back tears.

Linda reached over and flicked on the television. The six-o'clock news was just getting started.

There was Grover McCain all over the screen, talking to Christie O'Conner about Sandra Coulthard. "This was a tragedy," he was saying, "because this young woman did not need to die. The hospital had ordered an arsenic test, it had come back positive, and if the hospital had just made sure those results got to the responsible physicians, Sandra Coulthard would be alive today."

The story indicated that Sandra Coulthard's family had

won a considerable settlement, because of the muffed arsenic test. As soon as the interview had concluded, Linda reached over, turned off the television, and picked up the phone. "Chapel Hill, please. A business listing for Grover McCain, an attorney."

Chapter Sixteen

"Hello?" a male voice answered.

"Hello, my name is Linda Reid Sykes. Is Grover McCain in?"

"No, I'm sorry, Mr. McCain is not in. May I help you with something?"

"Yes. I just saw Mr. McCain on television talking about the Sandra Coulthard case. My family happens to be in a similar situation with regard to my ex-husband, Raymond Reid, who died three years ago at Baptist Hospital in Winston-Salem."

Forty miles away in a half-darkened office, a shirt-sleeved young attorney named Frank Hallstrom was peeling back a yellow ruled sheet on his legal pad and preparing to begin a fresh page of notes. "Your ex-husband was one of the people Blanche Moore is suspected of murdering."

"Yessir."

By the end of their two-hour conversation, they had agreed to meet at the McCain offices the following afternoon.

The next morning at work, Linda asked some of the lawyers

at her company what they knew of McCain's firm. They all said McCain and his people were topnotch, among the very best in the Southeast. They urged her to keep the appointment. She called Stevie and Ray and asked them to meet her in Chapel Hill that afternoon.

She made the drive to Chapel Hill and found McCain's office, arriving a little early in spite of bad weather. The boys were already there, waiting. Grover McCain came out into the waiting area before she had even taken her raincoat off and ushered all three of them back to a long sleek conference room in the center of the building.

Once they were seated, had coffee before them, and had exchanged a few polite words with McCain, Frank Hallstrom and Bill Hamilton came in and joined them. McCain introduced his staff and then asked Bill Hamilton to say a few words about arsenic.

Hamilton ran through a quick explanation of the scientific means by which evidence of arsenic poisoning normally is gathered. Then he said, "In Raymond Reid's case, all of the classic indications of arsenic poisoning were present and should have been visible to the doctors even without a test, including one thing that has not yet been made public—a very clear set of what are called Mees lines on his fingernails."

Linda held up a finger for a pause. "I don't know what Mees lines are, and I assume you are about to tell me, but I need to know something else first. We just showed up here ten minutes ago. How would you know things about Raymond Reid if those things have not yet been made public? How do you know things we don't even know and our lawyer doesn't know yet?"

"I discussed Raymond Reid's case with John Butts, the chief medical examiner of the State of North Carolina, several days ago, at which time I reviewed some of Dr. Butts's findings, including photographs of the fingernails showing the Mees lines."

There was a long pause in the conversation.

"Well, I admit I'm impressed," she said at last.

"Mrs. Sykes," McCain said, "what do you want?"

"I think Blanche stole money from my sons. But I think going after her probably is a waste of time. Now it looks as if my sons' father should not have had to die. I think my sons should sue the hospital where it happened."

McCain again deferred to Hamilton, who had been think-ing about the case and preparing for this issue all night.

"Mrs. Sykes," Hamilton said, "under normal circumstances, you would have absolutely no redress at this point. The statute of limitations in a wrongful-death suit in North Carolina is two years. It has long since run out.

"There is, however, a window of opportunity. The person whose responsibility it would have been to bring such a suit before the two years elapsed would have been the executor of the estate. But in this case, the executor of the estate may also have been the murderer.

"The murderer, obviously, had a clear motive not to ask the kind of questions or seek the kind of information that might have turned up the muffed arsenic test in time for a lawsuit to be filed.

"Obviously, if she killed him, Blanche wasn't going to go around the hospital saying, 'Now wait a minute, did you guys ever test Raymond for arsenic?' There is a principle in the law that would allow us to argue that the statute of limitations should not be imposed on you in your quest for rightful dam-ages in this case, because you were fraudulently prevented from the truth by your executor—"

"—who was the murderer," Ray finished for him.

"Yes," Hamilton said.

"Then you would have to prove that Blanche was the mur-derer," Ray said. "I thought that was up to the prosecutor."

McCain leaned forward. "You'd be surprised. You might find we could prove this lady was the murderer a whole lot better than the prosecutor could prove it. In a civil case, we're not all tied up in the restrictions that apply in a criminal case."

"How would that affect the criminal case?" Ray asked. "If there's any question of our doing anything that would wind up letting Blanche get off, then I'm sure I speak for Stevie, too, in saying we would rather not get a nickel."

Hamilton shook his head. "A criminal case for murder by poison is very, very difficult to make, because of the nature of the crime. Nobody sees the killer do it. The state has all kinds of restrictions on the kinds of searches it can make and the questions it can ask.

"If we go out there first and prove civilly that Blanche is

the killer, and we assemble a body of evidence establishing that fact, then it's just like a Christmas present for the state. We turn everything we have over to them, and most of the normal restrictions on how evidence can be gathered do not apply. They get the case handed to them."

"You need to realize one other thing," McCain said. "This case is a big deal to you and to the press right now. But when it gets to the prosecutor, it's going to land on the desk of some young assistant DA who may or may not know what he's doing, and anyway he's going to have a stack of dope cases and hot-check writers a mile high sitting there that he's got to spend time on, too.

"If we go after this, you have the advantage of some very good lawyers and support staff working full-time and bringing a great deal of specialized expertise that the DA won't have."

Stevie said: "How much?"

Grover McCain looked at Hallstrom, who opened a folder and removed a detailed printout several pages long.

"The case would be taken on a contingency, but you would still have up-front costs," Hallstrom said. "Here is a detailed projection of what those costs probably would be."

The Reids spent several minutes going over the printout. They nodded to each other and then nodded to McCain, Hallstrom, and Hamilton. A moment later they were all shaking hands around the conference table and talking about what sort of records the lawyers would need.

The weather outside had cleared. Linda and the boys stepped out into a bright North Carolina afternoon and took a deep breath of fresh air blowing in off the pines nearby. They all felt better than they had in weeks.

The six police cars took Blanche to the Alamance County Jail in Graham, where she was strip-searched, fingerprinted, and processed. A female jailer took her to the five-by-nine cell that would be her home for more than a year. The bail hearing was to be held in the morning.

That evening Blanche's daughters filed into the tiny waiting area at the front of Mitch McEntire's law office just down Elm Street from the jail.

Bear McEntire had a reputation for winning tough cases. In the mid-1970s he had gained a certain amount of local fame for winning the acquittal of a woman who had shot her husband in the back seven times with a semiautomatic rifle.

His day-to-day practice, however, was much less sensational. He helped the ordinary working- and middle-class citizens of the area with their ordinary difficulties—traffic tickets, fines for illegal dumping, the daily commerce of the lowest courts, as well as a smattering of civil work.

He had made a good living for himself and lived with his wife and daughter in an old rambling white house on a substantial acreage on a rocky hill outside Graham, surrounded by dogwood trees and thousands of bulbs that blossomed every spring. His wife was a teacher. Their teenage daughter was a bright kid, a talented writer and musician.

Cases like the wife-of-seven-shots didn't hurt his business, but that sort of thing was not his main act. He was one of the people. He came from native stock. Born in 1945 to a Scotch-Irish sawmill operator in the mountains of North Carolina, Mitch had been the seventh of nine children. There was no electricity or modern plumbing on the little farm, and the school was a long hike up a steep road. Yet every one of the seven McEntire children went to college. They ended up in law, medicine, education, business, or the arts.

He listened carefully as the Taylor girls spoke to him about their mother. He read their faces, their gestures, the expressions they chose. It was not Bear McEntire's habit to rush himself to any important conclusion. For hours he encouraged them to keep talking.

The next morning Mitch appeared with Blanche for the bond hearing. The judge refused to set any bond. Under North Carolina law, no bond could be set in a capital murder case. It was not yet clear what the charges were going to be, but the judge decided to err on the safe side and keep her locked up until the various DAs got their acts together and decided what kind of charges to seek. Mitch assured the family he would work to get her out of jail as fast as possible.

By now, with Blanche in jail and the exhumations on the front page and the network news, the public mood concerning the case was approaching frenzy. The rumor mill was grinding even more furiously than the news media: suggestions of child abuse were linked with lurid rumors of what really had gone on at Kroger before her sexual harassment suit. She emerged as the perfect witch, touched by evil in infancy, ingeniously duplicitous, Christian and kindly on the outside but a practitioner of black magic in the dark secrecy of her cell, and, most of all, a slut.

The Blanche Moore story leaped out of the news and began infecting other areas of life. Blanche's image spread into the malls, where merchants sold Blanche Moore T-shirts depicting her as a witch in a pointed black hat. The music selections on radio broadcasts all over North Carolina suddenly were crowded with lyrics alluding to witchcraft:

"Raven hair and ruby lips, sparks fly from her fingertips..."

"I got a black magic woman, I got a black magic woman..."

"Devil woman, devil woman, let go of me..."

In Greensboro, talk radio personality Brad Krantz watched the bodies come up out of the ground with growing incredulity. A University of Ohio graduate who had worked in Chicago and New York before coming to WKRR Rock Radio, Krantz thought the whole business of arsenic and clans and accusations of witchcraft was something from a nineteenth-century newspaper serial.

For a while he satisfied himself with a lot of banana-pudding jokes on the air, but as the story grew bigger and interest in it more intense in his station's large broadcast area, Krantz decided the Blanche Moore case deserved a more concerted effort on his part. With some musician friends for backup and using the station's mixing equipment, Krantz put together a musical replica of the theme from *The Mary Tyler Moore Show*. The musical accompaniment and overall sound of the song he recorded was exactly like the familiar theme. Only the lyrics were different:

> How will you make it out of jail?
> Like they've all abandoned you,
> and girl this time you're all alone.
> But it's time you started paying;
> It's time you let someone else do the slaying;
> Blanche is all around, her family's wasted;
> When she makes a meal, no need to taste it,

Old Dwight might make it after all.
Old Dwight might make it after all.

WKRR can be heard from Raleigh-Durham all the way south to Charlotte and west to Statesville—the larger portion of the entire state. The song was an instant and wild hit and was picked up and played on other stations everywhere. Reporters came and made videotapes of Krantz lip-synching the song in his broadcast studio.

A nurse came to the litter in the Alamance County Hospital emergency room where the ragged little man lay waiting.

"You should spend the night, Garvin," she said.

"By which I assume you mean that I am free to go," he said.

"You should stay here."

"Ah, fair lady," he said, lifting his bloated black-and-blue legs off the side of the litter and down to the floor, "I would love nothing more than to pass this long night with you, believe me..."

"But, I know," she said. "Who would feed your cats?"

"Precisely."

He had a bad coughing spell while he was pulling on his clothes.

"You are a sick man, Mr. Thomas. If you keep drinking and smoking, you will die soon."

"A great loss to my many loved ones," he said. He walked down the corridor to the cashier's window and signed for another night of bills he would never pay. Then he walked outside, wrapped in an unlined raincoat, and hobbled the twelve blocks to the little room he and his fifteen cats had shared since his stepsister had kicked him out.

Along the way, he hiked up the collar of the raincoat and ducked his face down in it as far as it would go. It wasn't really cold out, but he often tried to hide his lower face in his collar. A nervous disorder he had suffered since childhood caused Garvin Thomas's tongue to loll out of his mouth when he was unaware of it, and he still stuttered from embarrassment and self-consciousness in front of strangers.

Once he had fed the cats and heated himself a hot dog,

Garvin Thomas collapsed on top of a mound of newspapers on
his torn sofa and turned on the television in time for the network news. He wondered whether the eye of the world had
been turned toward Burlington that day and whether he would
catch a glimpse of his beautiful Blanche.

The prospect of bringing the Blanche Moore criminal case
to trial in Graham was not at all appetizing to District Attorney
Balog. He argued from the beginning that the Dwight Moore
case was the weakest of all the charges against Blanche, was
only an attempted murder charge, and would never hold water
as attempted capital murder. He wanted to see the Blanche
Moore case moved to Winston-Salem, where Raymond Reid
was killed, safely away from his own jurisdiction.

The Burlington police and the Alamance County Sheriff's
Department disagreed. They wanted to see Blanche brought to
justice on their turf. They argued that the James Taylor murder
clearly was a capital case—premeditated and carried out in
order to achieve a pecuniary gain.

Balog and his staff did some quick research and found that
the North Carolina death sentence had been thrown out by the
United States Supreme Court a few years before James Taylor
died. The state later fixed the things the high court had said
were wrong with the North Carolina penalty and enacted a new
law, but not until after Taylor died. Taylor, therefore, died in
the interim, when North Carolina did not have a working death
penalty. His case could not be a capital case.

If the charges against her were not capital charges, then
bond would have to be set. That meant, Balog said, that if
Blanche Moore continued to be his case, she would get out of
jail until her trial. He pointed out that Raymond Reid had been
killed after the death penalty was fixed. Therefore, Balog argued, the main case against Blanche should be Raymond Reid.

Raymond Reid had died in Forsyth County. If the Forsyth
County DA in Winston-Salem would agree to take over the case,
prosecute Blanche, and handle all the publicity, Balog would
be only too happy to ask the Alamance County sheriff to keep
her in his jail until the trial.

Barely an hour's drive down the freeway, Winston-Salem
is very different from blunt working-class Burlington. Created
in 1913 by the consolidation of the small towns of Winston and

Salem, the city had been dominated through most of this century by the R. J. Reynolds Tobacco Company. Reynolds named two of its most famous brands of cigarettes after the city and showered beneficence on the city's cultural institutions, especially on Wake Forest University. The stamp of the company had left the city genteel and conservative.

There were always some aspects of that gentility and conservatism that chafed slightly on Warren Sparrow, the Forsyth County district attorney. He was a very atypical Southern district attorney. A former high school gym rat, too gangly and uncoordinated for varsity basketball but a tiger later on the YMCA team, Sparrow spent several years as a sports reporter on North Carolina newspapers before going to law school at Wake Forest. His friends called him Bird. He became a good general-practice lawyer, even if he never seemed to get rich doing it.

In 1986, Warren Sparrow was the only person in Winston-Salem willing to run against the incumbent DA. Everyone in town was mad at the incumbent for losing a controversial murder case. In addition, the incumbent had driven off his supporters at Reynolds by getting involved in a public incident that combined booze, driving, and a girlfriend—considered to be three strikes in Winston-Salem.

Sparrow won narrowly and then set the law enforcement community on its ear immediately afterward by marching in an NAACP-sponsored parade. He hired people from outside the law enforcement old-boy network, including a tough, good-looking labor lawyer whose husband had supported Sparrow in his campaign.

Janet Branch, whom the courthouse regulars dismissed as the ditsy-dame wife of a rich businessman, had never practiced criminal law. She leaped into the fray and immediately began winning difficult cases, including an especially tough one in the random shooting of a woman in Rural Hall, a small community north of Winston-Salem where Janet Branch had grown up.

Sparrow himself won a conviction in a very difficult case against a nurse at Baptist Hospital who had killed a comatose patient.

None of it helped with the courthouse crowd. Sparrow's manner was loosey-goosey; he drove a down-at-the-heels little silver Mazda RX7; he lived in the West End, where a lot of former 1960s people were redoing old homes, rather than in one of the serious rich-people neighborhoods. None of the Forsyth County Courthouse crowd trusted him an inch.

While he and his staff won some big ones, they also had lost a huge one. In early 1989, Sparrow tried a man named Michael Charles Hayes who had barricaded himself at a busy intersection and sprayed traffic with bullets, killing four people and injuring many more. Hayes was so obviously crazy that he could barely speak coherently.

Sparrow and his assistants urged the jury to do exactly what everyone in Forsyth County wanted them to do—ignore Hayes's insanity, forget about the law, and send the bastard to his death. But the defense lawyers held the jury to the law: the jury found Hayes innocent by reason of insanity.

All anyone in Forsyth County knew about the case was that Warren Sparrow—that liberal—had let a mass murderer go free.

It also happened at about this time that the *Winston-Salem Journal*'s courthouse reporter, John Downey, launched a series of stories damaging to Sparrow's tenure. Downey discovered that Sparrow's modest abilities as an administrator were showing up in a zooming backlog of cases—from 736 to over 2,000 in one year.

Sparrow argued it was because he was really trying cases, instead of freeing his friends and plea-bargaining everyone else. It was a point that was lost on the public.

Sparrow had been doing his best to keep up with the police investigation of the Blanche Moore case—always a tough trick for him, because of the basic hostility toward him from the police fraternity. He had picked up enough to know that the most important witnesses in the Raymond Reid case, Reid's sons and ex-wife, were mad at the police because the police had lied to them about the existence of an arsenic test on Raymond Reid.

In spite of all these difficulties, the Sparrow staff wanted the Blanche Moore case. Their mood was the opposite of Balog's. There was a frank appetite for adventure, glory, and new ground in the Sparrow office. Janet Branch in particular relished the notion of trying the hottest case in recent North Carolina history and looked forward exuberantly to the publicity it would bring.

Sparrow fretted about the damage a case like this would

do to his budget, let alone to his reputation, if he lost it. He was pressed on one hand by Balog and his own staff to take it, tugged on the other by his responsibilities as an administrator and the pressure Downey's stories were putting on him.

The other specter haunting Sparrow was what he suspected had chilled Balog on the case. The courthouse gang were adamant. This time it didn't make any difference if it was Sparrow or someone they happened to like better. No one, they said, would ever win a conviction of Blanche Moore.

This was the courthouse, after all, that had seen Blanche in operation in her sexual harassment suit. In that case, she was smooth, tough, a great actor. And in this new case, nobody ever saw her put that poison in anybody's pudding. She would never be convicted, the courthouse gang agreed.

Sparrow vacillated for weeks.

Bear McEntire had been sitting quietly in his little office across the street from Chadwick's in Graham, watching all of this unfold. He was not a lawyer who found his principal arsenal in scholarship or in the esoteric principles and precedents of the law. He was a lawyer who succeeded by knowing exactly how the people around him would act, given a certain set of circumstances and the fact that this was North Carolina.

Carefully and quietly, he had been moving his own pawns out onto the board. He allowed the news reporters to discover, rather than telling them, that he had hired retired North Carolina medical examiner Dr. Page Hudson as a consultant. The news had the desired effect: Balog and Sparrow saw right away that this case was not going to be some kind of hayseed rout.

Hudson was one of the most respected authorities on arsenic poisoning in the country. After a lifetime of service to the state at modest pay, Hudson seemed to be ready to make some money as an expert witness. He could take the stand and say he had taught John Butts everything he knew. Hudson was a genuine and serious threat. His presence meant that nothing would be easy in this case, in terms of the forensic proofs that would have to be made.

Mitch had the gift of seeming to resist publicity just enough that he made the reporters want to hear more of what he had to say. Balog and Sparrow often were not even quoted in the stories now filling the local newspapers and newscasts, but Mitch seemed to be in every single one, making the same earnest speech over and over again: this entire scenario was the playing out of a mysterious plot; someone else would turn out to be the killer; Blanche was a kind and generous woman, beloved by all who know her; she had been the victim of a cruel and tragic fate; she had been viciously abused at Kroger; now the liars and the gossips were suggesting she had been abused as a child, and for this the community wanted to burn her at the stake.

In his handling of the press, McEntire was quietly, earnestly, slyly devastating. Balog and Sparrow could barely stand to pick up their newspapers in the morning.

Finally, after weeks of waiting and sliding the pieces slowly into play, Bear McEntire picked up the phone late one evening. He found Balog at home.

"It's time we talk turkey," McEntire said.

Balog agreed. The whole thing was dragging on too long. The indecision alone was becoming a bad political problem for Balog. People in Alamance County wanted the damned thing taken care of one way or the other. Balog admitted there were serious problems with proof. He wasn't sure how to read Sparrow, but he thought Sparrow was as afraid of the thing as he was.

In exchange for a guilty plea, Balog could offer a life sentence—no death penalty. He was fairly sure he could bring Sparrow along. It might take a couple of life sentences to make it wash politically, but Blanche was no nut-case machine gunner. She attracted a lot of sympathy in the community. Of course, the other half of the community thought she was a witch. But that would all die down with a plea and a couple of life sentences.

McEntire got up and walked the two dark blocks over to the jail. The deputies ushered him straight into her cell.

"Hello, Mitchell," she said sweetly. "What news do you bring me?"

Blanche's hair was a little unkempt, and she had not bothered to put on makeup that day. Her orange jailhouse jumpsuit was soiled, and her fingernails were cracked and dirty. She looked five years older than she had two months earlier.

McEntire sat beside her on the cot and outlined the offer briefly. Then he took her hand in his two huge hands.

"Blanche," he said solemnly, "as your attorney, I have a number of responsibilities toward you, several responsibilities. But they all run toward helping take care of you.

"And it is my responsibility, as part of taking care of you, to tell you about this offer and ask you to think about it. I don't want some quick response, because you feel like fighting all those dumb people. I want you to think it over."

He looked deep into her eyes. "Blanche, I can take the death penalty away. We can just take the death penalty away from you, and you can have a life.

"You can do whatever you want. Read, write, pray. Of course, you'll do it in confinement. But you will have a life."

Blanche was quiet and emotionless. She stared at the floor for a moment, then looked up at Mitch.

"Mitch, I'll do whatever they tell me I have to do, and if they tell me I have to die, I'll do that. I won't fight death. I will lay down and die. But I will not confess to something I did not do, and have my family have to live with that. I didn't do it. And I won't confess to it. I will lay down and die, but I will not confess."

She stood and turned away. When she turned back there was a flash in her eye.

"Mitch, I want you to fight."

He shrugged.

"If that's how it is, I will, Blanche. I will." He turned to leave and then turned back. "Almost forgot," he said. "Did the jailers give you a teddy bear today?"

"Yes," she said, shaking her head and smiling.

"From your secret admirer?"

"That's right. Mr. Garvin Thomas again."

"Ha!" he laughed. "None other. Well, you see, Blanche, you have a lot of fans out there."

Garvin Thomas had been sending her long block-printed letters for months, professing his undying love. She had not responded, which was causing Garvin Thomas some chagrin. He needed at least a single letter from her to show his drinking companions at Pine Hill Cemetery.

He had been telling the few people who would still listen to him that he and Blanche had become lovers through the mail. With his God-given gift of eloquence, he had won her heart, he told everyone. She was spilling her guts in the letters she returned to him, he said. He bragged that he would sell the letters to the *Greensboro News & Record* for a fortune.

His few acquaintances—mainly the riffraff and bums with whom he drank cheap wine in the alleys and at the cemetery—listened and snickered. Nothing Garvin ever said was true. He was all talk. It was good-sounding talk, true enough, and he might have made a fine snake-oil salesman if he'd had an ounce of ambition anywhere in his body. Instead, Garvin Thomas had spent his life in and out of jail for burglary, a crime he invariably committed while drunk and in search of more money for booze or for booze itself.

He knew much more about this case than he could ever tell, he said. They were all barking up the wrong tree. But he would die with his secret. Most of his drinking companions could agree only that he would die, and, from the looks of him, any minute.

Sparrow and Balog were in the same boat they had been in for over two months. In the absence of a plea bargain, one or the other of them had to try this case. Sparrow still could not make a decision.

Then one day two dapper civil lawyers from Chapel Hill appeared in Sparrow's office. From the shine on their shoes to the cut of their cashmere overcoats, Frank Hallstrom and Bill Hamilton looked like freshly minted money. Sparrow knew of the Grover McCain firm, of course.

These two young bullets had a deal for Warren Sparrow. They needed some help proving Blanche Taylor was a murderer in order to win a civil suit against Baptist Hospital. They intended to devote tens of thousands of dollars, maybe hundreds of thousands, to a painstaking gathering of evidence. The final product would be a stack of depositions and investigation reports a mile high, all of it gathered out in the open, unfenced by all of the restrictions the court had imposed in recent years on criminal investigations.

The constitutional protection against forced self-incrimination—the rule that says a person cannot be compelled to testify against himself—had been expanded by the courts in the last quarter century to include a long list of things no one could make an accused person do. But all of those protections had to do only with criminal proceedings. Few of the many rights and protections of the accused in a criminal proceeding extended into civil law.

The Grover McCain firm could go into court and get subpoenas Warren Sparrow couldn't even dream of getting. Hamilton and Hallstrom were ready to begin immediately pounding Mitch McEntire with subpoenas ordering Blanche herself and many of her most intimate associates and witnesses to appear for sworn depositions.

When Warren Sparrow had swept into office, a good many of Forsyth County's experienced felony prosecutors had left for private practice. He was short on experienced big-case talent, and he knew it. He had no one at all on the staff who had any experience with the kind of very sophisticated forensic and scientific evidence this case would involve. His budget was already stretched.

The McCain firm was a successful firm. It had major cash reserves it could invest in a case like this. It had Bill Hamilton— a crack lawyer and a forensic pathologist. Because it would proceed civilly, it would have no obstacles before it, just an open road. The McCain firm never went to court without an enormous battery of evidence behind it, and the McCain lawyers and investigators were already in the process of building their case. It was an incredible windfall.

It was all his. It would all come to Warren Sparrow. The kind of case a harried district attorney almost never has time, money, or opportunity to make would be put together for him by one of the best civil firms in the Southeast. They just needed a little help up front getting to the kind of criminal evidence that would help prove Blanche was a murderer. Once they knew who the main witnesses were and where the trails pointed, they would take care of all the drudge work.

As an added attraction, they told Sparrow they would impress upon the Reid family the importance of cooperating with law enforcement officials, especially with the district attorney and his staff.

Sparrow told Balog it was a deal. He and his people would try the case in Winston-Salem; Balog and his sheriff would keep her up there in Burlington until the trial; the civil boys would do all the work; Blanche would get the death penalty; and everyone else would go home happy.

That afternoon Garvin Thomas appeared at Mitchell McEntire's office. He was one of a parade of geeks and crazies who came to see McEntire almost every day now to talk about the Blanche Moore case. McEntire heard him out as he heard them all. He had a special interest in this one, because this one was persistent and sent gifts.

Thomas said he was in love with Blanche and had something he badly needed to tell her in person. McEntire made an assessment that Thomas was probably not dangerous and then sent him on his way.

Suddenly the task of making the case against Blanche was on the shoulders of Bill Hamilton and Frank Hallstrom. And suddenly it looked less simple. The hospital had a perfect case for itself going in. The statute of limitations protected it. It didn't matter who had made what mistakes. Time had run out, and that was supposed to mean the Reid boys could not claim anything, any way, no matter what.

In order to get off the dime, Hamilton and Hallstrom had to shoot a fatal hole in the statute of limitations. They had to make it disappear. There were ways to do that. But in this case it was going to take some very fancy shooting.

Early in the campaign, Frank Hallstrom became ill. He withdrew from the case until he recovered. Hamilton, meanwhile, was putting tens of thousands of miles on his car and compiling a mountain of notes, affidavits, and depositions. Sparrow had wired him in directly to the criminal file.

Hamilton knew all about Blanche's failed lie detector test, and as soon as the police investigators in the Dwight Moore and James Taylor cases brought in anything new, Hamilton saw it.

He also saw something in the Raymond Reid investigative files that caught his eye. One of the ICU nurses had told a sheriff's deputy that Blanche often brought in food for the nurses. The nurse had volunteered that Blanche brought grocery sacks full of Tupperware containing little treats for the nursing staff every night.

Playing slowly through his mind were all of his own long hours prowling hospital corridors in his years as a research scientist, sipping coffee in the labs in the dark hours of morning, shooting the breeze in the break rooms with nurses and residents so whacked out from fatigue that they went giddy as soon as they were away from the patients and attending physicians.

Food. She brought them food. She took food to her victims. Food of death. She took food to the nurses and the residents. Food of life. The staple of the hospital family, the common currency, the lifeblood. Food. She cooked food. That was how she did it.

He realized all at once who was going to send Blanche to her death. Not he. Not the DA or the SBI or the families of the victims. Not the doctors, who were all scared to death of malpractice suits and scared to death of the hospital administration.

The nurses would convict Blanche. The women. The tenders and the curers of the ICU. Blanche had fed them, had slowly wormed her way into their tight little tribe, had made herself one of them. And then she had killed one of their charges. She had betrayed them.

Chapter Seventeen

Bill Hamilton got the names and set up the depositions. The hospital's lawyers were present, of course, for each deposition, making objections and raising their own questions. The nurses all acted very suspicious and even hostile toward Hamilton. That was natural. They had to show their employers, who were sitting right there, that they were not aiding and abetting this malpractice lawyer who was suing their hospital.

But as he asked the questions, teasing out each little bit of anecdote, asking the right questions at the right moment, the nurses began providing a solid, almost cinematic portrait of Blanche entering the hospital every night, carrying her bag of goodies, handing out this Tupperware dish to nursing and that one to the residents, this one to the family of another patient, and, finally, that one to her victim.

The nurses knew exactly what had happened. They knew exactly what they were doing, exactly what they were giving Hamilton. They were giving him the rope. They were handing it to him right there in front of their bosses. They were making damned sure Blanche Moore would swing for what she had done in their hospital.

Warren Sparrow had been carefully considering the matter of whom to give the Blanche Moore case to. He was getting advice from everyone he knew.

They would let her off for reasons of chivalry, several people said. She would come across as a pretty, sweet, Christian lady. With the exception of the last one, most of her boyfriends and husbands would probably turn out to be wife-beaters. Especially if the prosecution put some big old DA up there to beat up on her, the jury would feel sorry for her, even if she was guilty, and they'd let her off.

People who knew Blanche said she was undefeatable unless you could get through her act and make her lose her temper. If somebody could push Blanche's button and make those black eyes start whirling, the jury would see her for the witch she was.

Sparrow had a staff of lawyers experienced in prosecuting murders to whom he could give the case. He gave it instead to a woman who wanted it desperately—Janet Branch.

Born in 1953 in Rural Hall, an outlying part of Winston-Salem, Janet Branch had moved with her parents to an even more rural area in Davidson County when she was six. Her father was a tobacco farmer, and her mother worked in the Haines Hosiery Mill. She had a sister twelve years older than she.

Small, pretty, with red hair and glittering green eyes, little Janet was always the apple of her parents' eyes. They tried to accomplish the parental miracle of spoiling her and keeping her modest at the same time. When her mother took her to the store for new clothes, she always said, "Janet, you have nice things for a poor child."

By the end of the summer following the graduation of her class from Ledford High School, the entire cheerleading squad had gotten married. Still small, still very pretty, little Janet had other ideas. She enrolled in Pfeiffer College near Charlotte, and graduated magna cum laude four years later. She married her high school sweetheart the day after graduation.

She took a master's degree in social work in one summer and decided anything she could learn that fast was not worth making a life's work. With her husband's encouragement, she enrolled in the University of North Carolina Law School at Chapel Hill.

She had something in common with Warren Sparrow. She, too, had grown up in the very conservative political climate of North Carolina, and she, too, had always chafed a little under it. When she completed law school and passed the bar, she stayed away from the corporate recruiters and the big firms and applied instead to the National Labor Relations Board.

Soon she was out in the field, driving down dusty roads and interviewing witnesses in the same sweaty, fan-cooled mills her mother had worked in. Her NLRB district included the J. P. Stevens Company—object of a long and bitter strike. The woman on whom the movie character Norma Rae was based was one of the witnesses Janet Branch handled.

She was tough, and she enjoyed tangling with men who thought they could push women around. Once while she was at Pfeiffer, a boy had slapped Janet Branch across the face because she told him she wasn't going to go out with him any-more. She leaned across the seat of his sports car and socked him in the mouth with a closed fist.

In 1978 she was a new young lawyer. It gave her immense pleasure to be a small, pretty, twenty-five-year-old whip of a girl in the eyes of men ... and go into court and break the knees of a fifty-year-old pinstriped son of a bitch making six times her government salary.

By the late 1980s, however, government work was wearing thin. She left the NLRB in 1985, worked at a couple of private-practice jobs, and then ran for a local lower-court judgeship in 1986. She had absolutely no chance of winning the post, but during her campaign she did make one terrific speech, which happened to be overheard by Warren Sparrow, who was run-ning that year for DA. Sparrow introduced himself later, and he and Janet and Janet's husband all hit if off famously. Warren Sparrow's first hire, after he was elected, was Janet Branch.

From the moment she got the Blanche Moore case, Janet made up her mind she wanted the death sentence. Sparrow was still hedging. They met one day in the living room of Janet's home. An extra BMW was parked in the back by the garage, and one of her husband's several large boats was in front on a trailer, waiting to be hauled somewhere. Inside, a beagle scrabbled across the hardwood floors, carefully avoiding the cascades of ruffled chintz bedecking the furniture.

They were going to watch a videotape Janet had paid someone to make of Dwight Moore in the convalescent home where he was living. Sitting stooped forward with his elbows on his knees, working his fingers in a ball before him, Sparrow was still worried about the risks of a major trial.

"Well, of course, since I'm facing reelection, I should be delighted to have this trial dragging out and have my face on page one every day right up to election day. But then I have to balance my responsibilities as the chief administrative officer of this department. We have a caseload here full of cocaine dealers and other murderers and thieves and all manner of people who need prosecuting. I have to say that if McEntire were to show up over here tomorrow and he wanted to talk about a deal, I would listen to him."

Janet, with her long red-blond hair combed down over her back, dressed in soft gray tweeds that set off the sparkle of her green eyes, watched him speak and then, when she spoke back, wagged a finger at him.

"Well, of course, Mr. Sparrow, you are my superior, but I for one would not be very interested in a deal. I want to see her get the death penalty. I want to see her sizzle on the griddle."

Sparrow waved both hands at her, muttering, "Easy now, easy. Look, Janet, if McEntire is going to give up a stroke, then you have to give him something. If he's going to hit a give-up stroke, he'll expect something in return."

With the disastrous Hayes case on his mind, Sparrow said, "Frankly, if I thought there were a way to avoid another six-week trial, I'd jump at it. And that would represent some kind of political sacrifice for me, but I'd do it anyway."

Janet was shaking her head no as he spoke. "I have been going through this evidence," she said, "and I want you to know that this is an especially horrible way for a person to die. Look at this tape. This is Dwight Moore, and he's the one she did the least harm to."

The tape showed Dwight sitting on a metal bed in a large bleak ward of other beds and linoleum floors. For some reason there was no sound. Dwight sat on the edge of his bed with his slippered feet on the floor, and a middle-aged woman in a white uniform leaned over him. She pointed to his hands. He lifted them up. The camera bumbled forward to show a close-up of the flapping tremors in both hands.

Then, with the white humming of the tape machine and the scrabbling feet of the beagle the only sound in Janet's large living room, she and Sparrow watched as the woman in white stuck needles deep into Dwight's arms. Dwight smiled.

"No feeling," Janet whispered to Sparrow.

Dwight's face was gray and haggard. His hands were gnarled and crabbed and had a pasty-waxy look of death about them. The woman in white motioned for Dwight to rise and walk. While the videocamera bumped backward out of his way, Dwight tiptoed and minced awkwardly across the ward, still smiling gamely. He sat back down, obviously tired. The woman in white handed Dwight a Bible. He tried to turn the pages with his half-dead hands, but he could not turn them, and in a moment the Bible fell to the floor. Dwight smiled lamely at the woman and at the camera.

"God," Sparrow whispered.

"What she did to this man, who loved her," Janet said, shaking her head with tears in her eyes. "I can't think about this, about poor Reverend Moore, and Raymond Reid who never did anything but love her with all his heart. I can't think about it without getting emotional."

Sparrow got up, walked over, and patted her on the back. "Just make sure you get emotional in ways that help you win the case."

"Oh, don't worry about that, Mr. Sparrow. We are going to win this case."

Sparrow gave Janet a clean desk. She would have no other assignments or duties until the conclusion of the Blanche Moore trial. He also gave her Vince Rabil, a young lawyer on the staff with a flair for organization and scholarship. Sparrow had made up his mind that Janet Branch was right. This was a go-for-broke case.

"I want it in court and going by the first of July," he said. "If we try it any later, they'll say I'm grandstanding for the November election. If we put it off, they'll say I was afraid to try it before the election."

"Mr. Sparrow, July is too soon."

"I'm doing it your way on the plea bargain, Janet. You will do it my way on the timing."

"Yes, sir."

The McCain lawyers had presented their suit against Baptist Hospital on behalf of the Reids in mid-summer. They presented all of their arguments why Baptist Hospital should not be allowed to claim the statute of limitations.

Now, a month later, the judge was to rule. Hamilton and the lawyers for the hospital all sat quietly in the courtroom while the judge read papers in a file before him. Finally, only half-lifting his head, the judge announced he was setting aside the statute of limitations.

It was a staggering loss for the hospital. The hospital lawyers retired from the courtroom and drove across town to confer with their client. The decision was made quickly. The hospital and its insurance company would settle with the Reid family.

The McCain firm had scored yet another brilliant victory. And now the evidence Bill Hamilton had amassed could all be boxed up and shipped to the eagerly awaiting Janet Branch.

That night Garvin Thomas staggered on his bloated blue diabetic legs from the hospital toward his room and the cats. He realized a third of the way home that he was not going to make it. He stopped at the room of a friend who often had wine, but the friend growled through the door that he had nothing to drink.

"I am not looking for drink," Thomas said. "I am in a bad way and need to lie down."

The door opened slowly. Garvin Thomas plunged in and collapsed on a torn and stained overstuffed chair. He fell into a deep sleep almost immediately.

The next morning his friend walked up to him, stared at him for a moment, and then touched his cheek with a dirty fingertip. "Shit," the friend muttered. "Old Garvin done died in my chair."

He had been a funny, strange little man, so filthy and grotesque physically, so eloquent and amusing when he spoke. Tough and mean in one moment, childishly ashamed of his lolling tongue the next. All of his relatives and near-relatives had kicked him out or driven him off at one moment or another. But they got together and gave him a modest, decent funeral, and they saw to it that his obituary was published in the local newspaper. It said he had died of chronic diabetes.

Janet Branch and Vince Rabil were working long hours, putting together their densely woven fabric of law and fact. Rabil's challenge was to find a way to put all of Blanche's murders together in the same case. The danger was that the judge might allow evidence for the Reid murder only.

If they could present all of the murders, then it would be obvious to the jury that the only common element in all of them was Blanche. But if they could present only one murder—Reid alone—then, in spite of all Hamilton's work and their own efforts, it might be very tricky.

All Mitch McEntire would have to do is say, "Yes, someone murdered Raymond Reid with arsenic. And yes, my client tried to comfort her dying husband by bringing him food, the same food she brought all of the nurses and the doctors, none of whom seem to have suffered ill effect. And yes, people in a superstitious culture like ours have a tendency to accuse women of being witches. But no, Blanche Moore, like the nurses and the doctors, had no idea what was killing Raymond Reid. The reason why no one saw her put arsenic in his food was that she did not do it."

The one thing Janet and Vince dreaded most, as they worked their way through all of David McDougall's work and the massive pile of evidence Bill Hamilton had put together, was that they would stumble on someone else who could be construed as a common denominator.

All the evidence they had gathered had to be shown to Mitch before the trial, under the rules of discovery. No matter how good their case against Blanche might be, they knew all too well how hard it was going to be to persuade a jury to convict this kindly Christian grandmother and send her to her death. The jury would be looking hard for a way out of it. If Mitch could point to a single other person who could serve as a reasonable suspect, then the prosecution would be dead in the water. They assumed Mitch probably was asking Blanche every day if she could come up with anyone else who might have done it.

But no other reasonable suspect appeared. Janet's confidence grew as she plunged through the factual evidence. She needed to be confident, in order to ward off Sparrow's continuing worry and continuing hints about the virtues of plea bargaining.

Rabil, on the other hand, was beginning to develop some private worries that had less to do with the facts in the case than with North Carolina law. The way to put the cases all together was through a legal principle called joinder. In order to allow joinder, the judge would have to find Blanche's crimes were part of a seamless fabric of events, unbroken in time. The problem was that the early deaths—her father, her mother-in-law—were clearly too far back in time for joinder with the others. Even James Taylor's murder was separated in time from Raymond Reid's. And the defense certainly would argue that Reid's death in 1986 was a distinct and separate event from Dwight Moore's near-death in 1989, worthy of a separate trial.

If the cases could not be joined and all Mitch had to do was defend against the Reid case alone, then it might be impossible to beat him. Janet was continuing to tell Sparrow that a plea bargain would be a foolish mistake, that they had Blanche cold. Rabil was less certain. If Mitch managed to talk Blanche into a deal and showed up with any kind of reasonable offer, it might still be a good idea to talk to him about it.

In fact, Mitch McEntire was sitting at his desk in the law office across Elm Street from Chadwick's thinking about another appeal to Blanche for a plea bargain, and simultaneously thinking a little about lunch, when the phone rang. It was one of the jailers. He told Mitch he had been inspecting Blanche's mail and had come across something Mitch needed to see right away.

Mitch told his assistant, Carol DiLello, that he would be out for a few minutes. He walked the two blocks to the jail, stopping twice to chat with other lawyers who were on their way to court. Fifteen minutes later he reappeared at his office, short of breath as if he had run back. He rushed past Carol DiLello in the outer office without speaking. He sat down hard on his squeaking swivel chair behind his desk and read the letter the jailer had given him, whistling low under his breath.

"What is it, Mitch?" Carol asked in the door.

He held up a finger for silence. "I don't know yet." He studied the letter intently, muttering.

He put the letter down flat on his desk and shoved his chair

away. He stared straight ahead into the unfocused distance for
a long time without speaking.

"Carol, please get me Janet Branch on the phone right
away."

Janet and Vince were huddled together in her tiny office.
Vince had bought a personal computer just for this case. He
had used sorting and data-base software to organize the incredible jumble of facts and dates and legal details, and he was
showing Janet how it worked when her phone rang.

"Sure," she said into the phone. "Put him on. . . . Hi there,
Mr. McEntire. Now listen, I hope you're not calling up here to
cry uncle and ask for a big old plea bargain for her, because
we are not in a plea-bargain mood this morning. . . . Oh fine,
go ahead, tell me all about it. What amazing new discovery do
you have, then?"

Rabil watched her face closely. She was rolling her eyes
and snickering at first, but the snicker quickly disappeared. She
grew suddenly very grave. She sat motionless, frozen like a
statue, for some moments.

"Oh shit, Mitch!" she shouted at last. "This is bullshit! This
is utter bullshit! I will see you very, very soon, my friend!" She
slammed the phone into the receiver. She shoved her hands
across the desk spastically, knocking files and pencils to the
floor. She rose, walked halfway out into the hall, crouched low,
and began beating the air with her fists.

"Oh, son of a bitch! Son of a bitch!"

Warren Sparrow came bolting out of his office, joined by
a crowd of secretaries, other assistant DAs, and some detectives
who happened to be in the office that day.

"What is it, Janet?" Rabil shouted.

"Oh, he has a letter! A bullshit letter! Oh, I can't believe
it!" There were tears in her eyes. It was several minutes before
anyone could get her calmed down enough to tell them what
was in the letter.

It was written in a long, jagged cursive hand, in ballpoint
pen over several pages of cheap white paper:

my dearest darling:

you received many letters from me during your confinement at the ala. jail in Graham. and earrings honey. you do not even know me. but i have loved you for years. i saw you the first time at Krogers in Burl. I thought you looked like an angel to me. I may have a few days to live and I need to right my wrongs to you and others involved.

You see i am responsible for these deaths. I can hardly write I am so nervous from med. I knew James from the antique shop and went there often and know his brothers. Blanche I was so jealous of you and you might say obsessed also. I followed you all the time and knew everything you did. When he died and you were free, I was so happy.

Then there was Raymond in Kernersville, and I hated him. he loved you too much. I used to follow you to his house in Kernersville when he got sick i followed to the hosp.

finally i couldn't take it no longer all that attention you gave him so i went in to visit him as a hosp. chaplain at Wesley Long. He was thirsty i got a coke and filled it with arsenic. i kept following you to the hosp. then to Bapt. did this for many months. then he got better and the jealousy took over again so again i went in as a chaplain. this time he was in a room with a T.V. I did not have to make a coke or anything when I saw how paralyzed he was. I went back later and injected the arsenic in his legs. Hope i can finish this letter my arm and chest hurt real bad.

This was the last time i went in his room. Blanche this was the last of Sept. I kept following you there. I even sat in the lobby one night when you stayed to make sure no one would hurt you. Later he died and I was happy.

I'm so tired and this is not easy. Later there was Dwight and I hated him even more but you married the bastard. I still rode by that parsonage everyday. then i followed you to his hosp. you did not know me so i was able to see when you went and read the name on the door. Later in the night and told him the nurses wanted me to give him water so i gave him arsenic and i also put more in his pitcher it was late and he was sleepy and did not even notice me.

Later he went Chapel Hill hosp. I just thought he would die like the others but he didn't and then has gotten you in a lot of trouble and hurt you a lot. I am sorry. I never meant harm to you I love you too much. but this plan failed me. when i came by the jail with the bear i wanted to see you and say i'm sorry even though you would not understand.

You see, i had been to the hospital that day and they told I would die soon. then i went to see your att. and started to tell him and could not do it. i have been in trouble before and did not want to die in jail. You see i have been obsessed and could not bear the thought of someone having you. I am very sorry and wish I had something to give you to help compensate somehow.

I have asked for this letter to be mailed after my funeral by a friend. God knows I pray this last request is granted. I prayed and asked for forgiveness, so darling, please forgive me with me gone you can at least have a life.

My final plan was to get everyone that has hurt you like both DAs in W-S, the Reid family, dwight moore, dr. butts and others even the man in your sex case.

My baby i must go please forgive me at least now you know what happened this will be mailed to your atty. keep them pretty brown eyes sparkling. this is the same handwriting i wrote your others this time sloppy because i was so sick. Goodbye my darling forever scared don't want to go to hell.

This letter is 100 percent truth and I'm ashamed of it. My step mom is Lois thomas but me and lois do not like each other, but it is my fault she is a good woman too my darling how i would like to hold you in my arms and kiss your lips take off your clothes and kiss your breasts and run my tongue through your pussy and suck up those sweet juices from your body and fuck fuck till morning. I'm sorry but this has been my fantasy for years please keep the teedy bear that I left for you bye bye baby.

Chapter Eighteen

Justin Catanoso walked into the large street-level lobby of the
Forsyth County Courthouse that afternoon to do some basic
scut work, following up on questions his editors back in Greensboro had been pestering him with, but halfway across the lobby
he ran into one of his favorite police sources, coming off the
elevator after a visit to the prosecutor's office.

"Tell you what, my friend," the source said. "There is a
major new development in the Blanche Moore case, and I do
mean major."

"Hey," Justin said as the man began to walk away, "you
can't do that! What is it? Don't just lay that on me and walk
away!"

With his back to Justin and both hands in the air, the man
laughed and said, "Do what you do, Mr. Reporter, do what
you do." He disappeared through the door to the police parking lot.

Catanoso rushed to a pay phone and called Sarah Avery,
the Alamance County bureau reporter for the *Greensboro News*

& Record. "I have no idea what it is," he told her. "I think it's big, but I'm sorry, I just have no idea."

Avery rushed immediately from her little office near the courthouse in Graham to Mitch McEntire's office. Just as she got to the door, Mitch came out in a hell of a hurry.

"Mitch," she said, stepping in front of him to stop him, "we know about it. We don't have the details, but we know you've got..." Her mind was speeding, trying to think what to say she knew he had. "We know you've got major new evidence or a new witness. Or something."

Mitch stopped dead in his tracks. His eyebrows went to the top of his forehead. He looked her up and down.

"From where in the hell do you know that?"

"From Winston-Salem," she said.

"Well, if that's how the lady DA wants to play it, then fine. C'mon in here, Miss Reporter. I'll show you just exactly what we have. We have the solution to this damned case."

The *Greensboro News & Record* was trapped against a tight afternoon deadline. It ran a brief story on the letter, and the rest of the media came unglued. All of the local and regional print and electronic media flooded back into Graham and Winston-Salem, and the networks and the national papers began calling again.

By the following afternoon, Catanoso and Avery had put together a detailed description of the letter and a full biography of the strange little man whom Mitchell McEntire now was touting as the principal suspect. The lobby of the Forsyth County Courthouse and the street out front was a circus of microwave dish-trucks, cables on the ground, reporters with notebooks buttonholing everybody who walked by.

Far above the madness in the silence of her seventh-story office, Janet Branch sat with a copy of the letter before her. She had read it at least twenty times. She leaned forward with her elbows on the desk and put her face in her hands. There was something in it. A hook or a voice. An echo, an accent, a trace of a song. Something wrong. A crack. She took her hands away from her face and allowed the words of the letter to run through her mind unexamined. All the voices and the cadences of her people ran along behind the words of the letter—the sound of the country, the sound of the city, the sound of North Carolina.

She slammed her fist on her desk. She leaped to her feet, threw open the door, and shouted down the hallway, "Vince Rabil, come here right now!"

Rabil hurried in. He stood. He had become wary of Janet in the last twenty-four hours. "What is it, Janet?"

Janet was sitting again, nodding yes, pointing to the letter. "She wrote it," she said.

"Who did? Blanche? How in the hell do you—"

"Yes, Blanche."

"But how do you know?"

"Vince, all this Bible stuff, asking for forgiveness, afraid to go to hell, and all about how Blanche is the poor dear darling center of the universe and all these other people hurt her and that's what this is all about and that's why they all had to die a horrible death. And then, from there, right into the tongue in the pussy and the sweet juices of her body.

"This is just exactly what all of the people who know her have been telling us about her. It's what does not add up about Blanche. It's what makes Blanche weird. It's the crack.

"The goody-goody and the self-centeredness and the church-lady talk, that's one thing. That's fine. The pussy talk and the oral sex obsession, that might be fine, too, in a totally different person.

"But when is the last time you heard of a nice little Christian North Carolina grandmother who could be talking the Bible out of one side of her mouth one minute, and the next thing anybody knows she's talking about cunnilingus and fellatio as if there had never even been a break in the conversation? When did you ever hear of somebody like that?"

"Never," Vince said soberly. "Once. One person."

"Blanche."

A huge smile broke across Vince's face. "Blanche!" he shouted.

Janet threw open her office door again.

"Blanche!" she shouted. "Blanche!"

Warren Sparrow and the other assistant DAs came bursting out of their office again to see what the ruckus was all about. "Oh God," Sparrow said, "I sure hope this time it's good news."

"The best," she said.

They all crowded into Janet's cubicle and brainstormed for the rest of the day. Garvin Thomas probably had written her some other letters. He was one of the geeks who had seen her on TV, maybe even had seen her at Kroger in her prime, and had become obsessed. Mitch probably had been pressing Blanche to come up with anyone else who could be a common denominator.

"This guy's dead, right?" Sparrow said.

"Right," she said.

"Was there an obit?" Sparrow asked. "Let's say there was. She has nothing to do in there but read the paper. She sees the obit, recognizes this as the weirdo who has been writing her, and she gets a bright idea to fake the letter."

Bill Hamilton called while they were in the middle of their meeting. Janet took the call. Hamilton had just seen the story on TV. He was laughing when Janet picked up.

"I had something I thought you'd like to know," Hamilton said. "Just before Coulthard was supposed to go to trial for arsenic-poisoning his wife, a letter appeared from another guy taking credit for the crime. Turned out Coulthard wrote it himself. It's standard jailhouse bullshit. They all tell each other in there how to do it. Bunch of geniuses."

In the weeks ahead, Janet Branch and Mitch McEntire engaged in a complex legal battle over custody of the letter. In the middle of that skirmish, Mitch added to the flames by demanding a change of venue out of Winston-Salem. He cited the heavy press coverage, the songs on the radio, and the overall atmosphere of witch-hunt as reasons why the trial needed to be moved to some remote rural county.

Janet charged, meanwhile, that the jailers at the Alamance County Jail had begun treating Blanche as if she were Mother Teresa. It was not, Janet said, that she wanted Blanche to be treated badly. It was that in trying to investigate the "chain of custody" of the letter—in exactly whose hands the letter had been and into whose it had passed—Janet had discovered that the Alamance County Jail was suspending most of its normal rules of procedure in Blanche's case.

It was true. The jailers in Graham were allowing Blanche's family to pass in and out of her cell at all hours, without even logging their visits. The problem for Janet was proving what Blanche had seen in the newspaper, when she had seen it, when she had sent out mail, and when the so-called Garvin Thomas letter had arrived at the jail.

Normally visitors and mailings and so on would be carefully noted for any prisoner. But in jail, as she had in the ICU, Blanche was making herself a part of the jail family. Blanche led prayer meetings in which she guided prisoners and jailers alike through long, tearful quaking sessions, all kneeling on aching knees on the concrete floor. The jailers were coming to think of her almost as one of the staff.

Her family gathered behind her with all the ferocity and unshakable loyalty a North Carolina clan can muster. Her daughters visited her often in jail and fielded inquiries from the press outside. Blanche was visited often by her brother, P.D. the barber, who had sold his shop and made himself Mitch's full-time unpaid assistant and gofer on the case. She also had visits from her brother Sam, a salesman who still performed religious music and had made a few recordings.

Sam was writing a series of songs about her trials which he hoped to record and sell, in part to raise money for the defense and in part as a way of doing battle with the rash of scratchy, hissing, home-taped witch-songs popping up now on every little two-bit radio station in the state. He often brought his guitar to jail and sat across the glass partition from Blanche, strumming and singing softly into a worn black telephone cocked on one shoulder.

Blanche sang into her own telephone on the other side of the glass. They looked deep into each other's eyes as they sang, sometimes frowning, going back over phrases and harmonies again and again until finally their eyes met and both nodded happily, acknowledging that they had it right at last.

The question of joinder was still unresolved. Vince Rabil was less confident than ever that they would persuade the judge to tie the cases together formally in one charge. Without that ruling, he wondered whether Blanche might not walk out of the Alamance County Jail a free woman and a hero.

The odds were steep. If they tried her and they won, then they would achieve a major legal victory, a blow for justice, and a neat lick for Warren Sparrow's political career. If they tried her and they lost, then all the dynamic of the witch business would come spilling back over them. If Blanche was found not guilty, then clearly the question would be how and why a community could have convinced itself that a woman like Blanche was a witch.

Sparrow was still telling Janet he wanted a trial in July, in order to stay well shy of his election campaign in the fall and avoid all the accusations one way or the other. But Warren Sparrow was the only person in North Carolina who believed the trial possibly could take place that soon.

All of the pending questions—joinder, change of venue, custody of the letter, whether the jail was treating Blanche like a queen, and the setting of a trial date—finally came to court in early June in North Carolina Superior Court in Winston-Salem. The judge was William H. Freeman, now forty-five—the same judge who had heard the early motions in Blanche's sexual harassment case.

Still youthful, handsome in a rugged Lincolnesque sort of way, thoughtful and wry, Judge Freeman had changed in only one way. He was even more experienced on the bench. He had heard four solid years' worth of criminal and civil cases since he last set eyes on Blanche Moore.

The media focus on the case had grown more intense as the trial had grown imminent. The Blanche Moore story was a long, complex, rambling saga—difficult to render in a twenty-five-inch newspaper story or a thirty-second bite. The trial would provide the media with a stage from which they would be able to capture the story in a tidy format.

That focus was beginning to settle on both Mitch and Janet in a way that rendered them both catatonic, whenever they stopped to think about it. "Oh, I hear she's spending ten thousand dollars on her wardrobe just for this," Mitch would say.

"Well, you just know this is going to be Mitchell McEntire's one great shining hour," Janet would say.

But both of them were scared to death at times, each begging the visiting troops of reporters for predictions of what it would look like, what the mood would be, what they should expect when the full media treatment began.

When the omnibus hearing on issues finally arrived, Mitch showed up in court with a team. To his own services he had added the expertise of Thomas Loflin, a noted criminal attorney from Durham, and David Tamer, a Winston-Salem lawyer who was considered to be extremely bright, a fine legal scholar, and the kind of lawyer who could find grounds for an appeal in the way the judge parted his hair.

All of a sudden it was no longer a case of Country Mitch, the affable bear from Graham, cozying up to the jury to paint Blanche as everybody's grammaw. It was Country Mitch, it was ace criminal attorney Loflin, and it was legal scholar and steel-trap tactician Tamer—all of them being paid out of the pockets of Blanche and her family, who never had tried to claim indigence or seek court-appointed counsel.

On the first day of the hearing, Warren Sparrow floated in and out of court like the bird his friends called him. Janet was dressed to the nines and had hair that would have earned admiration in Hollywood. Vince Rabil, who was stoop-shouldered for a young man, intense and brooding, sat between Janet and Sparrow poring over law books and looking very much as if he were the one facing the death penalty.

Early in the hearing, Judge Freeman began hitting the ball straight to the prosecution table. It was clear from his questions and his manner that he thought the defense motion for a change of venue was silly. Gazing out over the courtroom, he waved his hand at the media and said he couldn't imagine a worse circus atmosphere than what would ensue if he inflicted this trial on some shy little hamlet in the mountains. That was just what the media thirsted for—a village full of mountain yokels in whose faces they could stick sound booms.

Winston-Salem might not be New York, but it was a fairly sophisticated little city anyway, he said, and that sophistication was the best blanket of security the defense could hope for. Sparrow and Janet were winking at each other and nudging each other's shoulders.

It was clear Judge Freeman had not even been following the case very closely in the newspapers. When Janet made her pitch for custody of the letter, arguing that the letter would be a key piece of prosecution evidence if it turned out Blanche had written it, Freeman waved for her to stop talking.

He leaned forward over the bench and peered at her in silence for a moment. He looked at Blanche, who was sitting at the defense table sandwiched between Tamer and Mitch.

"Do you mean to tell me," Freeman said, talking to Janet but gazing toward Blanche, "that you are going to contend that the defendant wrote that letter herself?"

"We think it's a very strong possibility," Janet said.

Freeman's eyes opened wide. He shook his head. He looked at Blanche again. Then he ruled in Janet's favor.

A short while later, Freeman set the date of the trial for November. Warren Sparrow was not pleased, but Janet was delighted. She felt strongly that she needed the extra time to prepare. Everything was going her way.

Then Freeman began to ask questions related to joinder. It was clear Freeman did not like what he was hearing from Vince. The crimes were too far apart in time. That would make it hard for Freeman, under the rules of evidence, to grant the prosecution's request for joinder.

Freeman shook his head. He said that he would call a recess and retire to his chambers to study the matter. Warren Sparrow was crestfallen. He had believed all along that joinder was an absolute necessity. Janet and Vince leaned over to him and tried to reassure him in whispers that they didn't really need it. They could get in all the evidence they needed under another rule, called 404B. Sparrow looked queasy and unconvinced.

Mitch saw it. He smiled broadly at Sparrow and gave him a little wave. Sparrow—always genial—smiled back, but it was a very weak, very wan little smile. That made Mitch beam all the more.

Mitch whispered into Blanche's ear. Blanche turned and smiled an angry slitted smile at Sparrow and at Janet Branch, especially at Janet.

The mood around the DA's office was suddenly somber. Janet continued to peck away at the evidence, sifting through the mountain of depositions Hamilton had provided, going out of the office to do things like tour the little house in which James Taylor had died.

One of the elements the prosecution was struggling to establish was motive. Why did she really do it? Vince had hired a psychiatrist to look over several descriptions of Blanche by other people and to go through the notes of Dr. Jesse McNiel, the Burlington psychiatrist Blanche had hired when she was compiling evidence for her sexual harassment suit. He came up with a profile of Blanche that depicted her as a combination of "histrionic" and "narcissistic" personality types, meaning she was self-centered, egotistical, and so unable to communicate with other people that she would rather kill them than tell them an unpleasant truth.

Janet waved it all away with a flip of the hand. That kind of stuff wouldn't mean diddly to a North Carolina jury, she said. She thought it would just make them look as if they were reaching.

But that left the question of why Blanche did murder people. Because she was abused as a child and hated men? That was the last thing Janet wanted to tell a jury.

She was sifting through the evidence piled on her desk one day. An out-of-town reporter had dropped in to visit—one of the crew who were making regular swings through Winston-Salem now to keep up with the case. Most of the other people on the prosecution side of the case kept their distance from the press, for fear a leak or some other slip would provide Blanche with the escape route she needed. Janet was always careful what she said to reporters, but she also enjoyed talking to them, and over the long year of preparation she developed close relationships with a few writers. She liked using them as sounding boards for ideas.

"We could say all that stuff to them about her being abused," Janet said to the reporter. "I sit here and I read these notes and this evidence," she said. "And some of it's just so awful. Old James Taylor throwing food at her in front of her children and dragging her down the street with the car in front of all the neighbors.

"She lies so much. Everybody we talk to says Blanche would lie when there was no need to lie. So you don't know if the things she told Dwight about her childhood were true or something she made up."

She got up and walked over to look down on the street. "I grew up here. I know. There's something in the culture. A certain type of man. There are men in North Carolina who just need killing. Women aren't supposed to do anything to defend themselves. Little girls..."

She sat back down. "If we say all that garbage to a jury, we're just handing them a reason to feel sorry for Blanche. We're giving them an excuse to let her off. You know who I keep thinking of? I mean, it's all so tragic. Raymond Reid was a good man who never did anything but love Blanche. But I

think of Reverend Moore. I suppose I think of him because
he's still alive.

"I think of him palsied and living up there in Reidsville on
the charity of his sister. He has lost everything he cares about
in life. And why? Why does such tragedy and meanness have
to take place in the world?

"Everybody has problems. Lots of people. Lots of women
especially. Girls are abused. But it's not an excuse. You just can't
make it an excuse, you can't say, all right, because she was
abused as a child she has the right to torture and murder every
man who ever loved her or wanted to help her. The way these
men died was horrible, horrible, horrible.

"I'll tell you what my own psychological theory is. Blanche
is mean. Blanche is pure through-and-through one hundred
percent grade-A mean. She killed these men because she's
mean, she's greedy, she's a criminal, and she should pay with
her life for what she did. And that's what I am going to tell
that jury. If I ever get the chance. If Mr. Sparrow doesn't
bargain it away because we can't get joinder.

"Oh!" she said, sighing and shaking her head. "I hope we
get to trial with this."

The next day Janet went to Vince's office. She stood in the
door for a while, staring. Vince's office looked like a hurricane
in a library. There were boxes of evidence, books, notes, tapes,
and charts strewn and mounded almost literally from wall to
wall. Janet was suddenly very depressed.

Janet was the lead trial attorney on the case. But Vince
bore the all-important responsibility of writing the briefs. If
Freeman wound up tossing joinder in the trash can, then the
case would rise or fall legally on Vince's ability to get the evidence from the Taylor and Moore cases into the Raymond Reid
murder trial on some other basis.

She watched Vince at his desk, toiling away. He was an
unlikely executioner. Born and raised in Winston-Salem, Vince
had wanted to paint. After finishing undergraduate school in
1975, Vince had gone to New York to study painting and to
become a great artist. One day, while he was working at his
part-time job as a salesman in the Barnes & Noble remainder
store, a typical young hotshot lawyer came in and asked for a
book. When Vince looked up, the young lawyer stared at his

face for a moment and then said, "Vince!"

The lawyer had been his brother's college roommate. The roommate had gone straight to law school after graduation and now had a high-paying job with a big New York firm.

"Vince, what in the hell are you doing here?" the young man said, after Vince had just finished explaining what he was doing there. "New York's got ten thousand guys just like you trying to be artists and working at crappy jobs like this. Go home, man. Go to law school. Get a life!"

Somewhere over Vince Rabil's little corner of the Barnes & Noble remainder store, the leaden gong of unpleasant truth sounded. Not too many months later he headed back to North Carolina with a law school admission letter in his pocket.

Janet had great respect for Vince. A stranger would look into this office at this moment and see a typical lawyer-grunt, grinding his way through mountains of minutiae out of sheer doggedness, with little sense of where he was going or why. But she knew that Vince's real gift was synthesis. He would spend a certain amount of time swimming in this incredible jumble of paper, and then he would step back and see it all in some new, simple, and very valuable way.

He looked up finally and saw her standing there. He raised his eyebrows to ask what she wanted.

"Vince, we have to get the other cases in. If he denies joinder, then we're going to have to bet all our chips on 404B."

Rule of Evidence 404B, originally a provision of the federal court rules of evidence and now also included in the North Carolina rules, provided that prosecutors could bring in evidence from other crimes, even without joinder, but only under certain circumstances.

"How does 404B look to you?" she asked.

"Good. Strong. The identity exception is the best one. If we can find strong patterns of similarity in all these crimes showing a clear idiosyncratic modus operandi, then we can get all the evidence in under the identity rule..."

"Showing ...?"

"The same person did all of them."

"So what do you show the judge?"

Vince gestured around the room with his hand and shrugged. "All this," he said.

Janet shook her head and sighed. "Keep thinking, Vincent," she said, already walking back down the narrow hallway to her own office. "Please keep thinking."

Finally, with the trial date hovering ever closer on the horizon, Vince walked down to Janet's office with three pieces of paper in his hand.

"It's a simple chart," he said. "It will take Freeman five minutes to read it, five more to digest what it means."

Running down the left-hand side of each page was a column of circumstances: "Stated cause of death," "Victim received many small or chronic doses," "Victim restless, unable to sleep at night," "Victim poisoned in hospital," "Victim had diarrhea," "Defendant stated she hated victim or that they were cruel or evil," "Defendant stated victim was just like her father."

There were forty-three circumstances in all.

In three more columns toward the right sides of the pages were three names: J. Taylor, R. Reid, and D. Moore. Beneath each name and across from each circumstance was written "Yes," "No," "N/A" (for not applicable), or "Undetermined."

The sheets were a sea of "yes" notations. Yes, yes, yes. Tied together and reduced to this simple format, the similarities between the cases and between Blanche's behavior in each case were overwhelming and extremely damning.

Janet studied the sheet for a while. Even if Freeman did not give them joinder, and he almost certainly would not, Vince's sheets would give Freeman the comfort level he would need to grant 404B. With this kind of bulletproof argument in favor of 404B, Freeman would be in more danger of reversal if he denied it.

For the first time since she had been assigned the case, Janet was beginning to feel the creeping tingling sensation of possible confidence. Things were definitely falling into place.

The question of motive was still hanging out there, apparently unresolved, but Janet could handle that problem herself in trial. In dealing with a lady like Blanche, she would argue, you don't look for normal motives, rational motives, intelligent or even coherent motives. Blanche's motive, she would argue, was evil. Evil pure and simple.

Chapter Nineteen

W ith Mitch at one side and an agent of the State Bureau of Investigation at the other, Blanche sat in the lawyers' conference room at the Alamance County Jail and wrote out "exemplars" of her writing for three hours, while the agent dictated words, phrases, and sentences she was to write.

When they were finished, the agent said, "Mrs. Moore, you've been very nice. Is there anything you would like to write yourself?"

She squinted her eyes and bit her lips together. Looking up slowly at him, she said, "Yes. This sucks."

Blanche turned back slowly to the desk and carefully wrote from memory several verses from the Bible.

The exemplars were put together with more than forty letters Blanche had written to friends and family from jail and were sent to the SBI's own handwriting experts.

Days went by, then weeks, finally a month passed, and still the SBI was not ready to make its report to the prosecution. Both Janet and Vince called often to check on the findings, until Janet began to feel that perhaps the SBI people thought she was too pushy.

Finally, with the November trial date only a scant few weeks away, the call came from Raleigh that the SBI was ready to make its report. Janet waited on the phone for the report. Her heart sank as she realized the agent who had called her to tell her the analysis was complete was asking her to come to Raleigh for a "presentation."

She didn't have time for a "presentation." The trial was weeks away. The hearing on joinder was days away. The media were all over town. Why couldn't they just say what they had to say on the telephone?

But it was not a good idea to ruffle the feathers of the North Carolina State Bureau of Investigation. It had its way of doing things, and it had a definite taste for ceremony.

Two days later Janet jumped into her BMW and exceeded the speed limit all the way to Raleigh, trying to get there far enough ahead of noon so she could get the results and escape before the dreaded lunch opportunity arrived.

Her heart sank again soon after arriving when she realized they already had planned a mini-tour of the headquarters to be followed by a major outing to a local barbecue restaurant for grilled pork ribs, all before she could get the report she needed from them. She nodded and smiled her way through the tour.

On the way to lunch, the SBI people gushed over the barbecue restaurant where they were taking their guest. In the South, knowledge of a really good barbecue restaurant is tantamount to knowledge of a magnificent universal truth. A person who can lead the way to good barbecue is a person of wisdom and power.

As soon as she entered the restaurant, Janet's sensitive nose picked up the unmistakable whiff of tomato sauce. She could not believe it. There is a line that runs diagonally across North Carolina and into South Carolina that separates the region where barbecue sauce contains only hot pepper and vinegar from the region where sauce also contains tomato. People from the non-tomato region are revolted by barbecue sauce with tomato. Putting a non-tomato barbecue eater down in front of a platter of tomato-sauce barbecue is like feeding an American eight-year-old a living eel.

Janet was a non-tomato person. In addition to everything else, they were going to make her eat a platter of tomato-sauce barbecue. She was very depressed.

She got the food down, for the most part. Finally they brought her back to a small room at SBI headquarters. With a pointer in one hand and blowups of the exemplars and Blanche's letters on an easel, a young gentleman agent went through the details of what the SBI had found.

First there were the abbreviations, which Janet found quite interesting. In the Garvin Thomas letter, "Alamance" was written as "Ala." In Blanche's own letters, she wrote "Alamance" as "Ala." Thomas called "Burlington" "Burl." Blanche called "Burlington" "Burl." Garvin wrote "hosp.," "Bapt.," and "W-S" (for Winston-Salem). Blanche wrote "hosp.," "Bapt.," and "W-S."

Then there was the evidence of Garvin Thomas's own exemplars—samples of his handwriting taken from his home. There was the matter of his not being able to write in cursive at all. He printed all of his letters and notes in large block letters. The confession letter was in cursive handwriting.

"So you can say, no matter what, that Garvin Thomas is not the person who wrote the letter," Janet said.

The agent, a little offended because she was anticipating him, said, "I'll get to that, but, basically, yes, we will be able to say that in testimony."

The agent went on at some length about the work the SBI had farmed out to a linguist, who had studied the phrasing, grammar, and usage in Blanche's letters, the confession letter, and Garvin Thomas's known exemplars. In a lot of fancy terminology, the agent basically told Janet that Garvin Thomas was an eloquent speaker and writer who never used bad grammar, that Blanche used double negatives and bad grammar all the time, and that the author of the confession letter wrote like Blanche.

Janet felt herself cooling to this part of the evidence. She was not eager to give the members of the jury a schoolmarm lecture on why and how double negatives mark a person's social and ethnic heritage.

From there the agent launched into a long, very technical description of the handwriting similarities between Blanche's exemplars and the confession letter. According to the technical measurements handwriting experts use to identify writing, Blanche probably was the author of the confession letter.

"What do you mean, 'probably'?" she asked.

"Eighty percent."

She was silent.

"What's the matter?" he asked.

"I'm sorry. But eighty percent sucks."

He stiffened. "Well, I am very sorry, too," he said. "But that happens to be an extremely high correlation and degree of certainty, given the nonscientific nature of the discipline."

She stared at him without speaking. He stared back.

"Thank you," she said. "I believe I must be going."

"Very well. But, uh, oh yes. There is one other thing."

"What?"

"The confession letter. Here it is. The original." He held up the envelope with the folded letter inside. He held the envelope open with a finger and showed the inside of it to her. "What do you see inside the envelope?"

She stared at the envelope and then at him. "I see the letter inside the envelope," she said. She was beginning to wonder if this was an IQ test.

"No. Not the letter. What do you see on the inside of the envelope?"

She bent forward and looked again. "I see . . . I don't know. I see those squiggly lines they put on the insides of certain envelopes so you can't see there's a check inside."

"Yes. Now." He reached and picked a letter randomly from the middle of a stack of letters Blanche had written from jail to a woman in Dwight's church in Carolina. He held it open with his finger. She peered again.

"I see . . . I see . . . oh, son of a bitch. You are kidding me! You saved this for last?"

The agent smiled back with a wicked glint in his eye.

"The same pattern!" she squealed. "Was she so stupid she actually used the same envelopes? You are kidding me!"

"No, I'm not. You think she said to her brother, 'Bring me in a single envelope from a different store so I can mail a fake confession letter'?"

The answer obviously was no. All of the investigators and the DA's staff had come to realize that Blanche's family believed in her innocence devoutly. She could not have enlisted any of them in a trick. She had used the same envelopes they had brought her for her regular correspondence because she had to use the same envelopes. Or because she was stupid.

Janet sat turning the envelope over again and again in her hands.

"I'm sure the police in Burlington can trace the envelopes," the agent said.

"Hmm?" She looked up. "Oh, I don't think so."

"What do you mean? You don't want to trace them?"

"No, I don't think so. We get into all that, it all has to be shown to Mitch before the trial. He goes out and finds the envelopes somewhere else. No. I think we'll just leave this as it stands."

"But you'll use the envelope."

"Certainly. I love the envelope. I think I'll present it to the jury just the same way you did to me."

"Don't you have to tell the defense about it?"

"Yes," she said. "We have to tell the defense that we have the letters. We have to show all the letters to the defense. We don't have to tell them what we're going to say about the letters. I assume the defense will notice that the letters all came in envelopes."

"But you don't have to tell them what you're going to say..."

"...about the envelopes."

She got up and squeezed his hand. "Thank you so much. The barbecue was delicious."

"Really? I thought you Winston people hated tomato sauce."

She laughed. "I love these envelopes. I truly love them."

The trial was less than two weeks away. The clans began to gather in their camps. In New Jersey, Doug Moore was preparing to leave his career as a chemist to become an investment broker. He explained to the people he would be working for that he would have to wait until after the trial to begin their extensive training program.

In Virginia, Debbie Moore, who had lost a lot of time from work the year before to her father's illness, nevertheless had been promoted by the national automobile rental company for which she worked. She already had told her superiors she would have to be absent during the trial. They were supportive and wished her well.

In Pennsylvania, Dwight's sister Nellie made preparations to be away from her home. In Reidsville, his sister Nola and her husband, Howard Halbrook, worked ahead on various chores and jobs in order to be free.

Dwight spent long hours sitting by himself in the breakfast nook at the end of Nola's kitchen, staring out across the back yard to Howard's bee stand. There was enormous pressure on him from the family to be tough, to go for broke, to help Janet send that woman to her death. Blanche had broken his heart and deprived him of his ministry.

But as he sat and stared out over the back, he struggled with two difficult feelings. In the first place, his personal religious and moral convictions were absolutely opposed to the death penalty. In the second place, he knew that whatever Blanche had done, it all had some connection with what had been done to Blanche.

Steve Reid was beginning a new job. He shopped for a small portable fax machine so that he could stay in touch with his office from his mother's house in Burlington.

With his share of the settlement money from Baptist Hospital, Ray Reid, Jr., had bought his own small Christmas-tree farm in the mountains. For the last six months he had been working hard, all alone for the most part, laboring for long hours every day rehabilitating an old house on the property, clearing land, and planting trees.

He stood in his field one day and gazed out over the incredible beauty of the haze falling down like cream around the gentle peaks of the Appalachians. With a sudden ache he realized that he was going to have to go back down into the city and take part in the trial.

None of it was real. Not here. Here, Ray still half expected to look up at any moment and see his father's car come crunching down the long dirt road from the highway, see him waving and grinning from the open window.

Ray walked back to the house slowly with tears in his eyes and began bringing tools in from the weather, preparing the place for his absence.

In Burlington the Taylor family gathered over coffee and Moravian Christmas cookies—flat, unleavened ginger crackers sold the year round in Winston-Salem. They were solid citizens of Burlington. They suspected the prosecution was going to paint James as a drunk, a gambler, and a wife-beater, in order to provide Blanche with a motive. They also had learned the prosecution would seek no charges in the suspected murder of their mother, Isla Taylor.

There was some doubt whether the arsenic found in Isla Taylor's body had been a provably fatal dose, and the prosecution, still hoping for joinder, was afraid Isla Taylor's death might be too distant from the others. If Blanche was to be painted as a man-hater, then her possible involvement in the murder of Isla Taylor might muddy the picture.

Sitting in a pretty white house on Country Club Lane in Burlington, reflecting on the years of hard work and loyalty that had built their clan, it was hard for the Taylors to see justice in what was about to happen to them.

The Kiser clan was gathering in Burlington. Blanche's brothers, Sam and P.D., were working furiously to run any errand or carry out any task Mitch needed done. Blanche's daughters and former sons-in-law all put away their differences and gathered to give whatever support they could.

Never, in anything they said or in any action, did the Kiser clan ever give any indication they believed Blanche was anything but totally innocent. There was never a visible crack in their ranks.

P.D. Kiser, Blanche's brother, was extremely anxious about the prosecution's clear intent to call him and grill him on the stand about the haircut he had given Dwight in the hospital. He turned it over constantly and repeatedly asked Mitch how Mitch thought he should handle it.

Finally one day, as the two of them were driving to Winston for the joinder hearing, Mitch said, "P.D., I am afraid that if you don't find a way to calm down and put this out of your mind, you are going to have a heart attack. I'm afraid for you."

P.D. shook his head and was silent for the rest of the ride.

At the hearing, Vince and Janet sat at their table with folded hands. Tamer, Loflin, Mitch, and Blanche all sat quietly at their own table. Blanche glanced around at the reporters in the small courtroom, but the lawyers stared up silently at Judge Freeman, who sat high above them at the long raised bench.

Judge Freeman was hunched forward, leafing slowly

through law books. Each time Freeman turned a page, the crackling of the paper resounded through the silent courtroom.

Finally Freeman looked up with an expression of quizzical impatience. He began asking a rapid-fire series of questions about the kind of witnesses Janet and Vince would be able to produce and what the witnesses would say they knew or had seen. Janet tried to dance around the questions, but Freeman held up his hand to show he was not going to brook any kind of evasion or cleverness on the point.

"Miz Branch," he said, "you do not have anybody who can say, 'I saw her put poison in his food.' Is that right? All you have is people who can say, 'I saw her feed him dinner.' Am I right on this point, Miz Branch?"

Tamer, Loflin, Mitch, and Blanche sat at attention, staring at Janet, who was on her feet. Janet started to say something, thought better of it, looked at the defense table, and then looked up at Freeman, who was waiting.

"That's basically it, your honor," she said. She turned back and stared at Vince, who managed to remain perfectly expressionless.

Freeman turned pages again. Finally he looked up.

"The motion for joinder is denied," he said. "I am not going to rule on 404B at this juncture. I will listen to arguments on it as evidence is presented in the trial."

Blanche looked at Mitch. Mitch lifted his eyebrows up high over the heavy frames of his glasses and gave her a barely perceptible nod. She turned back toward Janet and shot her a quick grin.

Freeman adjourned.

It had not been a disastrous day for the prosecution, but it had not been a good day at all. The defense, on the other hand, was buoyant. Mitch and Tamer began handing out interviews before they even got up from their table. Janet and Vince walked to the back of the courtroom and slipped away down a long private corridor where the reporters were not supposed to go.

In Graham, the courthouse rabbits at the long table at Chadwick's gathered over their noon salads and wondered how the Bear was holding up. As the trial drew close, Mitch had withdrawn more and more into his office, arriving early, leaving late. They assumed he was burying himself in work.

Carol DiLello sat in the outer office working through her lunch hour to organize the vast mountain of briefs, motions, and lists of citations Tamer and Loflin had been sending over. A few feet away behind a closed door, Mitch sat by himself in his own office staring at his desk.

They had been preparing Blanche for her testimony. Tamer had been playing the role of DA, peppering her with the questions they assumed Janet Branch would ask.

"Did you feed banana pudding to Raymond Reid? Did you feed banana pudding to Dwight? Did James and Raymond and Dwight all have identical rashes on the trunks of their bodies?"

To each question Blanche had answered with denial. She denied she had fed any of them in the hospital. She denied she knew anything at all about Raymond Reid's will or Dwight's retirement benefits.

"Blanche, the prosecution has testimony in sworn depositions from the nurses at Baptist saying they saw you feed Raymond on many occasions."

"They're wrong. I never fed Raymond nothing."

It was clear, after hours of work with her, that that was how it was going to be. Blanche was designing her own defense. She wasn't going to listen to the lawyers. She believed she knew better than they. She was smarter.

There would be no plea bargain. She would deny the truth of any testimony that incriminated her. When the nurses and the doctors and the members of the other clans began marching through the dock, all pointing their fingers at Blanche and swearing they had seen her feed the victims, Blanche would sit stolidly in her place and deny it all.

She would deny it to her family. She would deny it to the court. It appeared she would deny it to herself.

It did no good for the lawyers to explain that denying all of it would seal her doom. She had to admit some of it. Yes, I fed my dying men, but no, I did them no harm. Then Mitch could say, "Show me the man or woman who saw my client put poison in the food."

But if she simply denied what many honest citizens were prepared to swear was the truth, then she would make an obvious liar of herself. If the Garvin Thomas letter fell the wrong way, if it fell against her, then the jury would see her as a liar, a conniving woman. A witch.

Blanche, for her part, believed she could seduce them all. She had taken James's life. She had held it in her hand and squeezed the light from it. She had rotted James Taylor from the universe. And no one had ever suspected a thing.

She had done it again in the sexual harassment trial. She had seduced her own lawyers, the judge, the Kroger private eyes, the jury, the shrinks. Later, when she was killing Raymond Reid, she had seduced the doctors—diagnosed the disease for them as Guillain-Barre syndrome. And they had believed her. The fools. The fancy educated fools.

She had seduced the nurses—fed them, talked them into lifting all the rules for her, talked them into treating her as if she were a nurse herself. Told the doctors there would be no autopsy. Led the boys around to the banks by their ears and taken the money out of their hands.

She held Dwight's life in her hand and squeezed and squeezed, and he was dying, too. Those stupid doctors kept dragging his bowels out of his belly looking for kinks. She was killing Dwight and getting away with it.

But Dwight, the stubborn mule, the relentless ox—Dwight would not die. Dwight was not human. He was not normal. She had fed him gobs of the stuff, great heaping tablespoons, much more than all of the poison she had used altogether on all the rest, and still he would not die. Dwight had done all of this to her. Dwight. He was the one who had brought her to this.

And so her plan was what it always had been. She would seduce. She would seduce the jury. She would appear before them, and they would see a Christian lady, a God-fearing woman, a kindly grandmother. They would see her beauty. They would love her. And want her. She would have them. She would have them all. She would admit nothing. She would see them all rot, and she would live.

Chapter Twenty

With the sun going down outside his office on Elm Street, Mitch McEntire realized suddenly it was time to go home to his wife and daughter.

A lawyer in Mitch's position had three choices. He could yell and scream and browbeat the client until finally the client did what the lawyer wanted. He could dump the client. Or the third choice. Having done the very best he could, having spent her money on expert counsel instead of paying it all to himself, having offered her a plea bargain at the right moment, having tried to show her what needed to be done, he could fold his hands—and stand by her.

He had tried being smart, and it hadn't worked. Now he could be loyal. He wouldn't look good. He would lose. When he lost, the reporters would blame him, not his client, because he was the lawyer, the one who was supposed to do the winning.

Mitch drove out under the freeway and down the long two-lane blacktop, past the lake and up the steep hill at the light, down the dirt road that led to his front door. Lights were glow-

ing from the den and kitchen of his house. He hoped he would
get some sleep in these last few nights before the trial.

Judge Freeman was all too aware the trial was going to
garner an enormous amount of attention, from both the walk-
in public and the media. For several months before the trial
began, he had been considering how to make sure the case's
notoriety would not become an issue in the trial. He had to
devise a way to allow enough media access so that access would
not become an issue, without allowing the media to get out of
hand so that decorum would become an issue instead.

For this trial he chose the largest courtroom in the Forsyth
County Courthouse—a broad ungainly hangar of a room on
the top floor of the courthouse, patched together from two
smaller courtrooms in a remodeling effort. It was used normally
for major civil trials in which lots of lawyers and evidence were
involved.

The room's finish was not up to the standard of the rest
of the courthouse: inexpensive paneling and a lot of varnished
plywood. The room was already beginning to looked frayed
even though it had been rebuilt fairly recently. A huge square
pillar at the front of the public area blocked the view of the
bench from a good many seats. The pillar was covered with
cheap vinyl wall covering.

The massive raised bench was at the west end of the room.
Windows were at the south side farthest from the public entrance to the room, which was on the north wall almost at the
northeast corner of the room. At the extreme southwest corner,
farthest from the door, was the jury box. It was a long box,
running from the west wall all the way to the railing that divided
the public area from the official deliberative area. A center aisle
and two side aisles divided the large bench area at the back of
the room into four sections.

At Judge Freeman's order, workmen brought a single
eight-by-four-foot sheet of gypsum wallboard into the room
and leaned it against the railing so that it divided the jury box
from the section of public benches on the south wall, creating
a visual barrier between the jury box and the first several rows
of benches in that section.

It was here that Judge Freeman intended the media to sit.
The workmen removed the first three ranks of benches just
behind the wallboard. In this space, television and still photog-

raphers would be allowed to stand and shoot. They would be able to shoot anything they liked of the public area; they would be able to shoot the backs of the prosecution team; they would have a fairly good profile shot of the defense team; and they would have a full-face perspective on the witness box and the bench. But they would not be able to take a single picture of the jury, and the jury would not see them working.

On the first morning of the trial on October 22, 1990, the several clans filed nervously into the room from the public door at the back and hovered nervously about without lighting on any bench. In a few short minutes, without a single word being spoken, they began sitting, having divided themselves perfectly into camps.

The Kiser clan sat in the north section right behind the defense table. No other clan sat in the next section over, which was the section whose view was blocked by the ugly vinyl pillar. In the first section on the far side of the center aisle, the Reids sat, a few rows back from the railing. Right behind the Reids, the Moores sat. Across the next aisle, in the south section just behind the media area, the Taylor family gathered.

The whole process of staking out separate turfs in the room had been instinctual and almost instant. After the lunch break, when people filed back into the room, they found that a helpful court employee had gone about the room sticking little yellow Post-it notes on the ends of the benches codifying the arrangement in penciled words: "Taylor Family Section," "Reid Family," "Kiser Family," and "Moore Family."

When the clans were all gathered together in clusters in the courtroom, the physical similarities among family members were striking. Especially in the Kiser and the Taylor clans, family members all looked alike. Several of the older Kiser women looked as if they were Blanche's twins.

The street wisdom—and indeed a great deal of the expert legal advice being proffered to Janet—was that the prosecution should go for a highbrow jury. Mitch, according to this theory, would look for just plain folks. His own appeal would be folksy, and it was beginning to be clear that the defense strategy would be to woo the jury with Blanche's grandmotherly personality.

The evidence against Blanche, on the other hand, would be circumstantial, technical, and voluminous. Janet's advisers told her she needed a college-educated jury—one that would stick with her expert witnesses and see through Blanche's Bible-smooching act.

Janet said little. When jury selection came, she and Mitch seemed almost to be working together. He did indeed want just plain folks. But so did she.

They wound up with six men and six women of whom only one was a college graduate. Their average age was thirty-eight. Their occupations included shipping clerk, heavy equipment operator, maintenance mechanic, electrician, warehouse worker, mail carrier, and beautician. Nine were white, three black.

Only three subscribed to more than one magazine. Five subscribed to none. Several said they watched between twenty and thirty hours of television a week. Their favorite TV shows were *Matlock, The Cosby Show, Knots Landing, 20/20,* and *60 Minutes.* Ten were parents, seven were churchgoers, of whom six were Baptists. All said they could vote for conviction based on circumstantial evidence, even if the prosecution failed to present a witness who actually saw Blanche poison someone.

The trial was slow and solemn. It opened with mumbled desultory speeches, one by Mitch and one by Warren Sparrow. Speaking so quietly the jury could barely hear him, Mitch meandered through a long, apparently extemporaneous speech about Blanche's superior qualities as a human being. He had planned a better opening statement, but he had run out of time in which to prepare it. In addition, on the first day of trial Mitch was struck by a terrible flu, so serious that he almost asked the judge for a postponement.

He decided the request would look bad, and he pumped himself full of cold medicine and did the best he could. The jury was so cowed by the entire setting and proceeding that they stared everywhere but at Mitch and seemed not to hear a single word he said. So much the better. Mitch seemed to forget his mission at times and almost seemed to be painting Blanche as a loose woman: "She asked me to tell you that her life has not been above sin," he mumbled. "Sin has touched her life, but her life is free of any guilt concerning these crimes."

While Janet and Vince sat meekly at their table, workmen came in and installed a large church-style podium directly in front of the jury, a few inches from the forward row of jurors.

When the podium was in place, Warren Sparrow stepped up to it, arranged the sheaves of a prepared speech before him, and then launched into a long florid diatribe.

"This trial is about secrecy," he said. "It's about pride—good and evil. It's about a woman who took on the power of deciding who shall live and who shall die."

But Sparrow was distracted, lost his place often, and never sustained a mood. He had a lot on his mind that day.

Things were not going well for Warren Sparrow in the world beyond the courtroom. In midsummer he had still believed he might run for reelection against only token opposition. But by fall, North Carolina had become politically inflamed by the Harvey Gantt/Jesse Helms senatorial race.

The national pundits and the network news shows were talking about the possibility that Helms could be upset by a man who would then become the first black senator from the South since Reconstruction. But right-wing Republicans in North Carolina were talking about a Jesse Helms cakewalk with coattails.

A credible well-financed conservative Republican lawyer in Winston-Salem, Thomas Keith, had emerged to oppose Sparrow. Keith had opened his campaign by ridiculing Sparrow for failing to win a conviction of Michael Hayes, the psycho who had killed four people and wounded five others in a shoot-out in 1988. In recent weeks, Keith had been slamming Sparrow for using the Blanche Moore trial as a campaign vehicle. Warren Sparrow's strategy for proving Keith wrong was to suspend practically all campaigning.

The weekend before the trial began, Keith's campaign put its television ads up for the first time. They were gut-punch slam-bangers. Thomas Keith snarled at the camera, "I have no intention of being fair to a bunch of hardened criminals."

On the day the trial opened, Warren Sparrow's political friends called him and told him to worry about the election, which would fall exactly midway in the trial as things were scheduled. Sparrow could not believe it. All of a sudden he was in danger of getting thrown out of his job in the middle of the Blanche Moore trial. He was beside himself.

During the recess after his fumbling speech, Sparrow caught Justin Catanoso in a back corridor behind the courtroom. "Listen, Justin," he said, tugging him by the elbow. "I don't care what you write about me. Just vote for me, will you?"

Catanoso laughed. He looked at Sparrow more closely. He wasn't sure Sparrow was joking.

Finally it began.

The Taylors testified that Blanche had called Raymond Reid to the house the day James died. The Reid brothers testified about the money Blanche had taken from them. Some of the jury listened closely. Two jurors dozed.

Blanche watched with slitted eyes, working her mouth, tilting her head backward and staring down her nose through the large square frames of her glasses.

Janet walked to the rail in front of the jury box and smiled at the jurors—her way of waking them up. Then she asked Ray Reid to describe his father's final hours.

"He was writhing and wriggling in his bed," Ray said. He paused and swallowed to regain his composure, but tears had leaped to his eyes. "They had to tie him to his bed. His eyes..."

He stopped speaking.

She waited.

The jurors looked away from him, embarrassed, but they were riveted by every word he uttered.

"I had never seen anything like this before," he said. He paused again. "The actual lenses of his eyes looked blistered."

A juror coughed nervously.

Again, when Linda Reid Sykes took the stand, Janet made a sweep by the jury box to wake them up. She asked Linda to walk back through what she had seen of her ex-husband's final agony.

"It's the most horrible thing I have ever seen in my life," Linda said through tears. "He was huge. His eyes were sunken in his head. His head was huge. He had tubes in him."

The testimony of death scenes and suffering was compelling for the jury. But Janet and Mitch had been forced to schedule witnesses as the witnesses were available. Already in the first few days of the trial, the family-member witnesses were getting mixed in between the medical experts. The lady from the little chemical company that manufactured the ant poison and the nurses and all manner of police witnesses melted together in a long, muddy river of detail.

Each team presented its version of the Garvin Thomas letter. Each team produced a handwriting expert to argue its own version of the facts—one for the prosecution to say that Blanche had written the letter and one for the defense to say she had not.

Janet and Vince marched their expert through all of the technical points of his case carefully to make certain the defense expert would not steal a march on them anywhere. But it was clear, by the second day of the handwriting testimony, that the eyes of almost all of the jurors had glazed over and that every-thing the experts were saying was falling on the jurors' ears as unintelligible babble.

Janet waited until the jurors all looked hunched and frozen before she sprang her surprise. At that point she compared the envelope in which the Garvin Thomas letter had been received and the envelopes in which Blanche had sent all of her own mail in the same period. Obviously the envelopes had come from the same lot of the same line from the same manufacturer.

The jurors straightened up; their eyes lighted up; they passed the envelopes carefully down through the jury box, each juror holding the envelopes for a while and staring. When Janet had finished, the defense team raised a few muddled objections and tried to suggest that such envelopes were common and could be bought anywhere—which was probably true.

But the jurors sat staring out from the box at Blanche.

The pornographic passage at the end of the letter was not read aloud but was handed out to the jury on photocopied sheets. At one point, huge blowups of the letter were arranged on easels in front of the jury.

Judge Freeman sent the jury from the room for a lunch recess and was about to leave himself when someone asked if it would be all right for the crowd of observers in the public benches to come forward during the break and examine the blowups.

Freeman shrugged and said he saw no harm in it. The moment he had disappeared through the back door, a hundred people crowded through the two little swinging gates separating the public area from the trial area and pushed in around the easels as if viewing old masters.

The crowd was quiet and intent. As soon as their eyes found the obscene passage, there rose a clucking and whistling sound.

Then the crowd filed out into the large lobby outside the court-room and erupted into a spirited roar of the kind one might hear during the intermission of a very good play.

After the break, it was Dwight's turn on the stand. At one point during his testimony, Janet asked Dwight what he would do with the rest of his life. He looked out into the courtroom and saw his sister Nola watching him. Dwight cleared his throat and said that he would be dependent on Nola for the foresee-able future.

Janet rushed from the room, on the verge of losing her composure. Immediately, the jury was hustled out and a recess was called. It seemed Janet had allowed tears to come to her eyes during Dwight's testimony.

The next day, in the absence of the jury, Mitch and Tamer and Loflin all rose and made long speeches in which they de-manded a mistrial, on the grounds that Janet's tears constituted an improper and prejudicing statement to the jury.

Freeman was obviously unimpressed. While Loflin cited long lists of cases in which mistrials had been declared for things other than crying, Freeman got up out of his chair and paced back and forth behind the bench, wincing and straightening his back. Finally, when the lawyers were finished talking, Free-man sat and examined the stack of precedents they had handed up to him.

After almost ten minutes of silence, Freeman looked up from the stack. "I daresay, in all of your research, which I'm sure you thoroughly did last night, that you cannot cite me one case in this state, or before the Supreme Court of the United States, in which crying by a prosecutor was grounds for a mistrial."

Loflin sprang to his feet. "Judge, we have not been able to find a case recorded where the facts were that a prosecuting attorney engaged in the conduct we saw here yesterday. I've been in the courtroom twenty years, and I have never seen or heard of a case in which a prosecuting attorney engaged in that. I think this is a new fact situation, quite frankly."

Freeman's voice rose. "You've never seen a prosecutor cry in a courtroom before?"

"No, your honor, I have not."

The judge shrugged. "You must not have been in the same courtrooms I've been. I have seen numbers of prosecutors cry,

I have seen a number of defense lawyers cry. One of the finest district attorneys in this state is a man I have seen cry on a number of occasions. There's never been a mistrial out of it."

He denied their motion.

That evening in an off-the-record exchange with a reporter, Janet allowed herself to gloat over how bad the defense had looked during Freeman's speech on human frailty and her loss of composure. "But you know," she said, "that's exactly how judges have ruled in the other cases I have cried in."

Janet Branch, as it turned out, knew her mistrials backward and forward. For a long time, until Sparrow made her get rid of it, the vanity plate on her BMW read, MISTRIAL.

Unfortunately, none of the drama of her tears had reached the jury, who had been sent out by the judge the moment the first tear appeared. Polled on the issue after the trial, the jurors all reported they thought she had lost a contact lens.

Barely three weeks into the trial, on the night of November 6, Warren Sparrow was struck down politically. Tom Keith beat him in the general election. The people of Forsyth County had rejected Sparrow's bid for reelection by a substantial margin, and local courthouse watchers were taking it as comment on how the Moore trial was progressing so far.

Sparrow appeared briefly in court the next day looking cowed and confused. Vince Rabil was solicitous of him, trying to make a show of conferring with him on important points at the table. Janet's demeanor was just the opposite: she strained visibly to stay away from him, as if she were afraid a photographer might catch the two of them together in the same frame.

None of it registered on Sparrow anyway. He was shocked by his defeat. He paid little attention to what was going on, and then after a while he left, smiling wanly at the clans on the prosecution side of the room.

Blanche turned to watch him depart. A faint snicker rippled at the corner of her mouth.

The next phase of the trial was Janet's introduction of the nurses' testimony. They were composed and purposeful.

"Did you see Raymond Reid on October 1, 1986, after he had been moved to the intermediate care room?"

"Yes, I did," said Nurse Wanda Brendle Moss.

"Was Mrs. Moore feeding him?"

"Yes, she was."

"And what was she feeding him?"

"She was feeding him banana pudding."

"How did Raymond Reid appear to be doing?"

"He was doing real well, and he looked just great." Nurse Moss faltered, then said: "I was so proud of him."

"Did Blanche Moore offer you some banana pudding?"

Nurse Moss said Blanche had offered her pudding in a separate container, and she had accepted it.

Later in the day, Janet introduced medical records to show Raymond had experienced violent projectile vomiting the day after Blanche had fed him the pudding, that three days later he was returned to the intensive care unit suffering from kidney and respiratory failure, severe swelling, and sweating, and that a week later he was dead.

Nurse Hutchens described how Blanche would take over the complete feeding of Raymond every time he came off the ventilator. She described Blanche's grocery sacks filled with peanut butter milk shakes, corn bread and milk, iced tea, frozen yogurt, creamed soups, and the ever-present banana pudding.

"She never left anything behind," Nurse Hutchens said. "Once when she brought a large container of iced tea, I asked her if she'd like to leave it here so we could give him some later. She said no."

Karla Ruth described the way Blanche had talked her into copying the will. She also described how Blanche had talked the boys out of an autopsy for their father.

The jury listened closely. The nurses testified in outwardly flat, unemotional tones for the most part, as if mimicking the doctors and the experts, but the jurors were awake to something living in their words and voices.

The jury listened to the nurses with the same intent focus with which they had listened to the family members and to Dwight. The jury knew these were not experts: these were people whose own relationships with Blanche had been personal and were now quite painful.

Janet asked each nurse: "Did you trust Mrs. Moore?"

Each one lost composure for a split second at the question and then finally said haltingly: "Yes, I did."

Blanche watched with her head cocked back, working her thin lips and squinting, never showing emotion or response to what was being said.

They all knew that afternoon that Blanche's own testimony was near. The prosecution had completed its case. Mitch had almost no witnesses to present except Blanche, and Blanche would want to go first.

The prosecution team strategized during a long afternoon recess. Based on the psychological profiles he had worked up on Blanche, Vince was convinced that Blanche could be cracked wide open on the stand. Her outward personality was a construct that she maintained with difficulty. She lied all the time about little things because she thought she had to hide everything about herself. She could not afford to confront even small truths about herself. Therefore, if Janet could find a fissure or a crevice somewhere and simply pull and pull Blanche might lose her composure, her entire sense of self. Her contrived public persona would crumble, those eyes would flare, and the witch within would come screaming out.

Sparrow, who had been lost in the depths of his own depression all day, was becoming more enthusiastic about the prospects. It was clear, he said, that Blanche especially disliked Janet. In so many strange ways, they shared things in common. Each had a tendency to be dramatic, even histrionic at times. Both were very conscious of their appearance and their effect on men. Blanche hated Janet possibly because she sensed those similarities and felt competitive with her.

But there were more pressures on Janet. The Taylor clan was still bitter that no charges had been brought in the murder of Isla Taylor. In the lobby outside the courtroom, they buttonholed Janet and hissed in her ear that they hoped she would rip Blanche limb from bloody limb.

The Reid boys were beside themselves. They told Sparrow they were uncertain how their own testimony had affected the jury. They thought all the scientific stuff had gone right over the jury's head. Janet, they said, was going way too soft on Mitch, Loflin, and Tamer. They too hoped to see blood when Blanche took the stand. Sparrow passed all of this on to Janet as further proof of what needed to be done the next day.

What the world wanted to see was a biting and hair-pulling bitch fight.

That evening the television newscasts reported that Blanche Moore probably would take the stand the following morning. When the regular crowd of eighty or so showed up the next morning—the clans and the witnesses, the police and the press—the lobby outside the courtroom was already packed with two hundred onlookers, and more people were flooding through the front door of the courthouse every minute. Lawyers, secretaries, retirees from all of the surrounding counties, many of the people Blanche had worked with at Kroger, former neighbors in Burlington, women wrapped in mink, high school kids in black clothes and earrings playing hooky from school—the Romans were gathering at the Colosseum.

When the bailiff opened the door and the crowd pushed in, it was standing room only in the back. With difficulty, the families found their way to their accustomed seating areas.

Judge Freeman came in and pretended not to notice at first that the room was jammed to the rafters. He studied law books for several minutes. When he did finally look up, he said, "I want all of you in this courtroom today to be very, very quiet. I don't want any talking. I don't even want you to cough if you can help it."

Blanche took the stand wearing a black suit, black hose, and black pumps. A long white strand of pearls lay around her neck. Her stylish, medium-length salt-and-pepper hair was arranged perfectly.

Blanche delivered an hour-long monologue on her life, her strict Christian upbringing, and her enduring religious values, digressing here and there to provide illustrative examples of her own good works and generosity through the years. In every moment of her speech, the slitted eyes behind the large square frames of her glasses flickered back and forth across the public audience at the back of the courtroom.

She arrived at the James Taylor years: "I was always happy with James. I loved him very much. I did not like his gambling, but I loved him. I was very happy with him. We did everything together."

The clans on the prosecution side rustled in their seats and exchanged glances. There was something eerie in her voice. It was a perfectly normal voice. But it was not Blanche's real voice. It was not even Blanche's accent. The trilling bird voice and the impatient pestering intelligence were gone. Blanche spoke with a country accent much deeper than her own, in the bitten-off syllables and the lurching cadence of the mountains and the ancient folk. She was everybody's kind old country aunt.

She told a very strange story of James Taylor's last evening. She said a preacher, whose name she had difficulty remembering, had visited James at home that evening and had brought with him "a Dr Pepper bottle with water in it and holes punched in the top.

"He called it Dr Pepper holy water," she said. "He kind of sprinkled some of it on James, and James reached up and grabbed it and said, 'Here, if it's so good why don't I just drink it,' and he flipped off the cap like that and drank it down.'"

She told of finding James's body that terrible morning. "I was devastated. I was shocked. I thought James was getting better. Then I go to his bed and find him dead. I was shocked. I called the rescue squad. It was instinct. I did what I had to do. And then . . ."

She daubed at her eyes with a handkerchief as if crying. James's elderly sister Jessie, who was seated in the center of the Taylor clan area, turned to look at the other Taylor family members. Over the edge of the handkerchief, Blanche caught that slight movement instantly. She stopped speaking, dropped the hanky, and stared dry-eyed at Jessie Taylor.

"Ma'am?" Blanche said to her across the crowded room.

The courtroom was dead silent. Even Judge Freeman seemed frozen.

Blanche turned to the judge. "There is someone there trying to say something to me," she said.

Freeman stared back at Blanche with his lips locked.

"Should I answer her?" Blanche asked.

Finally, shaking his head as if waking from a dream, the judge said, "No! No. Just go on with your testimony."

Blanche launched into a long exegesis of her sexual harassment suit, what really had happened and why, all of the ways in which she had been abused by Denton. She then gave the jurors a densely detailed description of the fires she had suffered in her homes.

Half the day was gone, and the eyes of the jurors were beginning to droop.

She came to Raymond, and the jurors stirred themselves visibly, one even stretching his arms and shaking off a delicious yawn. They listened closely while she told of her love for him.

"We would've been married if he hadn't died. Raymond and I were very, very much in love, very much in love. We could not have been more dedicated to each other if we had been married. The piece of paper would not have made that much difference."

Then, before getting to the Dwight years, Blanche launched off in a new direction. While Mitch and Tamer sat glumly at the defense table, Blanche set out her own un-prompted refutation of the principal evidence against her.

It was not true. None of it. They were all mistaken. Or they were all liars.

In a voice that had now grown pompous, she said, "There has been some talk about banana pudding."

She surveyed the jurors, who stared straight back at her in candid anticipation of the words to follow.

"No, I did not bring him banana pudding. And I never made peanut butter milk shakes."

The room was as quiet as if it had been completely empty. In a back row of the courtroom, Nurse Hutchens was watching and listening intently.

"I know it's been announced in here," Blanche went on, "that I was pessimistic about Raymond's condition and that he wouldn't make it. But that's not true. I always thought he would make it, because he was a fighter.

"I do not recall anyone speaking to me about an autopsy. I would not have been opposed to an autopsy. If I knew what I know now, I would have definitely wanted an autopsy."

She had talked for the better part of two days. Mitch got up on his feet to close.

"You are aware, Mrs. Moore, that there has been a great deal of testimony in this trial to show that several of these people you are accused of murdering had elevated levels of arsenic in their bodies?"

"I know arsenic was found in these people," she said. "But I know I didn't do it. I did not put it there."

"The defense rests, your honor."

Lisa Sue Hutchens drew in a sharp breath of astonishment. "No!" she thought to herself. "That's it? That's all?"

Mitch turned the witness over to Janet. Feet shuffled, and there was an audible sucking in of breath in the room as Janet rose and approached her. Everyone in the room smelled blood.

Janet was quiet, calm, gentle with her. She reminded Blanche of the testimony of the nurses, who had said under oath that they had seen Blanche feed Raymond on several occasions.

Whenever Janet referred to the record and asked Blanche if she remembered the testimony she had cited, Blanche would say, "Well, if you say it's there. If you say so."

Janet worked her way patiently through the evidence, forcing Blanche to acknowledge each of the glaring discrepancies between her own testimony and the record of the witnesses. After an hour, Blanche was chewing her thin lips and moving irritably around in her chair. The eyes behind the glasses winced involuntarily every minute or so.

The clans were on the edges of their seats. Vince and Sparrow, Mitch, Tamer, and Loflin, all of the many police officers in the room, the silent crowd of onlookers, the press: everyone sensed at once that this was the moment when the two women would explode at each other. Downstairs in the television pool room, the reporters were silent, each with a finger on the controls of his own tape machine.

Janet walked a circuit around the room, from Blanche, past the jury, back to Blanche. Speaking very quietly and gently, Janet said: "A great many people have come in here and not told the truth. Is that what you're saying, Mrs. Moore?"

The eyes of the jurors clicked back to Blanche.

"A great many people," Blanche said, "have come in here and said what they recall as the truth. But not as I saw it."

Janet turned, started to walk back to the prosecution table, stopped, turned again, and faced the judge.

"Your honor, the state rests," she said.

An explosive grunt of shock erupted from the room. Sparrow and Vince started to jump up but, eyeing the jury, sat again quickly. A broad smile broke across Mitch's face. Blanche saw it from the stand and smiled back demurely at him. The judge hammered for silence, but the door had flown open and reporters were racing for telephones. There was chaos in the lobby.

That afternoon the phone wires burned all over North Carolina. Many of the police investigators who had helped build the case were furious. "That was her one chance to draw some blood on Blanche," a detective fumed, "and she just didn't have the guts for it! I halfway wonder if Janet rested the case because it was time for her aerobics class."

Janet kept her own counsel. That evening she and Sparrow and Rabil did some planning for the next day's closing arguments, and then they all went home. Very early the next morning before court began, Janet called a writer friend who had become a frequent sounding board and poured her heart out over the telephone.

"I know they're mad. Forsyth County especially. Those guys don't realize that this is not about punishing Blanche. Screw that. That comes later. And it is not my job or their job or anybody's job to achieve the vengeance of the families for them. I tried to explain that to the Reid boys in the corridor yesterday. That is not what this is about. It's about winning.

"Our job is to win. We go in there and we do what we do and we do the very best we can do, and the way we know we have done it right is if we win. I'm the DA. That's all. I'm not the judge or the jury. I'm the DA, and my job is to beat the pants off Mitch. I have done it.

"Listen. The woman has hung herself. She has denied every ounce of testimony that has gone against her. She's so stupid. She thinks she can hoo-doo that jury.

"She can't. She cannot. Those are smart people. I don't give a damn if they went to college or not. Those are my people. I grew up with those people. And Blanche grew up with those people. And that's what this is all about. That's what it's from. That's what made it happen. That is what is going to bring it to an end.

"I know a lot of the scientific testimony went over their heads. But we had to have it in. And let me tell you something. Not one ounce of Blanche has gotten by them. I have been watching them. They know exactly what she is.

"The woman has hung herself. The jurors believed every word those nurses told them. They believed every word the families told them. They were waiting for Blanche to pull a rabbit out of a hat. Instead she sat up there and lied in their faces.

"Blanche is dead right now. She is executed. Dead.

"I have as much anger against that woman as any human being on earth. It would have been very satisfying to me to go in and rip her guts out for everybody and have the Reid boys come kiss me after and so on.

"But she was already dead. If I got into some big emotional

battle with her, the outcome of that battle in the jury's eyes would have been totally unpredictable. If I kept on fighting her one minute after I had already won, I would have given her a chance, however slight, to pull it out. I just wasn't going to do that. I had it won.

"Maybe they would have felt sorry for her if I beat up on her. Who knows? They love me right now. Believe me. I've got them eating out of my hand. If I had lit into Blanche, maybe they would have decided *I* was the bitch."

There were two elements in Mitch's closing argument that morning: the letter, and Blanche's reputation as a caring person and devout Christian.

"If you believe that Blanche Taylor Moore didn't write the letter and that Garvin Thomas did," he told the jury, "it's not a stretch to say that this misbegotten man, who has spent time in jail, did this.

"It may sound farfetched, but it's not as farfetched as saying Blanche Moore, with her life of goodness and decency, is responsible for these crimes."

He quoted verses from the Bible about the importance of having a good name in the community. His speech was a slow-moving, shambling, plaintive effort. The jurors looked bored.

Janet took the floor confidently, smiling hello to the jury.

"Ladies and gentlemen, Mr. McEntire began his argument to you with a theme, and that theme was from the Bible, and I believe the verse went something like 'A good name is rather to be chosen than great riches.'"

She looked down at her feet. "Well, I have a theme for you, too, and my theme is something that Abraham Lincoln said."

She looked up at them. "He said this: 'It is true that you may fool all of the people some of the time. You can even fool some of the people all of the time, but you can't fool all of the people all of the time.'

"That is the theme of my argument, ladies and gentlemen.

"There are three men in Blanche Taylor's life. James Taylor. Raymond Reid. And Dwight Moore. Three men, all of them in love with her, all of them intimate with her, all of them dependent upon her for care, for companionship, all of them loyal to her, all of them trusting in her, all of them fed by her and all of them dependent upon her for their care when they were sick, all of them sick, two of them dead, all of them full of the same substance, all of them fed by her in her presence each and every time they became sick, all of them her victims, all of them full of arsenic."

She whirled on her feet, marched over to the defense table, put her hands on the table, leaned into Blanche's face, and said, "Blanche Taylor, this is your life."

Blanche's nostrils flared, and the eyes widened and blackened.

Janet went back to the jury box.

"Coincidence?" she asked. "What a great coincidence. Conspiracy? A conspiracy to convict her of a great coincidence. It would be the world's greatest coincidence topped off by the world's greatest conspiracy."

She turned and lectured Blanche.

"Fifty-three witnesses. All in harmony. Spread out over seventeen years. Spread out over four or five different counties, spread out from California, from Grand Rapids, Michigan, from Toledo, Ohio, from New Jersey, from Pennsylvania, all in harmony, the world's greatest conspiracy on top of the world's greatest coincidence.

"Ladies and gentlemen, the circumstantial evidence in this case is so strong that it is as though each little fact has taken on a life of its own and become a spirit, a living spirit in this courtroom surrounding us all, all of those spirits turning to this defendant..." She slowly raised a finger and pointed at Blanche. "...saying, 'It's you. It's you who's guilty.'"

With the finger still pointing in Blanche's face, Janet walked slowly toward her.

"And out of this throng of spirits steps the ghost of Raymond Reid. He comes to the defendant. And he calls her name.

"'Blanche. Blanche. Blanche. You murdered me, Blanche. All I ever did was love you. Why did you take my life?'"

Chapter Twenty-one

The jury withdrew in early afternoon. They spent five and a half hours shut in the room. They talked and talked, each of them taking a turn at summarizing what he or she thought had happened in the trial. At one point they remembered that Janet had told them to ask for the Garvin Thomas letter, so they did. When they realized they had failed to take even a single vote, it was already the dinner hour. There were families at home waiting and television shows to be watched. They sent out word that they had no verdict, and the judge sent them home, to resume deliberations in the morning.

That night David McDougall sat at a desk at SBI headquarters in Raleigh, working late on a new case. He got up and walked to the window. He tried to think if there was something else he could have done, something he had overlooked in the Moore case. Blanche was a litigious lady. He wondered whom she would sue first if she got off.

Ray and Stevie Reid gathered with their mother at her house to watch the news. The reporters from the room downstairs were on all of the stations speculating that Warren Sparrow and his team had blown another big one.

Mitch and his wife sat in the den of their home on the hill above Graham, staring at each other in silence.

"I have no idea," Mitch said, rising to get another beer. "I have no idea what they're going to do."

Justin Catanoso went to bed early, feeling ill. His wife shook him awake in the middle of the night. He was rolling in the bed, groaning and pouring sweat.

Blanche's brother came to the jail for a visit with her, bringing his guitar. He sat down across the glass-partitioned table from her. They had almost finished getting the songs ready, and he was eager to start on the business of looking for a record deal. Each picked up a phone, and they began to sing to each other, watching each other's eyes through the glass, nodding and smiling through the jagged Appalachian harmonies.

On the morning of November 14, the verdict came in. After brief deliberations and a single vote of the jury, Blanche Moore was convicted of capital murder in the death of Raymond Reid. She took the news placidly, staring at the jury while the verdict was read, barely working her mouth. She left the courtroom slowly, helped by Mitch, who took her elbow in his arm.

Under North Carolina law, the jury had to name a punishment for Blanche in a separate proceeding. It was during the proceedings of the next two days that Blanche's carefully maintained public posture began to come apart. During the breaks she spent her time in the small defense room across the corridor from the courtroom, sobbing uncontrollably. She barely managed to compose herself in time to return to the courtroom. Each time she left and came back, she was more disheveled.

At eleven-thirty on the morning of the second day of the punishment deliberations, the jury was sent to the jury room to decide whether Blanche Taylor Moore should live or die. At four-nineteen in the afternoon, the bailiffs waiting on the other side of the jury-room door heard a knock and opened the door. Jury foreman Patricia Graham was standing there. She said quietly that the jury had come to a verdict.

The bailiffs brought Blanche out to the defense table at four twenty-four. Her hair, so perfect during the long weeks of the trial, was ratty, greasy, hanging in coils, and her face was smudged. She wore a teal-blue suit. Beneath the smears of makeup her skin was ashen.

Judge Freeman looked at the jury for a long odd moment without speaking. "Madam Foreman," he said at last, "have the members of the jury reached a verdict?"

"We have," she said. She handed a sheet of paper to the bailiff, who carried it to the judge. He put the paper down in front of him on the bench and read it carefully. He lifted his face to the room somberly.

"Before I pronounce this verdict," he said, "I want to urge everyone here in this room to keep your emotions in check and to respect the dignity of this court and this place.

"This has been a long and difficult ordeal for everybody. I know you all appreciate the fine representation both sides in this matter have received from the several attorneys who were involved in this case, and I know you appreciate the hard work done, too, by the jurors.

"I will remind the press that there will be no interviews conducted anywhere on this floor of the building following the adjournment of this court."

Then Judge Freeman began to read from the sheet. The jurors had been asked to answer a set of complex questions, some questions designed to determine whether there had been mitigating factors, which would tend to prohibit a penalty of death, other questions designed to find if there had been aggravating factors, which would tend to invoke the death penalty. There could be both. If the mitigating factors outweighed the aggravating factors, she would live. If the aggravating factors were preponderant, she would die. In the end, it was up to the jury to decide which weighed more heavily—the mitigating or the aggravating factors.

One by one, Judge Freeman read the jury's responses to the questions about mitigating factors. The jury had answered yes to three of them. The jury agreed Blanche had no prior criminal record; she was a devoted mother and churchgoer; she had not resisted arrest. Three mitigating factors.

Judge Freeman then turned to the note that held the jury's responses to questions about aggravating factors.

Had Blanche Moore murdered Raymond Reid for profit?

"Yes."

Had Raymond Reid's death been especially painful, his murder especially cruel and heinous?

"Yes."

Blanche closed her eyes and bit her lip. Tears were streaming down her face. On the other side of the rail behind her, her sisters, daughters, brothers, grandchildren, aunts, uncles, cousins, and nephews all sat on the edges of their seats.

Had the mitigating factors outweighed the aggravating factors?

Across the center aisle, the Moores and Reids were sitting together in the same rows. Steve and Ray sat with their mother. Doug and Deborah sat with their father. On the other side of the next aisle, behind the press section, the Taylor family had gathered in force. The Taylors watched with flint-eyed intensity.

"No."

Judge Freeman lifted his face from the sheet of paper and looked Blanche square in the face. He spoke clearly, with absolute authority, with no emotion whatever.

"Blanche Kiser Taylor Moore, you will be put to death as provided by law."

A gasp ran through the back of the room.

"Oh no!" a woman shouted from the Kiser section of the room.

"Oh God!" a man shouted.

Blanche dropped her face and began shaking her head.

Judge Freeman waited. When the room was quiet again, he said, "May God have mercy on your soul."

Epilogue

After two months in prison, Blanche reported to her family that she was getting regular exercise and much better food than she had received in the Alamance County Jail. She said she felt better than she had in months. But a short time later, when Mitch McEntire asked her if she would give an interview to Justin Catanoso, she plunged into a depression and refused to see Catanoso or anyone else.

Her brothers continued to work in her behalf. Sam Kiser announced he was ready to record the songs he and she had composed about her plight and would soon be approaching record companies. All proceeds would be devoted to her appeal.

The appeal was handled by Tamer. He wanted to argue that Judge Freeman had been improperly chummy with the jury, engaging in prejudicial sidebar chats with jurors, but the appeals court refused to hear those arguments. At present Blanche is still involved in technical appeals. She is given little chance of success by most observers.

Mitchell McEntire, who had almost totally suspended his

normal law practice during the year of the trial, came back to
Chadwick's and suggested in a friendly way, in the best tradition
and manner of the noon salad bar, that he would be available
and more than happy to represent ordinary people with ordinary legal problems again. He was soon busy.

Bill Hamilton, Frank Hallstrom, and Grover McCain never
sought or gained any publicity for their role in the Blanche
Moore case, even though they certainly had more to do with
building the evidence against her than anyone else. They were
content to log their fees in the Raymond Reid civil suit and
move on to fresh challenges.

Warren Sparrow went into private practice as a bankruptcy
attorney. A severe downturn in the national and regional econ-
omies, especially in real estate, provided him with a flood of
business, and he was soon taking only major clients and referring smaller fish to other lawyers.

In the months after her spectacular courtroom victory, Janet Branch became a public pariah. The old courthouse crowd
resented the idea that a young woman labor lawyer had won
so much attention for herself. There was even sharp jealousy
of her within the district attorney's staff.

When she and her husband began to have marital problems, the local press jumped on it with both feet, reporting the
breakup of her marriage gleefully and on the front page, as if
it were a major crime story. She left the DA's staff, fell in love
with a new man, had a baby, and established what quickly became a successful private practice.

The new prosecutor, Thomas Keith, made Vince Rabil his
chief deputy assistant.

In all, five people had been exhumed. Two of them, Raymond Reid and James Taylor, were found to have died of
arsenic poisoning. Blanche's mother-in-law, Isla Taylor, was
found to have had elevated arsenic levels at the time of her
death. She was old enough and weakened enough by other
ailments that Dr. Butts was uncertain it could ever be proved
the arsenic had killed her. A large dose was found undigested
in her stomach, suggesting she had been given arsenic moments
before she died.

After the trial, Ray Reid went back up to the mountains to
work his Christmas-tree farm. He walked the farm and found
that almost all of the ten thousand trees he had planted that

summer appeared to be dead or dying. In panic, he called a fellow Christmas-tree farmer. The more experienced farmer told him everything would be all right in the spring.

The next spring, Ray Reid's trees burst into bud. Fewer than a hundred had died—far fewer than the normal 10 percent loss rate for new trees. He walked alone among his trees and allowed the green scent of life to fill his lungs again.

Stevie married. He moved to Maryland, went into the restaurant supply business, and built a new house.

Linda Reid returned to her job and her life.

The *Greensboro News & Record* closed Justin Catanoso's bureau in Winston-Salem as a cost-cutting measure and called him back to Greensboro to take the medical beat.

Deborah Moore, who had broken up with her fiancé in the year between her father's illness and the trial, met a new man and married him soon after the trial ended. They have since had a baby.

Doug Moore and his wife had a second baby boy.

The Taylor clan felt the system had ignored what they firmly believed was the murder of Isla Taylor. Because they lived in Burlington and because some of their blood was in the children and the grandchildren on the Kiser side, the case continued to be a source of pain and emotion for them.

Blanche's father, the old preacher, whose body had come up in bones and rotted flesh like a monster in a horror movie, was found to have had elevated levels of arsenic in his body. Before the trial, the prosecution had toyed with charging Blanche in his death. The proof would have been difficult. Trying too hard to get it in might have clouded the all-important argument for Rule of Evidence 404B. And bringing P.D. into the trial might also have ushered in stories of Blanche's childhood, which might have caused the jury to feel pity for her. So the question of the old preacher's murder was returned to the ground with his body.

Blanche was charged but not tried in the death of James Taylor and in the attempted murder of Dwight Moore. The new Forsyth County district attorney said after taking office that he did not think he could afford to put on expensive trials in those cases in order to win additional verdicts against a woman who already had been sentenced to death.

Dwight Moore took occasional trips—to attend his daughter's wedding, to see his new grandson, to visit his brother in Titusville, Florida, to see his sister in Pennsylvania. He often went up to the old tobacco farm to visit his father, who remained hale.

But for months Dwight spent most of his time sitting quietly with his books in Howard and Nola Halbrook's house in Reidsville. While Nola tended to her housework and Howard worked outside on small carpentry projects and tended his bees, Dwight voraciously consumed the works of modern theologians and ethicists. He was especially taken by the books of the French writer Jacques Ellul, author of *The Ethics of Freedom, Judgment of Jonah, Meaning of the City, Betrayal of the West,* and other works. Ellul argues that mankind is beset by "new demons," in materialism, secularism, and other distractions from God and morality.

When he was finally ready, Dwight went out looking for a little church somewhere. Almost a year after the verdict, he rose shyly from a chair in the sanctuary of a small church in Virginia and preached a try-out sermon. This little rural church in Virginia had a dwindling membership and a tiny budget and held services only twice a month. In the car by himself on the way back down to North Carolina, he thought about this new little church, and he hoped it would call him. He wanted devoutly to try again.

The church did call him. He now lives by himself in rural Virginia, driving the long winding roads of the country to reach his parishioners. He is able to get around, operate his car, and get most things done, even though he will never have normal sensation in his hands and feet.

He says he loves his church. He says he is reasonably happy. His view of Blanche has hardened and darkened with the passage of time. He still says he loved her deeply, however. He still wishes there had been a way to reach the good in her. But the evil was too strong.